Human Resource Management in China

The past 25 years of economic reform in China have led to impressive growth and significant integration into the global economy. These developments have, in turn, resulted in major changes in the management of industrial enterprises and hold considerable implications for HR practices in the nation with the largest workforce in the world.

This book examines the rise of a highly centralized command economy and dominance of public ownership during Mao's regime, and discusses the impact of different economic systems and ownership forms on management in general and HR practices in China's industrial enterprises in particular. Through four major case studies and two surveys, the book considers three specific questions:

- How were human resources in Chinese industrial enterprise managed before and after the commencement of economic reform with respect to major HR activities, including: human resource planning, recruitment and selection, performance appraisal and training and development?
- What impact do forms of ownership have on HR practices in Chinese industrial enterprises?
- What are the possible future development paths of HR management in Chinese industrial enterprises?

Human Resource Management in China explores the emerging role of HRM in China's industrial enterprises and enhances our understanding of HRM in the Chinese industrial sector. A significant contribution to the theory of HRM, this book will be essential reading for students and researchers of Business and Management, HRM and Asian Business.

Cherrie Jiuhua Zhu is Associate Professor in the Department of Management, Monash University. Her research interests include human resource management (international and domestic level) and cross-cultural management.

RoutledgeCurzon advances in Asia-Pacific business

人力资源管理在中国
Human Resource Management in China

Past, current and future HR practices
in the industrial sector

朱久华
Cherrie Jiuhua Zhu

BA (Nanjing Normal University, China),
MBA (Monash), PhD (Tasmania)

RoutledgeCurzon
Taylor & Francis Group
LONDON AND NEW YORK

First published 2005
by RoutledgeCurzon
2 Park Square, Milton Park, Abingdon, Oxon OX14 4RN

Simultaneously published in the USA and Canada
by RoutledgeCurzon
270 Madison Ave, New York, NY 10016

Transferred to Digital Printing 2005

RoutledgeCurzon is an imprint of the Taylor & Francis Group

© 2005 Cherrie Jiuhua Zhu

Typeset in Baskerville by
Bookcraft Ltd, Stroud, Gloucestershire
Printed and bound in Great Britain by
TJI Digital, Padstow, Cornwall

British Library Cataloguing in Publication Data
A catalogue record for this book is available from the British
Library

Library of Congress Cataloging in Publication Data
A catalog record for this book has been requested

ISBN 0-415-28667-0

To Lisheng, Jun, and Adrian

Contents

Figures

Tables

Acknowledgments

It is with great relief that I finally complete this book and realize another dream in my life. Without the strong encouragement from my former PhD supervisor, Professor Peter Dowling, I probably would not have embarked on this project, which found me heading back to China to gather the additional data needed to expand on my original dissertation. Although Peter was unable to share in the authorship due to other work commitments, his help in preparing some of the chapters was invaluable. Moreover, his intellectual guidance and support were a constant inspiration to me, and he is the first person I would like to acknowledge with my heartfelt thanks.

While conducting my field study in China, I was fortunate to receive the assistance of my friends, classmates and students, including Mr. Bill Ng from Pacific Dunlop, Professor Zhao Shuming and Professor Liu Hong from Nanjing University, Professor Song Hong from Mt. Eliza Business School in Beijing, Mr. Li Kaoshan from the Jingling Hotel in Nanjing, Ms. Sun Ying, Ms. Yu Jingqi, Mr. Qian Jianzhong, Mr. Lu Chen, Mr. Gao Shengli, Mr. Tang Deping, Mr. Li Zhengli, together with other Monash alumni in Shanghai, and Professor Zhang Wei from Shanghai Science and Technology Management College. I sincerely thank them for their time and generous support which enabled me to complete my empirical studies. I am also very grateful for the understanding, support and cooperation of managers and employees I interviewed for the case studies.

The completion of this book was greatly facilitated by Dr. Simon Moss and Mr. Brian Cooper who offered valuable data processing expertise, Ms. Carla Taines who assisted with editing and Ms. Fang Lam with formatting, Mr. John Button from Bookcraft Ltd who gave assistance and support with the production, and Mr. Alex Sharpe from Standard Eight Ltd who edited the final draft. I would also like to recognize the help of my colleagues, especially Professor Chris Nyland and Professor Russell Smyth, whose constructive feedback has made this a far better book than it would otherwise have been, and whose personal support will always be appreciated.

I also acknowledge with gratitude the financial support from the Department of Management and the Faculty of Business and Economics at Monash University, which enabled me to conduct the second survey in China and to progress with the publication of this text.

Throughout this journey, which has seen the basis of my PhD thesis evolve into the content of this book, I have received the full support of my family, including my husband Lisheng Yang, our daughter Jun Yang and her fiancé Adrian Mar, my mother, mother-in-law, and my brothers, sisters and their families. I wish to thank them all for their love, support and encouragement. In particular, I would like to thank Lisheng, Jun and Adrian for their understanding, patience and sacrifices made in helping me to see this project through to its completion. For these reasons I dedicate this book to them.

Preface

The past 25 years of economic reform in China have led to impressive growth and significant integration into the global economy. China is now the largest recipient of foreign direct investment in the developing world, and accession to the WTO in late 2001 has further accelerated China's market-oriented economic reforms. These developments have, in turn, resulted in major changes in the management of industrial enterprises and hold considerable implications for human resource (HR) practices in the nation with the largest workforce in the world.

Based on a review of the current literature, this book briefly examines the rise of a highly centralized command economy and dominance of public ownership during Mao's regime and changes that occurred in both the economic system and ownership structure since economic reform. It discusses the impact of different economic systems and ownership forms on management in general and HR practices in China's industrial enterprises in particular. There is a dearth of research that systematically examines current HR practices in Chinese industrial enterprises, especially across enterprises with different types of ownership. Given this, the book identifies three research questions:

1   How were human resources in Chinese industrial enterprise managed before and after the commencement of economic reform with respect to major HR activities, including: human resource planning; recruitment and selection; performance appraisal; compensation and welfare; training and development; and labour relations?
2   What impact does form of ownership have on HR practices in Chinese industrial enterprises?
3   What are the possible future development paths of human resource management (HRM) in Chinese industrial enterprises?

The three research questions were investigated and addressed through four major case studies conducted in four enterprises with different owner-ship forms in China and survey questionnaires with 440 respondents in 1994–5 and 447 in 2001–2. Each case study and survey result was discussed and analysed separately. This was followed by a comparative analysis between the qualitative (case studies) and quantitative (surveys) studies.

The book thus achieved its primary purpose, namely, to explore the emerging role of HRM in China's industrial enterprises with different types of ownership. It enhances the understanding of HRM in the Chinese indus-trial sector by offering empirical evidence of past and current practices across the major HR activities, and pointing to future HR trends within the sector. It also contributes to the theory of HRM by exploring HR practices across enterprises with four types of ownership to investigate the impact of owner-ship form on HRM. In addition, the study proposes a model of transitional HRM that indicates possible future development paths for HRM in Chinese industrial enterprises and discusses future HRM challenges, emphasizing the significance of training the workforce in China for such challenges.

1 Introduction

The objective of this book is to explore the emerging role of human resource management (HRM) in Chinese industrial enterprises through the examination of human resource (HR) practices prior to and during the continuing economic reform that has been occurring since 1978, the evaluation of future HRM trends, and the analysis of the impact of the form of ownership on HRM. This objective is achieved by conducting systematic research through both a review of current literature and field investigations, including case studies and surveys. This introductory chapter first provides background for the book, including the rationale, objectives and significance of the research; and then outlines the structure of the book.

RATIONALE FOR THE RESEARCH

The Third Plenary of the 11th Central Committee of the Communist Party of China (CPC), held in December 1978, was regarded as a turning point in the history of the People's Republic of China (PRC) because it initiated a major programme of reform of the Chinese economy. The meeting 'started all the processes which put an end to the excesses of the "extreme left" policies over two decades and finally led to the emergence and consolidation of the policies of reform and opening' (Talas, 1991: 67). Two major components of the command economy – central planning and public ownership – were targeted for reforms (Dong, 1992; Talas, 1991). Reform in planning, also called operational reform, sought to substitute the mandatory central planning system with a market-oriented system. Reform in ownership structure aimed to change the predominantly public ownership of Mao's regime and to reform state ownership itself to establish a new form of public ownership that stimulates economic growth (Dong, 1992).

The economic reforms since 1978 have led to a 'socialist market economy with Chinese characteristics'. The operational reform has resulted in a shrinkage of the old centralized planning system and an increasing role for the market in areas ranging from control over prices to resource allocation. The ownership reform has resulted in a rapid growth of enterprises in the non-state sector and thus more intensive competition. In particular, the enterprise reform that is focused on state-owned enterprises (SOEs) has been at the centre of reforms since the early 1990s with the introduction of a modern enterprise system incorporating restructuring, corporatization, shareholding and marketization (e.g. Chai and Docwra, 1997; Dernberger, 1997; Lo, 1997; Smyth, 2002; Smyth and Zhai, 2003). As a result, ownership is gradually being separated from the administration of enterprises, particularly in those SOEs that have been converted into financially self-sufficient businesses rather than being administered and subsidized by the state.

The series of reforms have led to rapid economic growth in China. Between the late 1970s, when China opened its doors, until 1997, its economy sustained a growth rate in excess of 9 per cent (EIU, 1997). By 1997 GDP growth was slower than the blistering pace of the immediately preceding years because of the Asian financial crisis, but was still nearly 9 per cent in 1997 and exceeded 7 per cent from 1999 to 2003. China's open-door policy has accelerated its integration into the global economy, as evidenced by its accession to the World Trade Organization (WTO) in late 2001.

The past two and a half decades of reforms and impressive economic growth have witnessed an unprecedented enthusiasm for the establishment of foreign-invested enterprises (FIEs) in China. Many foreign companies have expanded their operations into China, attracted mainly by the sheer size of its potential market. Foreign direct investment (FDI) in China has grown from $US4 billion in 1990 to $US40 billion in 2000 and over $US50 billion in 2003. By the end of 2001, accumulative real use of FDI had reached over $US568.4 billion and employment in FIEs had increased to over 6.71 million from 550,000 employees in 1986 (*China Statistical Yearbook*, 2002: 629 and 121). China is the largest recipient of FDI among the developing countries and is second only to the USA in the world (Panitchpakdi and Clifford, 2002: 145). It is also ranked as one of the largest outward investors among developing economies, with a cumulative stock of outward FDI of over $US27.6 billion in 2001 (Wong and Chan, 2003). China is now considered to be the third biggest economy in the world after the USA and Japan. Its greater economic integration with the rest of the world, especially after becoming a member of the WTO, has further accelerated its market-oriented economic reforms, as it needs to open its protected markets and submit to the rule of international law.

The economic reforms and its increasing participation in the world economy have thus set the stage for significant changes in the management of industrial enterprises in China, especially in regards to HR practices. For example, the responsibility for labour allocation has been shifted from a centralized planning authority to the HR function or department within enterprises; production and reward systems are changing, with much less emphasis on egalitarianism and a stronger link to efficiency and individual performance. While China is in the transition 'from plan to market' (see Liew, 1997) and the reforms have substantially upgraded China's old-style 'command economy' to a new 'socialist market economy', a number of questions arise. First, to what extent have traditional management systems and practices, especially HR activities, been changed? Second, what is the impact of both operational and ownership reforms on the management of the workforce in Chinese industrial enterprises? In particular, what is the impact of different ownership types on HRM? Finally, how will HR practices develop as a result of the economic reforms and what issues are emerging for the future? To date many researchers have addressed only part rather than all of these questions, such as changes in management practices in general (e.g. Chen, D.R., 1995; Child, 1994; Laaksonen, 1988; Strange, 1998; Warner, 1999), and changes in some HR practices (e.g. Jackson, 1992; Sun, 2000; Warner, 1995; Whiteley *et al.*, 2000; Zhao, 1995). Many of these studies are qualitative rather than quantitative in nature. There remains a dearth of research that systematically examines past and current HR practices through both quantitative and qualitative approaches across industrial enterprises with different types of ownership. In order to contribute to this under-researched area, this research employs both qualitative and quantitative methodologies to explore these questions.

RESEARCH OBJECTIVES

The objectives of this research are threefold. The first is to enhance the understanding of HRM in China's industrial sector by offering both qualitative and quantitative evidence of past and current practices across the major HR activities, and by indicating future trends in HR practices. The second is to contribute to the research literature on HRM in China by exploring HR practices across Chinese industrial enterprises with four types of ownership and to investigate the impact of ownership type on HRM. The third is to construct a transitional HRM model for Chinese industrial enterprises to illustrate possible paths of development of Chinese HRM. To this end, three related research questions were identified for investigation:

- *Question 1.* How were human resources in Chinese industrial enterprises managed before and after the commencement of economic reform with respect to major HR activities, including: human resource planning; recruitment and selection; performance appraisal; compensation and welfare; training and development; and labour relations?

- *Question 2.* What impact does ownership type have on HR practices in Chinese industrial enterprises?
- *Question 3.* What are the possible future development paths of HRM in Chinese industrial enterprises?

SIGNIFICANCE OF THE RESEARCH

Given the size of its growing economy and its vast population, China has become increasingly significant in international business decisions and 'has become a focus of interest for Western organization and management researchers' (Shenkar and Von Glinow, 1994: 56). This is because the changes that have occurred in China hold profound consequences for different groups including managers, management researchers and policy-makers at both government and company levels.

This research is significant for managers, especially foreign managers who are working or going to work in China, as the escalation of FDI in China has resulted in greater involvement of foreign companies in technology transfer and in the injection of managerial expertise into China's economic development. FIEs, including foreign joint ventures and wholly foreign-owned ventures, have become the most widespread form of foreign investment in China. However, many FIEs in China have experienced substantial problems, which have prevented them from reaching the expectations of parent companies (e.g. Deng, 2001; Goodall and Warner, 2002; Skopal and Zhu, 2003). These problems often stem from differences in political, economic and social systems, national culture, and conflict with the traditional Chinese management practices that are a legacy of the pre-reform days (Deng, 2003; Vanhonacker, 1997).

Various researchers have pointed out differences between Chinese and Western work attitudes, behaviour and concepts such that cooperation between Western managers and Chinese local employees could be seriously hampered (Fung, 1995; Shenkar, 1994). Also, Chinese HRM policies and practices are quite different from those used in both developed and other developing market economies (e.g. Ding *et al.*, 1997; Goodall and Warner, 1997; Paik *et al.*, 1996). Careful consideration of local idiosyncratic practices is thus required to operate successfully in China. Current HR practices in China have a distinctive 'Chinese' flavour, as they have been grafted onto the old system (Warner, 1995; Zhu *et al.*, 2004). Therefore, the study of Chinese enterprise management 'promises not only to provide information of direct relevance to those who are active in that economy, but also to illuminate the relevance of Western thinking on management' (Child, 1994: 2).

The results of this research will allow better appreciation of the effect of transition to a market economy on management and HR practices. An understanding of China's past and present management, particularly concerning HR practices, will be of value to foreign managers and their local Chinese counterparts. The results of this research will assist their understanding of the changes that have occurred and the emerging role of HRM in enterprise management, and recognize the inefficiencies in current HR practices for future improvement.

This research is also significant for management researchers as China represents a most attractive site for research on management, especially in the area of comparative and international management. Shenkar and Von Glinow (1994) present three compelling reasons for this. The first reason is that, as China has the largest workforce in the world, current management theories and methodologies cannot claim to be universal unless 'they can explain the structure and processes of PRC enterprises, as well as the attitudes and behaviour of those who work in them'. The second reason is that China, because of its numerous differences compared with Western countries, 'potentially represents the most serious challenge to paradigms developed in the West'. Finally, China's integration into the world, albeit slow, has made the relevance of Western models 'a practical matter as much as a theoretical issue' (Shenkar and Von Glinow, 1994: 56–7). Though raised a decade ago, these reasons are still relevant today as China's period of reform towards a more market-oriented economy continues.

While moving from a highly centralized command economy to a more market-driven economy, China retains its socialist one-party government system as well as its socialist ideology (e.g. Burns, 1999; Pye, 1999; Starr, 1997; Story, 2003). It can be used as a test case for socialist and post-socialist economic reform. Its enterprises can be studied to assess the universality of the macro and micro theories of management and organization that have been developed largely in the West or derived from Western experience. In this research, the HRM function and major HR activities (as defined in the West by Schuler *et al.*, 1992) are applied to examine how Chinese employees have been managed both prior to and during the economic reforms. In addition, a survey questionnaire built upon the work of Western researchers (see Von Glinow, 2002; Geringer *et al.*, 2002) is adopted to study a range of HR practices in China's industrial enterprises. This study will facilitate management researchers' understanding of the application of Western-developed management and HR practices in the Chinese context and related problems.

This research, based on both qualitative and quantitative data, also explores the impact of ownership forms on HR practices in different types of industrial enterprises. The findings of this study will address the dearth of research on the relationship between ownership types and HR practices in China. Finally, this research constructs a model of HRM for Chinese industrial enterprises under transition. In this respect, the results of this study should add significantly to an understanding of Chinese HRM and its transformation.

Policy-makers will also find this research useful as the study reveals that the impact of economic reforms and subsequent changes in traditional systems and practices on the management of human resources are profound. It therefore offers some important insights for policy-makers in companies and governments. For example, foreign companies that might look to transfer their home country HR policies and practices to their subsidiaries in China will find that this research supports the argument that foreign companies should not assume that identical HR practices can be applied to their Chinese enterprises (e.g. Child, 1993; Fung, 1995; Huo and Von Glinow, 1995; Paik *et al.*, 1996). This research examines the degree to which some Western-style HR practices have been employed in Chinese enterprises and their perceived effectiveness, thereby providing a framework for ascertaining the extent of transfer of foreign company policies to their Chinese subsidiaries.

This research also highlights issues for government policy-makers in terms of the regulation of enterprises. These issues include the enforcement of social security policies, further reform of managerial appointments for senior enterprise managers, and consistency and transparency of regulations for private-owned enterprises to improve their business environment. An awareness of these issues could help government policy-makers re-evaluate their current policies to facilitate development of HR practices in industrial enterprises.

STRUCTURE OF THE BOOK

As the reform of the traditional command economy is regarded as a turning point in the history of the PRC, with a profound impact on management and HR practices in the industrial sector, it is necessary to understand the two major components of the command economic system (a centralized planning system and a socialist ownership structure), the transition of the economic system since the reform in the late 1970s, changes in ownership structure and government regulation of HR practices, and the consequent impact on management practices, especially HR practices. These issues are addressed in Chapter 2, which also compares the pre-reform personnel and labour administration with current HRM in terms of the categorization of human resources and a range of HR practices. A traditional PRC model of personnel and labour administration (built up from a literature review) is presented, which is in contrast to the HRM model proposed in the last chapter.

The research methodology of this study is detailed in Chapter 3. It includes the rationale for adopting both qualitative and quantitative approaches in the research, and discusses the design and conduct of four major case studies in 1995 and two questionnaire surveys 1994–5 and 2001–2 in China that examined HR practices. The results of four case studies are presented in Chapters 4, 5, 6 and 7. Each of these chapters focuses on an enterprise with a different type of ownership, ranging from state-owned enterprise (SOE) to collective-owned (COE), private-owned (POE) and foreign-invested enterprise (FIE). These four major case studies have similar objectives, that is, to examine past and current HRM in the enterprise with respect to six major HR practices (i.e. human resource planning; recruitment and selection; performance appraisal; compensation and welfare; training and development; and labour relations); to explore the impact of ownership type on HR practices; and to analyse probable paths of HRM development in the future.

While Chapters 4–7 provide qualitative results, Chapter 8 presents quantitative data obtained from surveys conducted in 1994–5 and 2001–2. The survey questionnaire is based on the work of Von Glinow and colleagues on best international HRM practices (see Geringer *et al.*, 2002; Teagarden *et al.*, 1995). It investigates the status quo of the HR function/department and the existence of HR activities in the industrial enterprises, examines the extent to which HR activities were conducted and were expected to be conducted in the future, explores the impact of ownership type on HR activities, and analyses future probable paths of HRM development.

In Chapter 9, the research findings obtained from both the qualitative case studies and quantitative surveys are analysed and discussed in relation to the research questions posed above. The comparative analysis across the four cases and surveys enables an integration of research findings obtained from different research methods. Implications of the research findings are drawn with regard to government regulation of enterprises, contribution to the literature on Chinese HRM, and HRM practices in China. This final chapter concludes with a strong indication that a role for HRM is emerging in China, albeit one still in transition along with the economic system.

2 Economic reform and its impact on HR practices

Since the late 1970s China has been going through a transition which has resulted in significant changes in the economic system and management practices. This chapter first reviews briefly the transition of the economic system and changes in the ownership structure in China. It then examines the impact of economic reforms on HRM in the industrial sector by comparing the pre-reform personnel and labour administration with current HR practices.

TRANSITION OF THE ECONOMIC SYSTEM AND CHANGES IN OWNERSHIP STRUCTURE

The economic system and ownership structure during Mao's regime

After the PRC was founded in 1949, the Maoist Chinese model was developed and maintained until the commencement of economic reforms in the late 1970s. The three major components of this model included a Stalinist 'big push' development strategy; a centralized or command economic system; and the radical principles of Maoist ideology (Dernberger, 1982). The Stalinist big push development strategy or 'leap forward type of heavy-industry-oriented development strategy' (Lin et al., 1996: 19) was adopted by the government in the early 1950s to achieve the goal of rapid industrialization. However, China's scarce capital and poorly developed economy could not support extremely capital-intensive heavy industries. To reduce the conflict between a capital-intensive heavy industry and a capital-scarce economy, a command economic system was established (Lin et al., 1996).

The command economy in China had two prominent features: central planning and public ownership (Pu, 1990; Riskin, 1987). Central planning before the reform involved the central government setting priorities and carrying them out administratively by distributing materials and finance to enterprises and ordering output from them, especially SOEs. Public owner-ship, including state ownership of the means of production (mainly in the form of SOEs) and collective ownership, reflects the control of state institu-tions over enterprises. This control includes 'the contractual power to deter-mine who will comprise the management and their remuneration, and the right to determine the allocation of residual gains and losses' (Hay *et al.*, 1994: 424). The ownership structure 'allows the state to maintain direct-authority relations over most of its output' and 'permits a command system to function unimpeded' (Naughton, 1996: 29). As central planning enabled the government to exert strong and direct control over industry and manage-ment, the enterprises acted as production units to fulfil state plans. The nature of public ownership also moulded the enterprise into a social unit or a mini-society that had to take on various social responsibilities (e.g. Chen, D.R., 1995; Kaple, 1994). These two major characteristics of the command economy later became targets of economic reforms in China.

Public ownership of the means of production was regarded as one of the most important characteristics of socialism in China and was referred to as the material foundation of the superiority of socialism (Hsu, 1991). Accord-ing to Maoist ideology, public ownership was always superior to other types of ownership. However, the Chinese concept of ownership is different from the Western one.

> The Chinese concept of ownership (*suoyouzhi*) is appreciably more am-biguous and is a political and ideological consideration rather than an economic and legal one. The term *suoyouzhi* ... implies an overall system of governance based on the ideological principles of socialism, such that all the means of production are ultimately a public asset and that the state acts as the custodian of this public ownership.
>
> (Child, 1994: 19)

Institutions of the state controlled managers through hiring, firing and compensation, and had the right to allocate residual surpluses, losses or risks (Hay *et al.*, 1994), thereby establishing their ownership of the enter-prises. As a public ownership structure paved the way for adopting cen-tral planning and implementing the big push strategy, the Communist Party of China (CPC or the Party) launched socialist transformation soon after it took power.

The transformation of the ownership structure experienced three major phases: (1) a mixed ownership structure (1949–52); (2) a primitive stage of socialist ownership (1953–7); and (3) the establishment and consolidation of a state ownership structure (1958–78) (Wang, 1994). The first two phases represented two important periods of economic development: economic rehabilitation and socialist transformation, which ran concurrently with the first five-year plan. The last phase covered two decades, which included three important periods of economic development. The first was the Great Leap Forward (1958–61), which ended in sharp declines in both agricultural and industrial output. The second was economic readjustment (1962–5) which witnessed the revival and development of the national economy. The final period was the Cultural Revolution and its legacy from 1966 to 1978. The major features of the Chinese economy (i.e. a highly centralized planning system and a public-dominated ownership structure) remained unchanged and unchallenged until economic reforms began in the late 1970s.

Reforms of the economic system and ownership structure

By the late 1970s, after failing to achieve its targets over a period of three decades, the Maoist development strategy was being critically reviewed. Evidence of failure was evident in China's technological backwardness, pervasive economic inefficiency, critical shortage of daily necessities, low income level of the urban population, persistent poverty of millions of peasants, and a huge gap in the economic development between China and its newly industrialized neighbours (Lin *et al.*, 1996; White, 1993). The breakthrough or turning point in China's economic and political strategy occurred at the Third Plenary of the 11th Central Committee in late 1978. The plenary officially 'declared that the era of turbulent class struggles was over, and turned the focus of party work to economic development' (Riskin, 1987: 284). Since China embarked on its economic reforms, the economic system has been under continuous transition with respect to its micro-management, resource allocation, macro-policy environment and ownership structure, each of which is examined briefly below.

The micro-management level

The reform in late 1978 started with changes in micro-management by offering the enterprise a profit incentive to improve its performance. Under the planned economy, the state centralized all earnings and expenditures of SOEs, profits were channelled to the central government, and losses were covered by the state. This practice robbed enterprise managers and workers of any incentive for efficient or profitable production. In order to improve the incentive mechanism, different types of profit sharing systems were experimented with from late 1978 to loosen the government's control over the economy and build a market regulatory mechanism (Chai and Docwra, 1997). However, this 'market mechanism' was far different from the Western-style market, because it was largely based on 'widespread practices of negotiation, consensus, compromise, administrative intervention, etc.' (Lo, 1997: 59). Since 1994, the modern enterprise system was introduced through marketization or shareholding and the objective of reform at the micro-management level was no longer only to provide incentives for improving efficiency but also to increase the market competitiveness of enterprises.

The resource allocation system

Under the central planning, market forces were totally ignored in the allocation and acquisition of material, capital and human resources and the distribution of output. The reform in the resource-allocation system was facilitated by the adoption of the *Decision on Reforming the Economic System* by the CPC in 1984, which focused on the marketization of the Chinese economy with the intention of reducing direct planning control over the economy (Dernberger, 1997). The *Decision on Issues Concerning the Establishment of a Socialist Market Structure* adopted by the CPC in 1993 further emphasized the role of the market by declaring that the market would 'play the fundamental role in resource allocations under macro-economic control by the state', and the dual-track price system for capital goods would be abolished as soon as possible (Liew, 1997: 85). As a consequence, the role of direct planning in resource allocation was reduced, while the role of the market was expanded.

The macro-policy environment

Reforms in the micro-management institution and resource-allocation system could not be sustained without reform in the macro-policy environment, which in a broad sense referred to price reform. Reform affected prices in five major areas: the prices of production inputs (raw materials, intermediate input, and energy), products (final products and services), capital (the interest rate), foreign currency (the exchange rate), and labour (wages) (Lin *et al.*, 1996).

Under the command economy, most prices were determined by the state and failed to reflect the value of social input, or market supply and demand, thus hindering the establishment of an efficiently functioning economic system. Profits, for example, were neither a good indicator of enterprise performance nor a reliable base for government taxation under the old system (Wong, 1993). Thus price reform was regarded as 'the key to the reform of

Table 2.1 Shares of gross value of industrial output by ownership sectors, 1980–99

Year	SOEs[a] (%)	COEs[b] (%)	POEs[c] (%)	Others[d] (%)
1980	75.97	23.54	0.02	0.48
1985	64.86	32.08	1.85	1.21
1988	56.80	36.15	4.34	2.72
1990	54.60	35.62	5.39	4.38
1991	52.94	35.70	5.70	5.66
1992	48.09	38.04	6.76	7.11
1993	43.13	38.36	8.35	10.16
1994	34.07	40.87	11.51	13.55
1999	28.50	38.50	12.00	21.00

Sources: Adapted from Lo, 1997: 4. Also *China Statistical Yearbook* 1990: 416 and 1995: 377; Xiao, Z.J. 2001: 17.

a   SOEs = state-owned enterprises.
b   COEs = collective-owned enterprises.
c   POEs = private-owned enterprises.
d   Others = enterprises of other ownership forms, mainly refers to foreign-invested enterprises such as foreign joint ventures and wholly foreign-owned ventures.

the entire economic structure' by the CPC in 1984, because 'the existing administratively set prices were like a "funny mirror" that distorted reality and sent economic decision-makers perverse signals' (Shirk, 1993: 299). As prices became decentralized, the market increasingly influenced production and management policies in enterprises, and 'striving for economic efficiency became an integral part of an enterprise's action' (Lin *et al.*, 1996: 161).

Ownership structure

Ownership reform, one of two major aspects of the economic reform, aimed to reform both the existing ownership structure and state ownership itself. As the result of socialist transformation and consolidation of socialist ownership, China's economy was basically dominated by two forms of socialist ownership on the eve of reform: state ownership by the whole people as in all SOEs, and collective ownership by the working people as in many small and medium-sized enterprises. In 1978, the state and collective sectors represented 98–99 per cent of the gross social product, gross national product, and national income of China, while the individual and private sectors were a mere 1–2 per cent (Talas, 1991).

Under the monopoly of state ownership, many problems occurred such as low efficiency and overstaffing of enterprises, short supplies of daily necessities and slow commodity circulation (Wu, Y. 1996). It was not until the mid-1980s that it 'became obvious that the key to the success of economic and political reform was a deep and radical reform of the ownership system' (Talas, 1991: 330). The monopoly status of the state sector was undermined by allowing collective and private enterprises to flourish, and by allowing foreign investment to support enterprises in many industries, especially manufacturing and tertiary industries. These different forms of ownership were granted legal status in 1988 and were supported by government policies such as low tax rates, the retention of all profits, and no restrictions on employee salaries. As many of these enterprises had a competitive advantage over state enterprises in that they could meet market demand, they soon flourished. The ownership structure of production has changed immensely during the reforms as indicated in Table 2.1. The share of gross value of industrial output by enterprises with private and other types of ownership rose significantly from 0.02 and 0.48 per cent, respectively, in 1980 to 12 and 21 per cent, respectively, in 1999. Meanwhile, SOEs' proportion declined steadily from 75.97 per cent in 1980 to 28.5 per cent in 1999 (Lo, 1997; *China Statistical Yearbook*, 1990–2000; Xiao, 2001).

THE IMPACT OF REFORMS ON HR PRACTICES

Under the command economy, central planners 'created a system in which property rights were vague or non-existent', so they could have maximum discretionary control (Naughton, 1996: 30). As they assumed no risk and had no right to allocate residual profits or losses, Chinese managers had no incentive to pursue efficient, profit-maximising strategies in their production and distribution activities. Furthermore, 'management and labour policies have, throughout the history of the PRC, been subject to changes in the ideological stance of the Party leadership' (Jackson, 1988: 338).

Changes in management policies and labour practices

The major changes in enterprise management policies and practices between 1949 and 1978 can be grouped into four stages according to Lee (1987). The first stage was in the period of economic rehabilitation and socialist transformation (1949–57), during which the one-man management system was installed with an emphasis on material incentives and regulatory controls. The second stage, during the Great Leap Forward (1958–61), was dominated by Mao's 'proletarian line' that stressed the commanding role of the Party, the importance of political ideology and the leading role of the workers. The third, which occurred during economic readjustment (1962–5), resurrected the practices and policies of the first stage and witnessed the implementation of the Seventy Articles for Regulations in Industry. The final stage, during the Cultural Revolution (1966–76), revived Mao's dominance and ended up eliminating the 'bourgeois line' advocated by the then Chairman Liu Shaoqi (e.g. Kaple, 1994; Laaksonen, 1988; Riskin, 1987).

Under the planned economy and state ownership, enterprise management was like 'the bird in the cage' as described by Naughton (1996: 57), or 'just like a puppet' (Lin *et al.*, 1996: 51). Regardless of whether managers were given autonomy for their operations as in the 'one-man' management practices or deprived of such autonomy as in the Cultural Revolution, they were constantly confined by a centralized command economic system. The state invariably 'set the norms of economic activities to be followed by enterprises' (Hsu, 1991: 76):

> … all required factors of production were allocated to enterprises by the state, all their products were submitted to the state, all their production costs were settled by the state, and all their profits were remitted to the state. There was no link between the expansion of an enterprise and its economic efficiency, or between its workers' income and their contribution.
>
> (Lin *et al.*, 1996: 61)

A highly restrictive and rigid set of constraints over the behaviour of managers was imposed, depriving them of any authority 'to shape the enterprise into a unique or idiosyncratic organization to match the output, market, or personality of that unit' (Naughton, 1996: 107). Fundamental changes in management practices began in the early 1980s with the adoption of different systems of management responsibility. Three major systems have been used since then: the factory director responsibility system (FDRS) (1984–6); the contract management responsibility system (CMRS) (1987–94); and the modern enterprise system since 1994.

The FDRS specified who within the enterprise could exercise decision-making power, and it was the first time a unitary management system had been officially accepted since the adoption of the Soviet one-man management in the 1950s. However, serious problems were identified with this system, such as an asymmetry between benefits and responsibility of factory directors as there was a persistent tendency for investments and bonuses to expand. The investment hunger of enterprises was caused by the fact that directors would receive additional benefits if they succeeded, but they risked very little if they failed. Bonuses expanded mostly through 'wage emulation' rather than productivity improvement (Lo, 1997: 109). Other problems (see Hay *et al.*, 1994) include a vague definition and flexible interpretation of 'responsibility'; lack of strong motivation and commitment for directors to meet profit targets and 'one-way' responsibility (i.e. the director was responsible to a higher authority, the higher authority could – and did – intervene without any responsibility for the consequences of such intervention). Because of these problems, the FDRS was replaced with a contractual management system in 1987 (for more details of FDRS, see Mackerras *et al.*, 1994; White, 1993).

CMRS swiftly became general practice among SOEs as it restored targets for profit delivery, and established a more explicit link between enterprise performance and the payment of bonuses to workers. Under CMRS, the government took into account the enterprise's business conditions and environment by negotiating individual contracts for each enterprise (Ishihara, 1993). Enterprise managers had more independence from higher level authority, more focused managerial objectives and a more business-like orientation. They also became more responsible in their investment behaviour, and were encouraged to reform their payment systems (Chen, D.R., 1995). However, while CMRS ensured greater stability in state revenue collection and capacity for increasing workers' income, it focused mainly on profitability rather than on developments such as technical innovation and enterprise expansion (Chai and Docwra, 1997). SOEs continued to be out-performed by other types of enterprises and incurred heavy financial losses. One way to enforce budget constraint was to increase the independence and competitiveness of enterprises, and to expose them to market forces rather than allowing them to be protected by the state (Lo, 1997). In 1994, the state implemented a new tax system which aimed to equalize the tax burden among different types of enterprises so as to equalize competition. This removed the foundation for the contract system and the CMRS was replaced by the modern enterprise system through corporatization and shareholding (e.g. Chai and Docwra, 1997; Ishihara, 1993; Jackson, 1992).

In its *Decision on Issues Concerning the Establishment of a Socialist Market Structure* of 1993, the CPC formally adopted a modern enterprise system through marketization and shareholding (CPC Central Committee, 1993). The four features as defined in the Decision included clearly established ownership (*chanquan qingxi*); well-defined rights and responsibilities (*quanzhe minque*); separation of enterprise from government administration (*zhengqi fengkai*); and management in a scientific way (*guanli kexue*) (Chen, Q., 1995). The first benefit stemming from the decision was the clarification of the assignment of property rights, which separated government administration from enterprise management, thus allowing the state to get away from its unlimited responsibility for enterprises. The second benefit was that marketization would encourage the infusion of new capital into state enterprises by other state corporations and private and foreign investors. The programme to set up a modern enterprise system was facilitated in 1994 with the implementation of the new tax system, the abolition of the CMRS and promulgation of the *Corporate Law* (Deng, 1998; Liew, 1997; Xu, 1996).

Although marketization has achieved a very high degree of separation between ownership and control, it is still not fully effective because of market imperfections. For example, while a free labour market has emerged, enterprises cannot retrench surplus employees at their discretion due to an enterprise-based social security system. Also, some government administrative departments were restructured into corporations without any alterations to their social obligations. Thus, the implementation of the modern enterprise system relies on further reforms in other areas, such as the divestment of SOEs of their heavy social responsibilities, and establishment of detailed legislation for implementing the *Corporate Law* (Zhang, D.Z., 1996). Nevertheless, the government's emphasis on implementing the modern enterprise system, and its strong desire for enterprises to 'become corporate entities and competitors adaptable to the market' (*Documents*, 1997: 20) have become driving forces for further reform in management practices, especially in the area of HRM, which is discussed in the next section.

HR practices

Since the founding of the PRC, human resources in the industrial sector were classified into two groups, cadres and workers (e.g. Laaksonen, 1988; Yabuki, 1995). Cadres are administrative staff or white-collar employees such as managers, engineers and senior technicians in government organizations and in enterprises. The two groups were administrated by different institutions and in many situations were subject to different rules and regulations. Because of this division, the management of personnel and labour was marked by differences in HR practices. For example, the pre-reform wage scales were designed separately for cadres and workers, and the criteria for performance appraisal also differed between them.

Since the economic reforms, the distinction between cadres and workers has gradually become blurred for three reasons: (1) the replacement of cadres with civil servants in the government departments after the promulgation of the *Regulation of State Civil Servants* in August 1993; (2) an official emphasis by the Minister of Personnel in 1994 on two-way selection and merit-based appointment to advertised jobs; and (3) the adoption of different types of management responsibility systems. All these changes have enabled managers to exercise greater autonomy in choosing people for particular positions.

With the blurring of the classification between cadres and workers, traditional personnel and labour administration has also undergone reform. The three-system reform launched in the late 1980s focused on reforms of the labour and personnel system, the wage and welfare system and the social insurance system. Old HR practices have undergone unprecedented changes: the responsibility for labour allocation has shifted from a centralized planning authority to forecasting and planning departments within enterprises; a contract labour system has replaced traditional lifetime employment; open competition replaced authority-nominated cadre appointments for managerial positions; and production and reward systems moved from emphasizing egalitarianism to rewarding efficiency and performance. Managers in China have started to show an increased interest in using HR practices, such as compensation and motivational systems, to increase productivity at the individual, group and enterprise level (Cyr and Frost, 1991). In order to systematically examine these changes in the management of human resources before and after the commencement of the reform process, the author has selected the five major HR practices as defined in the West (Schuler *et al.*, 1992), namely, staffing policies and practices, performance appraisal, compensation and welfare, training and development and labour relations for our discussion.

Staffing policies and practices

Planning was the dominant control mechanism during Mao's regime, with the market serving only a supplementary role. Industrial enterprises were under the control of government institutions at the relevant level according to their ownership, size and industry. Staffing or employment policies and practices in the industrial sector were characterized by four major features: full employment; lifetime tenure; low labour mobility and centralized labour allocation (e.g. Child, 1994; Warner, 1995). The traditional employment practices guaranteed that urban job seekers would belong to a working unit (*danwei*) with an 'iron rice bowl' (*tie fanwan*), but this guarantee in turn seriously undermined Chinese industry by contributing to problems such as overstaffing and low productivity. The problems of overstaffing and low productivity are major causes of losses in SOEs and addressing these issues has become the driving force for reform of the employment system.

Since the late 1970s, China's reforms 'have unleashed a process of growth and institutional change that has moved its vast economy to the brink of a market system' (Rawski, 1995: 1172). Driven by a socialist market economy, the pre-reform employment system experienced radical changes, which include the implementation of two-way job selection rather than central allocation, a move away from the policy of full employment, the adoption of the labour contract to help break the 'iron rice bowl' and the emergence of a free labour market. The adoption of the contract system was one of the most important changes. In 1986, the state issued regulations concerning four areas covered by the labour contract system: employment procedures, labour insurance and labour discipline, and the right to fire employees. From October 1986 all newly employed workers in the state sector were contracted rather than permanent (Howard, 1991), initially on three- to five-year contracts. The policy document issued in 1992, *Regulations for Changing the Methods of Operation of State-owned Industrial Enterprises*, required a labour contract to specify the terms and conditions of employment, and the rights and responsibilities of workers and employers (Yang and Wu, 1993). The contract can be signed by an individual or on a collective basis, and the contract period may be specified or unspecified, depending on the nature of the job. By 1996, the labour contract system had become compulsory in both public and private sectors, including for managers at different levels.

The introduction of the labour contract system was the most significant aspect of the labour reform because it revoked the long-standing tradition of lifetime employment and increased the authority and autonomy of enterprise managers in relation to both government and the enterprise workforce. The legislation clarified that the responsibility for employment of employees lay with the enterprise rather than with the state (Dang, 1991). This made it possible, in theory at least, for both workers and managers to be free to select each other (Warner, 1995). The contract system has facilitated the adoption of other types of employment, such as part-time jobs, casual, seasonal and hourly based work, as well as flexible working time (Qin, 1995; Yang, 1995). The contract system, however, has not really eliminated or reduced job security as most contracts were renewed automatically except in the case of a serious infraction of labour discipline (e.g. Howard, 1991; Howe, 1992). Some individual labour contracts merely 'clarify the nature of tasks given to workers and their rights in work as well as the responsibilities of employers' (Warner, 1996a: 41) rather than establishing new relationships and levels of participation.

The emergence of a labour market and subsequent high labour mobility is another major change in employment practices. Until the mid-1980s, under the official view in China, labour was not a commodity to be bought and sold, and hence there was no basis for the existence of a labour market (Chen, K., 1995; Porket, 1995). Only in 1987 did the government legislate that labour mobility should be encouraged and that an individual's discretion to select a job should be respected (Zhao, 1994). This legislation was aimed at promoting job mobility, or at least lessening impediments to job transfers. Government personnel exchange and service centres were set up in many cities, which sponsored personnel exchange negotiations and career development programmes, and provided information on job opportunities. Many skilled employees and managerial staff from SOEs were attracted to foreign-invested enterprises and private-owned enterprises by better pay and/or the opportunity to demonstrate their abilities (Zhao, 1998). The emergence of such a labour market would not have been possible during Mao's regime. The price for the creation of a labour market was a retreat from the commitment to full employment (Korzec, 1988).

Chinese workers can now move more easily from one unit to another as enterprises no longer have the same control over their personal files (*dang'an*) which normally held an employee's personal data, political history and performance records and was kept by the enterprise. Before enterprise reform, an employee could not leave an enterprise without obtaining official permission to transfer his/her personal file to another enterprise. Under the contract system, the personal file has become increasingly irrelevant. However, many workers have limited mobility because of residential restrictions and enterprise-specific housing, pensions and medical benefits. Reforms in housing and welfare benefits and further relaxation of the household registration system are necessary to further develop the free labour market.

As the government strengthens enterprise reform by pushing more SOEs into the market, more employees will be laid off because it is mainly the SOEs that have sheltered 'an army of redundant but tenured workers' and suffered from poor productivity (Rawski, 1995: 1150). In April 1993, the government's *Regulation for Reallocating Redundant Employees in State-owned Enterprises* specified that surplus employees reallocated by SOEs would receive financial assistance from the government to maintain their basic living standard. This Regulation sparked a nationwide re-employment project since the mid-1990s, and enterprises were required by the state to 'assist the redundant workers in finding placement in other trades and assist those who are laid off in finding new jobs' (*Beijing Review*, 6 April 1997: 9). In 1998 the Ministry of Labour's top priority was to continue this project with an aim of re-employing 60 per cent of those laid off (Hai, 1998: 32).

The pressure placed on enterprises, especially SOEs, to keep their surplus workforce or absorb redundant employees internally is strongly indicative of the legacy of a command economy where enterprises had to follow government instructions. Although employment practices have been decentralized since the reforms, a question remains as to the extent to which enterprises can hire and fire people. Child (1994) has observed that China claims to be a socialist market economy and government officials continue to play an active role in key policy decisions. In many SOEs, decisions are still affected by both social and economic factors such as the social security reform and the low skill base of many employees, which have contributed to the slow progress of reform in the SOE sector (Xu, 1997; Yao, 1998).

Performance appraisal

With the transition of employment practices from high centralization to merit-orientation, performance appraisal has also changed. Performance appraisal is defined as 'the process of identifying, observing, measuring and developing human performance in organizations' (Cardy and Dobbins, 1994: 1). Along with other HR practices such as staffing and reward systems, performance appraisal is an integral part of modern Western management systems and is currently used in the majority of large Western companies (Lindholm *et al.*, 1999). In its broad sense, performance appraisal aims to assist improvement in three areas within an enterprise: administration, development and communication (Butler *et al.*, 1991). In contrast to the West, performance appraisal during Mao's regime was mainly used to assist administrative tasks such as job transfer, promotion, rewards or welfare. It was also more commonly used for cadres than for workers, and practised more in large and medium-sized SOEs that had a 'consistent set of personnel practices' (Zhao, 1994: 7).

Cadres' performance appraisal was conducted by the personnel department that kept their personal files. Leading cadres who were Party members were under the control of the CPC's Organization Department of the Central Committee (ODCC) which issued many policies and regulations regarding the management of cadres, illustrating the direct control of the Party over its cadres. The basis for cadre appraisal relied heavily on political loyalty and seniority, and ideological purity and activeness were especially emphasized during political changes in China (Laaksonen, 1988). Although Mao maintained that cadres should be both 'red' (politically and ideologically sound) and 'expert' (technically competent), the dual criteria were difficult to apply as there was no objective benchmark to measure 'redness' and the weight given to each criterion fluctuated during political and ideological upheavals (Tung, 1982). All significant managerial posts, especially those in medium- and large-sized enterprises, were directly controlled by the Party and government through the nomenclature system. The appointment, promotion, and dismissal of cadres was normally determined by the Party (or its representatives) through the personnel department rather than relying on performance appraisal data (Naughton, 1996). This inevitably increased the Party's control over cadres and encouraged political soundness over technical competence.

The appraisal process was usually conducted annually by the personnel department of the cadre's enterprise. Each cadre received an appraisal form composed of three parts: self-evaluation, peer group opinions and assessment by the head of the department in which the cadre worked. For senior cadres, 'mass opinions' were often gathered from a wide sample of employees (the ratio could be one cadre to 20 or even 40 colleagues or staff) to strive for a democratic evaluation (Easterby-Smith *et al.*, 1995). Appraisal in the form of a narrative essay was adopted, which is mainly a 'superior-rating-subordinate' type of system and thus lacks specified criteria and other appraisal techniques commonly used in Western market economies such as two-way communication. These deficiencies increased the subjectivity of the appraisal process.

Performance appraisal for blue-collar workers was more sporadic and conducted in a much more informal way. It usually relied on the comments of the worker's peers and leaders who would make judgement based on their subjective impressions of his/her day-to-day job performance and cooperation. Personal relationships with colleagues, especially with the leaders, were thus the key to a good assessment (Brown and Branine, 1995). Such appraisals were characterized by vagueness, being open to individual interpretation, the potential for favouritism and the domination of political ideology. Sometimes three criteria were used for such an evaluation: seniority, skill and political attitude. It is difficult to assess how appraisers applied these criteria and how they weighed the importance of each one, casting doubt on the effectiveness of the assessment process. The purpose of workers' performance assessment was primarily for job promotions, transfers, distribution of welfare benefits such as housing or having a holiday at the trade union's sanatorium, and selection of 'model workers' (Walder, 1986). It was difficult to link individual performance to compensation because it was 'hard to weigh political considerations against work performance, and workers themselves had different perceptions of fairness ... the easy way out was seniority' (Jackson, 1992: 166).

In 1979 the ODCC issued the *Suggestion for Implementing the Cadre Performance Appraisal System*, which gave five reasons for establishing a formal performance appraisal system for cadres. First, it could identify cadres' professional training needs to increase their competency in building socialism. Second, it could distinguish between good and bad performers and assist decision-making in promotions. Third, it could help implement the socialist principle of distribution (i.e. from each according to his/her ability, and to each according to his/her work). The identification of high and low performers through performance appraisal would encourage the former and motivate the latter. Fourth, it could help to break the 'iron rice organization', as cadres would be promoted or demoted on the basis of performance evaluations. Finally, subordinates could evaluate their leaders in the appraisal process to reduce the superior's domination and put cadres under workers' supervision (Su and Zhu, 1992). This document was an important signal for the abolishment of the 'iron posts' (*tie jiaoyi*) of cadres.

The appraisal criteria for cadres typically covered four broad areas known as: 'good moral practice' (*de*), 'adequate competence' (*neng*), 'positive work attitude' (*qing*), and 'strong performance record' (*jie*) (Brown and Branine, 1995; Child, 1994). Cadres received a grade of excellent, good, pass or poor on each criterion. Good moral practice means virtue or moral integrity, which evaluates whether the cadre is politically in step with the Party and whether the cadre carries out government orders and regulations. Since Mao's regime, *de* (or *red* which was more commonly used before the reform) has always been listed at the top of a cadre's appraisal sheet. While Mao Zedong advocated 'Be both *red* (politically reliable) and *expert* (professionally competent)', Deng Xiaoping stated that '*Red* does not mean *expert*, however, to be *expert* must be *red*' (Chen, 1990: 352). Adequate competence covers three main aspects: educational background; ability in leadership, management, organization, negotiation, planning, forecasting and decision-making; and physical status, which also includes age. Since the Party Congress in 1982, the criteria for selecting and promoting cadres have shifted from pure political ideology and seniority to youth, knowledge, education and managerial capability. Thus, *neng* has become more strongly emphasized than before (Zhao, 1986).

Positive work attitude refers to diligence and usually assesses attendance at work, discipline, initiative and sense of responsibility. The final area, strong performance record, evaluates the cadre's work efficiency, including the quality and quantity of output as well as other contributions made to the enterprise. The last two criteria have been given particular attention since the economic reforms. Under the old system, cadres could keep their positions or be promoted irrespective of their work attitude and achievement. However, under the market-driven economy, production and reward systems place less emphasis on egalitarianism and more emphasis on efficiency and performance (Shenkar and Chow, 1989). As a result, performance appraisal has become the crucial link between performance and rewards, and achievement has been given high priority in appraisals.

Since the reforms, different assessment methods for cadres have been adopted (Chen, 1990; Su and Zhu, 1992). One approach is a computer-aided panel assessment. The panel at each enterprise draws up more detailed categories under each of the four major criteria (i.e. *de, neng, qing* and *jie*) and determines a weighting to each category. Panel members allocate marks to appraisees under each category and the data is entered into a computer to obtain final assessment results. This method aims to quantify performance assessment and improve the credibility of performance appraisal. Another approach is position-related yearly assessment, which is more results-oriented. It is mainly based on a cadre's job description and objectives set at either the time of appointment or the beginning of each year, including the quantity and quality of work and task fulfilment. These two assessment methods require detailed criteria to reduce subjectivity and informality as observed in traditional practice. However, the old methods of assessing cadres, such as 'superior-evaluating-subordinate' and comprehensive qualitative evaluation (i.e. self-assessment first, then peer group discussion and superior's final comments) are still being used by many government organizations.

Performance appraisal for shop-floor workers has become more widely used since 1978. Different assessment methods have been tried such as appraisal through 'position specification' where each job position has detailed specifications including quality control, technical requirements, quantified workloads, tools and machine maintenance, labour discipline, caring for the working environment, team cooperation and work safety. Management by objectives (common in Western market economies but quite new in Chinese enterprises) has also been used in work groups, where each individual has specific objectives to complete. 'Internal subcontracting' appraisal has also been used when the enterprise obtains a contract from the state, and the project or production work is subcontracted to internal departments or business units. Each unit is accountable for its profits or losses and the employees are appraised within such units for compensation purposes. These appraisal methods aim to break the old practice of 'eating from the big rice pot' which did not distinguish between high and low performers and did not link performance to rewards. However, these methods still suffer from flaws such as the emphasis given to political considerations, inconsistency in measurement, subjectivity, static rather than forward-looking attitudes and poor communication. They also tend to serve an evaluative rather than developmental or communication purpose.

The extension of labour contracts to the whole workforce has offered a more realistic basis for conducting performance appraisal in enterprises. According to the *Labour Law* of the PRC (1994), 'a labour contract is the agreement reached between a labourer and an employing unit for the establishment of the labour relationship and the definition of the rights, interests and obligations of each party' (Article 16). The renewal of contractual employment 'depends on employees' performance and/or the enterprise's need for their service' (Child, 1994: 165). Labour contracts with workers 'were more matter of fact and were restricted to mutual obligations vis-à-vis a set of defined expectations' (Warner 1995: 131), such as production targets and payment. The requirements specified in the contract can now supply basic criteria for performance appraisal and help enhance the validity of the appraisal process.

With increased FDI, Western-style performance appraisal has been introduced in many FIEs in China. According to the *Regulations for the Implementation of the Law of the PRC on Sino–Foreign Joint Ventures* promulgated in 1983, FIE wage and bonus systems should follow the principles of 'to each according to his/her work' and 'more pay for more work' (Article 39). This has facilitated the adoption of the Western-style reward system that relies more on performance than on age, length of service or political ideology (Child and Lu, 1996). When visiting some FIEs in China between 1994 and 1995, the author noticed that these FIEs all conducted performance appraisal on either a yearly or quarterly basis. The criteria used included knowledge of the job, quantity and quality of work, and managerial skills and the results of performance appraisal were used more for administrative purposes to break traditional 'iron practices', such as the distribution of a bonus, than for communication or development purposes.

In summary, the politically oriented performance appraisal used before the reforms failed to distinguish between high and low performers in the industrial sector, which not only facilitated practices such as the 'iron rice bowl' and the 'iron post', but also an iron wage system (fixed wage rates regardless of performance). In order to break these iron practices, a more performance-related appraisal system has been tried and developed since the reforms. These changes in performance appraisal, in turn, have facilitated a radical reform in China's compensation system.

Compensation and welfare

Compensation, as Geringer and Frayne define it, 'includes those rewards – monetary and non-monetary, direct and indirect – that an organization exchanges for the contributions of its employees, both job performance and personal contributions' (1990: 114). This definition, however, could hardly be applied to the compensation system under the command economy as it was strictly controlled by the state rather than the enterprise. The main feature of this system was its egalitarianism, which was reflected in five aspects: few incentives offered to managers to improve enterprise performance; minimal wage differentials; seniority-based wage promotion; an emphasis on moral-encouragement rather than 'bourgeois materialism' incentives; and low take-home pay but high subsidies and benefits.

The traditional compensation system became a major target of the economic reforms because it was incompatible with the principle 'to each according to his/her work' and failed as a mechanism to enhance productivity. Many enterprises began compensation reform by restructuring enterprises into relatively independent business units where compensation was linked to performance. The state fixed wage system was replaced by diversified wage packages with more emphasis on enterprise profitability and individual performance, and the significance of the bonus system as an important part of the wage package was restored and further developed.

Compensation reform has resulted in a shift from equal distribution to income polarization among employees working in different types of enterprises, especially in private sector such as FIEs.

Linking compensation to enterprise performance was the first important step in compensation reform. In 1984, the central government launched enterprise reform with the main objective to provide incentives for enterprises and individuals to be more efficient (Xu, 1996). A series of new policies and regulations such as profit retention and the separation of management from ownership were introduced. The *Enterprise Law* issued in 1988 and the *Regulations for Changing the Methods of Operation of State-owned Industrial Enterprises* issued in 1992 endorsed further autonomy for enterprises. This autonomy, as defined in the regulations, included assumption of four responsibilities of enterprises: the responsibility for their own business and operations; profits or losses; development and expansion; and legal compliance (*Economic Daily*, 25 August 1992). The *Enterprise Law* states that 'enterprises possess the sovereign authority over incentive award payments and the form of wages as appropriate to the conditions of the particular enterprise' (Article 3). The regulations stipulate that an enterprise's total wage cost should be related to its economic performance. This was the first legal confirmation of the sovereignty of enterprises over internal wage distribution.

As compensation became linked to enterprise performance, diversified wage packages emerged. This was the second main change in the compensation system. In late 1984, the government announced plans to develop measures to link wages and bonuses with improved enterprise performance (Harding, 1987). Since 1985, various changes to the wage system have been introduced, such as floating and structural wage systems. The former introduced a range of wage fluctuations to link individual wages to enterprise and/or individual performance (Takahara, 1992), while the latter covered four components: basic pay, position (job-related) pay, seniority pay (based on length of service) and bonus (Nyaw, 1995). In 1992, the Ministry of Labour introduced a new position-and-skills wage system to facilitate enterprise reform. This system was based on the four major work factors emphasized by the International Labour Organization in 1950: knowledge and skills required; responsibility assumed; work intensity (load) involved; and working conditions. To help eliminate egalitarianism in the old eight-grade wage system, enterprises were required to consider these four components when assembling wage packages. This system allowed enterprises to place different weights on each of the four factors – for example, the knowledge and skills factor has been weighted from 25 to 40 per cent of the wage package (Hu and He, 1992).

The restoration and development of the bonus system is another important change. Though the bonus system was restored in the late 1970s with the aim of ending egalitarianism and rewarding good performance, bonuses still tended to be distributed equally to all workers and managers in a given job grade because it was often regarded as part of the basic wage (Tu and Jones, 1991). Again during the 1990s, the government tried to encourage ways to 'improve the method of linking total wages to economic efficiency and performance' (Warner, 1996b: 218), but the problems of minimal bonus differentials and envy or 'red eyes' (a Chinese phrase for jealousy) remain as significant impediments to linking individual performance to bonuses (Branine, 1997).

Compensation practices in FIEs reflect another major change. FIEs were subject to significantly less stringent government regulations than SOEs but they were not totally free to set their own wage scales until the *Labour Law* was issued in 1994. Since 1994, FIEs have been free to set their own wage scales on the condition that they observe minimum wage requirements and typically have larger pay differentials and higher wage levels than SOEs and collective-owned enterprises (Zhu, Y. 1997). Lump sum allowances are also increasingly popular in FIEs as employers discard the traditional system of paying separate benefits, such as meal, clothing and shower allowances.

Training and development

As with other HR practices, training and development in the industrial sector has undergone transition from centrally planned practices to more job-related activities. Training practices in the industrial sector before the economic reforms were directly affected by a centralized economic planning and regulatory structure as was the education system. Under the planned economy, the education system 'enrolled all students according to state quotas and then all graduates would be assigned by the state' (Laaksonen, 1988: 249). Similarly, at the enterprise level there was 'a consistently high degree of state involvement in the provision and regulation of manpower training resources' (Nyaw, 1995: 202). The traditional education system placed emphasis on general education and obtaining high school certificates, which limited the employment opportunities of junior and senior high school graduates as they lacked vocational skills (Holton, 1990; Zhao, 1994). The higher education system closely followed the Soviet model, taking a narrow approach to course design and placing emphasis on abstract theories rather than practical or vocational training. As a result, many graduates were narrowly trained and lacked the ability to solve practical problems at work. This issue could not be adequately addressed in the training programmes offered by industrial enterprises as the training was centrally planned and usually uniform nationwide, and did not focus on the requirements of a specific job.

The employee training system in the industrial sector was generally divided along worker/cadre lines. The training programme for workers was planned by the Department of Training under the Ministry of Labour. The jurisdiction over cadre education and training rested mainly with the Department of Training of the Ministry of Personnel and the State Education Commission. The training for leading cadres who were Party members was often supplied by the Party's own schools. Training for blue-collar workers primarily took the form of apprenticeships and technical school education (Guan, 1990; Zhao, 1994). The number of apprentices and technical school students was decided by the state, leaving enterprises or technical schools no discretion in filling the quotas as required. Enterprises also had to offer apprentices lifetime employment once they started training. Technical school students would be assigned to an enterprise by the state after completing two to three years of study. Apprenticeships were offered to young people over the age of 16 who had usually completed primary school and would become junior-level skilled workers after one to three years of on-the-job training. Under a highly centralized planning system it was difficult to match each enterprise's training with its production needs, and training was provided mainly for the induction of new workers rather than for the career development of existing employees. This impeded the improvement of the education level of the workforce (Yu and Xin, 1994). The training for cadres was usually politically oriented, which led to a shortage of competent managers and became a serious problem during the reform period.

The economic reforms provoked dramatic changes in the work environment of most Chinese enterprises. Increased decision-making powers have changed the manager's role from 'merely an administrator responsible for carrying out government orders to a manufacturer and marketer of goods with full powers to decide on management matters and full responsibility for the enterprise's performance' (Sha, 1987: 699). Therefore, performance of Chinese managers no longer depends 'as much on political or technical aptitude as on the ability to pinpoint market opportunities, to solicit financing, and increasingly, to match competition from foreign enterprises' (Borgonjon and Vanhonacker, 1992: 12). Managers now need a new set of skills to be successful under the pressure of increased autonomy, competition and uncertainty.

The lack of adequately trained management became a major obstacle to achieving modernization and implementing industrial reform, which led to a demand for urgent training and upgrading of both managerial staff and blue-collar workers. Since the 1980s, many institutions for further education of adults have been established, such as TV Universities and Management Training Colleges. These institutions enrol part-time and full-time students and usually offer only a two-year college associate diploma (called *da-zhuan*).

The State Economic Commission has introduced a nationwide programme of management training, including an MBA programme and some enterprises have sent their managers overseas for training. A survey conducted by the State Planning Committee in 1998 showed that the education level of China's managerial staff was considerably improved by the 1990s: among the respondents (3180 senior managers from industrial enterprises), 40.1 per cent had achieved a *da-zhuan* diploma as compared with 35 per cent in 1990. In addition, 34.3 per cent had bachelor's degrees (four-year full-time university education) and 7.3 per cent had postgraduate certificates (Xie *et al.*, 1999: 70).

While training for managers has been emphasized, further training for vocational and professional skills has been carried out with equal vigour. The first change was a shift from post-employment to pre-employment training, which was implemented experimentally in some areas in the early 1990s and, following its success, was formally written into the *Labour Law* in 1994 (see Article 68). This change aimed to break the 'iron rice bowl' for apprentices by linking training directly to employment, and trainees would be offered a job only after the successful completion of their pre-employment training programme (Guan, 1990).

The requirement of double certificates (educational and vocational) for employment was another major change in training practice. In 1990 the Ministry of Labour promulgated the *Regulations for Worker's Technical Grade Examination* which defined examination content, including political and technical aspects (Zhao, 1994). This examination system, however, has been gradually replaced since the mid-1990s by a vocational qualification verification system. In 1993, the Party Congress adopted a resolution specifying that 'the state should stipulate the qualification requirement and employment criteria for different occupations and adopt the practice of double certificates, education certificate and vocational qualification certificate' (CVQDV, 1994: 8). This was the first time since 1949 that vocational training had been given the same priority as liberal education. The government recognized that the German model of a dual education system was appropriate for China (Guan, 1990), and aimed to achieve a similar outcome as that observed in Germany, where large numbers of young people attained vocational knowledge and skills.

The requirement of double certificates has been not only implemented in most vocational education institutions such as technical and vocational schools, but also introduced to the workforce training system to replace the technical grade examination. This enables workers to take the training course of their choice and offers more flexibility in job selection. The double-certificate practice has also been extended to the private sector to increase the technical competence of self-employed people and the rural labour force (CVQDV, 1994). The adoption of double certificates was legitimized in the

Labour Law in 1994. This clearly indicates that reform in the training system is striving 'to develop professional skills of labourers, improve their qualities, and raise their employment capability and work ability' (*The Labour Law*, Article 66). The new policy helps maintain a balance between theoretical knowledge and practical skills, supplying the labour market with technically competent graduates rather than with school-leavers lacking vocational skills.

Labour relations

Labour relations or industrial relations have been defined in the West as the study of the employment relationship in industrial and industrializing societies (Poole, 1998). This usually includes both formal and informal dealings between workers and managers and/or employers with respect to wages and welfare, conditions of work, unionization of employees, collective or individual bargaining, and the right to strike. However, according to Chinese sources (Xia, 1991: 544), labour relations represent 'different employment relationships in different systems'. Such sources view that in a capitalist economy an unequal relationship exists between employers (or managers as their representatives) and employees, with the former always exploiting the latter. In contrast, as part of the features of a socialist country, labour relations in China are supposed to involve a mutually cooperative and mutually beneficial relationship between the state, enterprises and employees. Therefore, the Chinese system of labour relations has characteristics quite distinct from those in the West. While trade unions in the Western market economy 'seek, through collective action, to give workers a formal and independent voice in setting the terms and conditions of their work' (Noe *et al.*, 1997: 562), and are viewed by workers 'as a citadel from which they can bargain with management from a position of strength' (Tung, 1982: 228), the unions in China served as a pillar supporting state power and were used to 'transmit the Party line to workers, encourage production, engage in political education, and execute a range of welfare chores' (Hoffmann, 1974: 134). The unions were also called the 'transmission belts' (Poole, 1986: 92) and were 'fundamentally different from the unions in Western democracies' (Lee, 1986: 159) in terms of their organization, functions and roles, and the members they recruited.

China's trade unions, under the All-China Federation of Trade Unions (ACFTU), were established in 1925. From 1949 onwards, the ACFTU undertook a national role except during the Cultural Revolution period when it went into abeyance. The trade union constitutions stated that unions were Chinese working-class mass organizations led by the CPC and formed voluntarily by workers and staff. However, the Party dominated from the outset, as it controlled the policy-making of unions, supervised policy implementation, and scrutinized and evaluated the performance of union cadres (An and Feng, 1991). The Party also appointed senior union staff and these officials sometimes exchanged roles with enterprise managers.

Trade unions were organized vertically with councils at central, provincial, municipal and organizational levels. The ACFTU had departments dealing with the economy, finance and accounts, international issues, propaganda, training, safety, wages and women's needs. The councils at lower levels handled similar activities with rules from above rather than below (O'Leary, 1992). The trade unions had to undertake endeavours in the four main areas of protection, construction, participation and education (An and Feng, 1991). First, the unions had to protect and defend employees' legitimate rights, safeguard their interests and act as caretaker. They needed to channel employees' opinions, needs or grievances about their work and life to the Party and higher authorities so policies could be adjusted. Second, trade unions had to organize employees to fulfil state production plans and stimulate employees' enthusiasm for work in order to raise productivity. This usually involved launching socialist labour emulation campaigns to encourage workers to participate in technical innovation activities and recommending outstanding employees as models for others. Third, the unions had to educate and prepare employees to exercise their democratic rights in management participation. Finally, trade unions were required to conduct ideological, cultural and technical education programmes for employees to raise their political consciousness, and enable them to act according to the Party's policies and be competent in their positions.

The trade unions' four broad aims covered two major functions: administration and representation. Under the planned economy, trade unions were always required to follow policies and regulations of the Party and the state and were thus disproportionately geared to the 'administrative function rather than representative' (Warner, 1995: 37). This is evident in the services provided by trade unions in the welfare system including various insurance and welfare benefits for employees. Furthermore, the representative function of trade unions for employees was reduced by their exclusive membership requirement, as only permanent employees could join unions and become eligible for welfare benefits administrated by trade unions. This restriction denied union protection to temporary and contract employees and was one of the reasons for the collapse of unions during the Cultural Revolution when they were criticized for their 'welfarism and economism' on behalf of urban employees who held tenured positions (Dixon, 1981: 130). 'Economism' meant that trade unions had put the short-term interests of workers before the long-term interests of the nation (Leung, 1989).

In brief, the most distinctive feature of pre-reform labour relations in China was an administration-oriented relationship among management, trade unions and employees. Without operational independence, trade unions could only act in a consultative manner and inevitably became part of the Party's organizational structures, in effect, another 'official department' (Zhao, 1995: 355) or 'another voice within the state and Party apparatus' (Chan and Senser, 1997: 113). Since the reforms, management (especially managers in FIEs and POEs) has been granted more autonomy to hire and fire employees, to determine employee compensation packages and to abolish lifetime employment. Labour relations in China now are no longer only between employees and the state, but also between workers and foreign investors or their representatives, and between private employers and managers who have become legal representatives of enterprises.

Many labour-relations disputes have occurred since the reforms due to unjustified dismissals, inequitable wage packages and even physical punishment (Chan, 2001). Ann (1996) argues that trade unions could play an important role in reducing such disputes and conflicts by participating in more activities. These include developing a series of labour-related laws and regulations, such as a 'Labour Protection Law' and 'Minimum Wage Law'; assisting and advising individual workers when they sign labour contracts, and supervising the implementation of contracts; advocating the adoption of a collective contract and signing the contract on behalf of employees; being actively involved in mediation of labour disputes; and supervising the implementation of Labour Law within the enterprise. Ann's argument raises the question of whether trade unions need to adjust their traditional practices to play a greater role when industrial disputes surface.

As the trade unions remain a non-Party apparatus to link the Party and workforce and to facilitate management, 'there is little comparison between Western collective bargaining and the Chinese model of labour management with the trade unions in a subordinate role in the enterprise' (Warner, 1993: 49). This is especially true when the Party endeavours to strengthen its position in enterprises, especially SOEs. In a document issued by the Party, the *Notice of Further Strengthening the CPC's Role and Improving the CPC's Construction Work in the State-owned Enterprises* (see *People's Daily*, 11 March 1997: 1), the Central Committee stressed that the political leadership of the Party over enterprises is always of great significance and the Party branch of an enterprise should be involved in major decision-making in areas such as business strategies, development planning, budgeting, and hiring and firing of middle-level and senior-level managers. The document also emphasized that all cadres of the SOE (i.e. managers and white-collar employees, including heads of trade unions) should be managed by the Party. It signifies that only the Party branch has the power to recommend higher level managers as the head of the trade union and to scrutinize the hiring and firing decisions made by the general manager or the board of directors. The Party branch is also responsible for training, appraising and monitoring managerial staff at all levels. Considering the emphasis placed on the Party's authority in enterprises, there is no doubt that the trade unions have to adhere to the Party's instructions.

However, while trade unions are still passive supporters of management in SOEs, in FIEs or POEs they may gradually become active defenders of workers' interests, as 'one unique aspect of the trade unions of joint ventures in China is that they deal directly with foreign partners or their representatives with regards to labour disputes or grievance' (Nyaw, 1995: 210). Trade unions are not mandatory in FIEs, but the *Labour Law* has legitimized the right of workers to form and participate in trade unions. The ACFTU announced a campaign to organize unions in all overseas-funded enterprises in 1994, and reported that 48,000 out of 120,000 such enterprises had been unionized by 1996 (Chan and Senser, 1997). Although Chan and Senser argue that trade unions have little or no impact even when they are in place, the government has still called for the establishment of trade unions in these enterprises to protect local employees from being exploited or unfairly treated by foreign investors or private employers. Therefore, trade unions will help the state to monitor and supervise foreign partners of joint ventures (when foreign investors hold the majority of ownership), owners of wholly foreign-owned companies or private owners in implementing the *Labour Law*, especially in areas of employee compensation, training and contract termination.

CONCLUSIONS

The previous discussion reveals how cadres and workers in the industrial enterprises were managed under the Maoist model which was characterized by its heavy industry-oriented Stalinist big push strategy, a socialist command economy system and the radical principles of Maoist ideology. These three major parts of the model formed key contextual variables in the domestic economic environment before economic reform, because China had adopted a closed-door policy and the global environment was ignored. The two major components in the command economic system were the planning system and the ownership structure. Under the command economy, a highly centralized planning system and public ownership structure deprived enterprises of any autonomy to manage their own operations, which led to 'puppet-like' enterprise management with extensive involvement of the government and traditional labour and personnel administration. Although the three parts of the

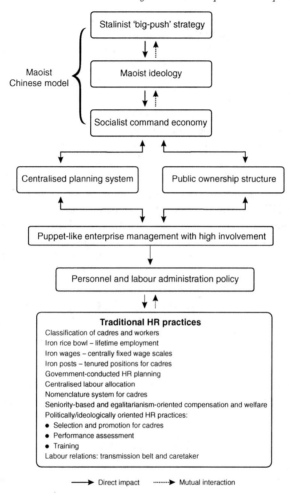

Maoist Chinese model

Stalinist 'big-push' strategy

Maoist ideology

Socialist command economy

Centralised planning system

Public ownership structure

Puppet-like enterprise management with high involvement

Personnel and labour administration policy

Traditional HR practices
Classification of cadres and workers
Iron rice bowl – lifetime employment
Iron wages – centrally fixed wage scales
Iron posts – tenured positions for cadres
Government-conducted HR planning
Centralised labour allocation
Nomenclature system for cadres
Seniority-based and egalitarianism-oriented compensation and welfare
Politically/ideologically oriented HR practices:
• Selection and promotion for cadres
• Performance assessment
• Training
Labour relations: transmission belt and caretaker

⟶ Direct impact ┈┈▶ Mutual interaction

Figure 2.1 Traditional PRC model of Personnel and Labour Administration

Maoist Chinese model were interrelated and interacted (as shown by arrows with both straight and dotted lines in Figure 2.1), their impact on enterprises and their management was generally one-way and top-down, as enterprise managers, especially HR managers, were merely instruction-followers and administrators. This model of traditional personnel and labour administration (henceforth referred to the traditional PRC model) is shown in Figure 2.1.

In Figure 2.1, traditional HR practices (listed in the bottom box) might exert some influence on the policy of personnel and labour administration (as indicated by the arrow with a dotted line). The traditional PRC model managed people in a way that was administrative and politically/ideologically oriented. Since the late 1970s, the central planning system and public ownership structure have been subjected to two types of economic reform: operational reform and ownership reform. Operational reform involved decentralization and deregulation of the central planning system and a gradual separation of enterprises from government administration. Ownership reform has facilitated changes within public sector enterprises and the establishment of enterprises with mixed ownership forms. With the introduction of the modern enterprise system, fewer constraints have been imposed by the government and enterprise management has greater autonomy. The management of human resources in the PRC has gradually moved away from the traditional HR practices, and there has been a sea-change in HR practices in Chinese industrial enterprises. These developments include the recognition of concepts of Western-developed HRM, at least in terms of policy, by Chinese professionals and practitioners, and the adoption of some HR activities such as merit-based recruitment and selection, performance-linked compensation, and job-related training.

Increased research into HRM issues in the Chinese context has contributed to an expansion of knowledge in this area (e.g. Ding and Akhtar, 2001; Leung *et al.*, 2001; Warner, 1998a, 1998b; Whiteley *et al.*, 2000). Most of these studies, however, were conducted through 'direct investigations by Westerners' and were 'qualitative rather than quantitative oriented', (Xie, 1995: 25). There has been very little research that systematically examines current HR practices such as planning, staffing, appraisal and compensation in Chinese industrial enterprises through both quantitative and qualitative approaches, and especially, across enterprises with different types of ownership. Furthermore, as a result of economic reform, ownership structure has changed significantly in China's industries. The economy is no longer dominated by SOEs, it enjoys different ownership forms, including collective-owned, private-owned, and foreign-invested enterprises, which coexist and compete. The number of people working in the private sector jumped from 1.84 million in 1991 to some 100 million by the end of 1999 (Wang, 1994; Xiao, 2001), while the number working in SOEs dropped dramatically from about 100 million to 49 million (*China Labour and Social Security Yearbook*, 2001: 524–41). This raises the question of the extent to which the type of ownership has an impact on HR practices. Since 'management processes are radically different in the different types of enterprises' (Shenkar, 1994: 21), external constraints such as 'ownership structure and the role of the State' should be integrated into the concept of HRM research (Brewster, 1995: 13) and are a focus of the study reported in this book.

3 Research methodology

This chapter outlines the rationale for the research methodology used in this book and describes the design and conduct of the case studies, and the survey research component of the study, including the development and distribution of questionnaires and techniques used for survey data analysis. The research questions examined in this book focus mainly upon the 'what, how and why' of HRM in Chinese industrial enterprises, especially those with different types of ownership. Given that HRM in Chinese industrial enterprises, especially in the non-state sector, is an under-researched area (see Chapter 2), the author concluded that an exploratory approach (Yin, 1994) was the most appropriate method of analysis.

FOCUS AND AIMS OF THE RESEARCH

This research focuses on HR practices in Chinese industrial enterprises with different types of ownership, including SOEs, COEs, POEs and FIEs. Pre-reform personnel and labour administration is examined primarily in the context of SOEs and COEs, as POEs and FIEs have only been established and developed since the post-Mao reforms. HR practices after Mao's regime (referred to as 'HRM' in this study to distinguish them from traditional labour and personnel administration) are investigated across the four types of enterprises and across the major HR activities. The aims of this research are threefold. First, it investigates and describes how human resources in the Chinese industrial sector are managed with respect to the six major HR activities as defined in the West (Schuler *et al.*, 1992). These activities include human resource planning, recruitment and selection, performance appraisal, compensation and welfare, training and development, and labour relations. The effects of economic and enterprise reforms on HRM are analysed and highlighted. Second, our research attempts to explore the impact of changed ownership structure upon HR practices in enterprises within ownership types, that is, SOEs, COEs, POEs and FIEs. Specifically, this exploratory empirical research tests whether ownership type has an impact on HRM and the extent to which HR practices are affected by ownership type. Third, this research suggests probable future trends for the development of HRM in China's industrial sector. Both qualitative and quantitative approaches are employed to gather data.

QUALITATIVE AND QUANTITATIVE APPROACHES

A qualitative approach can lead to 'an in-depth and rich description of specific cases based on the belief that this is the best way to know about some aspect of organizational life' (Schmitt and Klimoski, 1991: 117). As indicated by the research questions, this research is 'interested in insight, discovery and interpretation rather than hypothesis testing' (Merriam 1998: 28), and it intends to investigate a contemporary phenomenon (HR practices in the Chinese industrial sector) within its real-life context (enterprises that are in the centre of the reforms of economic system and management practices and belong to different types of ownership) when the boundaries between phenomenon and context are not clearly evident (Yin, 1994: 13). Given the exploratory, real-life and process nature of the research, the case study method is used.

Although the case study method can derive its rigour from 'the researcher's presence, the nature of the interaction between researcher and participants, the triangulation of data, the interpretation of perceptions, and rich, thick description' as noted by Merriam (1998: 151), its limitations (including issues of validity, reliability and generalizability) need to be carefully managed (Yin, 1994). One of the tactics to address such limitations is also to use a quantitative approach as it 'can indicate relationships which may not be salient to the researcher', while 'the qualitative data are useful for understanding the rationale or theory underlying relationships revealed in the quantitative data' (Eisenhardt, 1989: 538). Thus, the combination of qualitative with quantitative evidence can be highly synergistic.

In this research the author used survey questionnaires in addition to multiple case studies to collect data from relatively large numbers of managerial and non-managerial employees working in the four major types of enterprises. The survey questions covered the main HR activities and addressed those research questions that were more quantitative in nature, such as the extent to which current and future HR activities are and should be conducted and the perceived effectiveness of HR practices. These data support the case study analysis in several ways, as noted by Sieber (1982): the data help correct the holistic fallacy by guarding the researcher against the assumption that all aspects of a situation in the case study fit an emerging theory; the data can be used to support a generalization made from a single or limited case study; observations based on fieldwork can be verified. Finally, 'survey results can cast a new light on field observation, or more precisely, the serendipitous nature of some survey findings can illuminate a field observation that was hitherto inexplicable or misinterpreted' (Sieber, 1982: 187).

DESIGN AND CONDUCT OF THE CASE STUDY

This research used a multiple case or comparative case design, which is regarded as a powerful means of creating theory because it permits replication and extension of individual cases (Eisenhardt, 1989, 1991). Replication helps researchers to perceive patterns more easily and eliminates chance associations. Extension enables researchers to develop a more elaborate theory. Multiple case studies can also help strengthen the validity and stability of the findings (Miles and Huberman, 1994).

Case studies were conducted in four manufacturing enterprises to investigate current HR activities, to compare these activities across the four types of enterprises and to explore the impact of reforms and ownership on these activities. The protocol was prepared at an early stage to help document the entire research procedure, and more importantly, to facilitate the comparative study across major HRM functions in this multiple-case design. It contains four main parts: case study objectives and questions; the selection of case enterprises; data collection strategies including documentation, interview and observation; and finally, a guide for the case study analysis and report. Each part of the protocol is detailed below.

Case study objectives and questions

Three major objectives were established for each case study: (1) to describe current practices of HRM in the enterprise investigated in terms of the six major activities as defined in Western-developed HRM; (2) to explore the impact of ownership types on HR practices; and (3) to describe and analyse probable paths of HRM development in the future as a result of reforms. With these objectives in mind, a list of semi-structured questions was prepared to use in each of the four case enterprises. The first group of questions covered background information on the enterprise, including its ownership type, history, size, structure, business strategy and the perceived role of the human resource function. The subsequent questions were related to management of human resources in the past (where available) and at present with respect to the six major

HR activities. The final questions tried to identify the perspective of managers and employees with regard to the future trend of HRM in the enterprise (see Appendix I – case study interview questions).

Selection of case enterprises

The unit of analysis in this research is the manufacturing enterprise. To select appropriate enterprises, a list of criteria was prepared, including accessibility; location (in well-developed industrialized cities so as to be representative); industrial sector (manufacturing); ownership structure (one for each major type, i.e. state, collective, private or foreign-invested); size (small to medium, because private-owned enterprises in China tend to be in this size category); and operational period (more than two years of operations to enable establishment of formal structure and business operations).

Initial access to the enterprises was obtained through a product division manager at an Australian company that had invested extensively in China. This manager, who was heavily involved in the establishment and businesses of CableCo[1] (a joint venture between this Australian firm and Chinese partners in Tianjin), showed great interest in the research project and agreed to introduce the first author to senior managers of CableCo in China. He also suggested that a SOE, TeleCo (owned by the Chinese parent company of CableCo), be considered for another case study. A comparison between these two companies was facilitated by the fact that they were located in the same city, of a similar size, involved in the same industry and manufactured similar products, and differed only in their ownership type. The researcher contacted senior managers of both enterprises to explain the purpose and nature of the research, and sent them the list of research questions to be used. Both enterprises indicated their willingness to participate in the study and structured schedules for a field study (one week at each enterprise).

After selecting CableCo as an FIE case and TeleCo as a SOE case, the author established access to two other enterprises through personal contact: RadioCo, a COE manufacturing radio products, and ElectroCo, a POE producing electronic equipment. These two enterprises, located in another industrialized city (Nanjing), were in a similar industry and of a similar size to CableCo and TeleCo. The heads and senior managers of the two enterprises promised full support of the research. The researcher was able to spend one week in each enterprise to conduct the case study. The details of each case study are presented in Chapters 4–7.

Data collection strategies

To enhance the validity and reliability of the study, three major data collection strategies were adopted in each of the four case studies, that is, reviewing documentation, interviewing and direct observation.

In the review of documentation, written information sources were studied, such as the enterprise brochure; employee handbook; enterprise policies and regulations, especially those relating to human resource practices (e.g. selection criteria and procedures, performance assessment guidelines and forms, and type of labour contract used); job description handbooks; internal newsletters; enterprise official history book (*chang zhi*) and news from published sources (newspaper, magazine or journal, where available) about the enterprise. Not all these documents were available for every enterprise, and the POE investigated (ElectroCo) had the least written materials of all four case enterprises. However, the documentary evidence that could be obtained helped the researcher to further understand the information obtained from other sources (such as interviews), which offered different perspectives and verification of the same phenomenon (Yin, 1994).

Interviews are used 'to gain insights regarding how individuals attend to, perceive or otherwise deal with some phenomenon of interest' (Schmitt and Klimoski, 1991: 139). They are one of the most important sources of case study information because of their dynamism, flexibility and convenience for follow-up questions or interviews (Marshall and Rossman, 1989; Schmitt and Klimoski, 1991; Yin, 1994). However, willingness to be interviewed is critical for effective interviews with local people in China, and gaining such willingness requires trust, rapport and cooperation between the interviewer and interviewees. The researcher acted as interviewer, because as a native Mandarin speaker with several decades of experience in China and a keen awareness of political and cultural issues, she was able to establish the requisite rapport. During the interview process, the researcher encouraged interviewees to actively participate in the interview and to be responsive.

The format of the interview was semi-structured to allow people to answer more in their own terms than a standardized interview permits and to provide information as they wished. A common set of questions was asked of all interviewees, while additional issues to be explored could be raised, according to the development of the interview. The researcher could thus respond to the situation in hand, to the emerging view of the interviewees and to new ideas on the topic (Merriam, 1998). Interviews were conducted individually for about an hour with all senior managers and middle-level managers, and for about two hours for groups of two or three people of similar occupation and status, such as production workers, supervisors or engineers. A group interview organized in this manner can avoid 'stylized response and deference to the senior member of the group' and encourage each individual to offer their private (or inconsistent) thoughts (Schmitt and Klimoski, 1991). Compared with individual interviews, the group interviews might produce different perspectives on the same issues, but they could 'provide a valuable insight into both social relations in general and the examination of processes and social dynamics in particular' (May, 1997: 114). This method was also efficient in the face of time constraints.

The final issue concerned the setting of the interviews. In order to be free from distractions and interruptions, and more importantly, to maintain confidentiality, all interviews were conducted in the enterprise meeting room behind closed doors. A tape recorder was not used as awareness of being recorded usually creates a mind set that everything said is 'for the record' and can have inhibiting effects (Schmitt and Klimoski, 1991: 145). This is particularly true in the Chinese setting where personal files are held and controlled by management. People interviewed included the number one senior manager of the enterprise (usually called a general manager in an FIE and POE, and a director in a SOE and COE), other senior managers (e.g. deputy general managers or deputy directors), department heads, some supervisors, technical staff and production workers. The details of interviewees are listed in the relevant case study chapter.

The last strategy used for data collection was observation. The researcher stayed for one week (six working days as was the practice in China in 1994) in each of the four case enterprises, visiting both department offices and shop floors, talking with employees at job positions (when permitted by line managers), attending meetings for management and employees, and whenever possible having lunch in the enterprise canteen with managers and employees to engage in informal and friendly discussion. These observations were recorded in the field notes, including descriptions, direct quotations and observer comments. The direct observation helped the researcher to understand each case individually and in as much depth as is feasible (Eisenhardt, 1989).

Data analysis and reports of case studies

The first step in the data analysis was to examine the case study database, which included relevant document records, interview transcripts, field notes and the researcher's own comments and memos. This procedure was followed by the categorization of collected data so that the events, relationships and interactions observed could be understood or explained within the context. This categorization enabled the researcher to substantiate, revise and reconfigure tentative findings identified at the initial stage of data analysis.

Based on the case study objectives and questions, a standardized outline for each case study was prepared. Following this outline and incorporating all categorized data, the case report was drafted. As each case report was completed before conducting the next case study, the researcher was able to become familiar with each case as a 'stand-alone entity', and the process of analysing and writing up the case allowed 'the unique patterns of each case to emerge before investigators push to generalize patterns across cases' (Eisenhardt, 1989: 540).

After each draft report was completed, the draft was sent to key interviewees (the senior manager of the enterprise and manager in charge of HRM) for factual verification and further comment. In some situations the researcher needed to seek further evidence because of discrepancies between the key interviewees and the data obtained. After the corrections and comments were incorporated, another draft was sent to key interviewees for a final review. Although this validating procedure was time-consuming, it enhanced the accuracy of the case study.

Cross-case analysis was conducted after the completion of the four separate cases. Each case study analysis was compared with the research questions and the literature reviewed, and then a comparison of the four cases identified their similarities, differences and emerging patterns. The data obtained from the survey questionnaires were also utilized for cross-case analysis. The combination of qualitative and quantitative evidence in cross-case analysis was used to avoid narrow and idiosyncratic theory and hence 'to raise the level of generality of the theory' (Eisenhardt, 1989: 547), and also 'to build a general explanation that fits each of the individual cases, even though the cases will vary in their details' (Yin, 1994: 121). The cross-case analysis is discussed together with the survey results in Chapter 9.

SURVEY RESEARCH

Survey research was utilized in this study to maximize the benefits of the combined qualitative and quantitative approaches. This part briefly introduces the development of the survey questionnaire, the conduct of two surveys and techniques used in data analysis.

Development of the questionnaire

The survey questionnaire builds upon the work of Von Glinow and her colleagues on best international HRM practices and includes a wide range of topics relating to HRM, such as staffing, performance appraisal, compensation and welfare, training and development, and employee participation (Teagarden *et al.*, 1995; Von Glinow, 1993). Some researchers have argued that the validity of questionnaires designed in the West for non-Western societies such as China is open to question, especially when translation is required (Shenkar, 1994; Xie, 1995). To minimize such problems, the researcher with bilingual skills and personal experience in China verified the translated questionnaire. Some alterations were made in the Chinese version to specify certain terms used (e.g. HRM is used together with personnel and labour administration, and interpersonal ability is specified as the ability to work with other colleagues) and to reflect local management practices (e.g. with regard to recruitment of employees, labour sources are included to see whether there is a legacy of the old allocation or replacement system, and the bonus system is also added as an important part of compensation). A simplified set of characters as commonly used in China was adopted.[2] The revisions in the questionnaire content and format helped the Chinese respondents to better comprehend the questions and increased the suitability of the survey to the PRC context.

The questionnaire covered three major areas, including background information about the enterprise and respondent, current status of the HRM or personnel and labour department, and practice of some HR activities. These items were all close-ended questions, but respondents could add their comments and suggestions at the end of the questionnaire (see Appendix II – survey questionnaire). The results of the survey questionnaire are discussed in more detail in Chapter 8.

Conducting the surveys

The first survey was conducted during 1994 and 1995 (hereinafter called the 1994–5 survey) and survey questionnaires were distributed to 850 managers and employees in the manufacturing enterprises with four types of ownership in three major Chinese cities (Shanghai, Nanjing and Tianjin). A follow-up survey was conducted at the end of 2001 and early 2002 (hereinafter called the 2001–2 survey) and 900 copies of the questionnaire were distributed to people working in the similar industrial enterprises as in the first survey in the cities of Shanghai, Nanjing and Beijing. These cities were selected because of accessibility and their representativeness of most industrialized cities in China.

In both surveys, the author visited the industrial enterprises and had a short meeting with both the general manager and manager in charge of human resources (called the HR manager in this study) in each enterprise, explaining to them the nature and purpose of the survey and giving each of them a copy of the questionnaire to fill in. Then, as agreed, the HR manager recommended 10 to 20 people (depending on the size of the enterprise) to participate in the survey, including managers, engineers and workers from different departments of that enterprise, and arranged a time for them to meet with the researcher.

At the meeting, the researcher outlined her background, explained the purpose and importance of the survey and answered participants' questions. The most typical concern of the respondents was the disclosure of their views. This fear is understandable considering the frequent political purges that people have suffered since the founding of the PRC and the cultural impact of these purges and traditions on people's behaviour (e.g. the emphasis on collectivism and harmony; see Xie, 1995 for example). To reduce such fears and avoid any uncertainty, it was stressed at the meeting that all answers would be kept strictly confidential. Anonymity would be achieved by sealing each questionnaire in an envelope to be collected personally by the researcher or by the respondent's friend (who then forwarded the sealed envelope directly to the researcher).

The 'snowball, chain or network sampling' method (Merriam, 1998) was then introduced at the meeting for further distribution of the questionnaire. This meant each participant was given an extra three to four questionnaires to give to (and also collect from) their friends or acquaintances through their network who met three requirements. First, these people had to work in a manufacturing enterprise with any type of ownership. Second, it was preferred that they worked in different enterprises, and respondents were asked to write down the name of the enterprise. Finally, these participants were asked to pass on the researcher's explanation about the survey to other participants. The researcher revisited each of these enterprises after two weeks to collect those completed questionnaires.

In both surveys some questionnaires were also distributed to managers attending MBA courses at Beijing, Nanjing and Shanghai where the author was involved in the delivery of management training courses. The same method was used for these respondents except that questionnaires were circulated, completed and then collected on the spot. Final response rates for the two surveys were 51.8 per cent (440 out of 850) for 1994–5 and 49.7 per cent (447 out of 900) for 2001–2.

Techniques used for analysing the data

Analysis of survey data was conducted using the Statistical Package for the Social Sciences (SPSS) computer program. In addition to calculating frequency and means of some descriptive items, a factor analysis was utilized to identify clusters of related items (Kline, 1994) when groups could not be categorized in advance. This helped to combine some items that were highly correlated rather than to examine them individually, and to construct informative scales. Various techniques were employed for a range of analyses.[3] For example, paired-sample *t*-tests were conducted to compare the gap between the current and ideal practices of some HR activities, and *t*-values obtained to test whether reported differences were statistically significant. Spearman rank-order correlations were calculated between perceived effectiveness of some HR practices and enterprise performance. In order to explore the impact of ownership on HR practices, a multivariate analysis-of-variance (MANOVA) and one-way analysis of variance (ANOVA) were conducted based on the values (means and standard deviations) of variables. Where only the percentage of HR practices was available, chi-square tests were employed to analyse differences among the practices across the four major types of ownership. For ease of reading, statistically significant values (e.g. *F* value, *t*-value, etc.) are indicated in the tables when their *p* value is smaller than 0.05 or at a better level (i.e. statistical significance is demonstrated) and then discussed in the body of the text. Respondents' comments and suggestions for HR practices in China are categorized and incorporated into the discussion of the survey results.

Limitations of the data

Although the overall response rate at nearly 50 per cent was quite high, the data have two major limitations. First, some HR practices noted in the questionnaire were not used in the enterprise, or employees were not aware of these practices, so they left some questions unanswered. For example, in some enterprises (e.g. the CableCo case study) performance appraisal was solely conducted by managers without employees' knowledge (see Chapter 7).

Second, in the survey there were many questions asking about current practices (classified into 'is now' questions) and ideal practices in the future ('should be'). If only one part of the question – 'is now' or 'should be' – was answered, then the answer was incomplete and was excluded from some processing such as the paired-sample *t*-tests. Some respondents had no opinions about what should be ideal HR practices in the future, and only answered the 'is now' questions. As a result, sample size varies for some items because of missing data.

CONCLUSIONS

This chapter has explained why and how both qualitative and quantitative approaches were used to gather data. Multiple case studies were conducted to provide firsthand evidence on how human resources were managed in terms of the major HR activities. Survey questionnaires were used to gain more information on the situation of HR practices in the industrial sector, to help explore the impact of ownership on such practices and to track trends and changes between the two survey times (1994–5 and 2001–2). These methods provided empirical evidence to enhance our understanding of HRM in China, to explore the impact of ownership on HRM, and to provide the base data for a HRM model for the industrial sector in China.

4 Case study 1

HR practices in a state-owned enterprise (SOE)

This chapter presents the case study of TeleCo, a state-owned enterprise. As in all the case study chapters, a brief review of the enterprise with a particular type of ownership is presented first, and then the data collection methods are detailed. The actual case study begins with an overview of TeleCo, including its history and ownership, size and structure, and business strategy as well as the emerging role of the human resource function in the enterprise. Then follows a description and analysis of HR practices in TeleCo, with emphasis on the six major HR activities.

STATE-OWNED ENTERPRISES (SOES)

As outlined in Chapter 2, private ownership of the means of production was transformed to public ownership soon after the founding of the PRC in 1949, and 'a hegemonic state-owned sector' emerged in the mid-1950s (Jackson, 1992: 55). In 1980, SOEs possessed 90 per cent of the nation's total industrial fixed assets, employed 69 per cent of the country's total industrial population and produced 76 per cent of the national gross industrial output by value. State-owned (*guoyou*) enterprises, referred to officially as 'enterprises owned by the whole people', were called 'state-run' or 'state-operated' (*guoying*) enterprises before 1990, which reflected the true nature of SOEs before the reforms as they were under the direct management and administration of the state. Assets in SOEs are legally owned by the people of the nation, who in theory are represented by the state. Being the owner and administrator of state assets, the government maintained an administrative rather than economic relationship with SOEs under a command economy. This relationship was characterized by three 'unified practices' conducted by the state: unified purchasing of materials and selling of products (*tonggou tongxiao*); unified receipts of earnings and allocation of expenditures of enterprises (*tongshou tongzhi*); and unified allocation of human resources to enterprises (*tongbao tongpei*).

These unified practices led to Chinese SOEs having several distinct features. First, an SOE's 'financial performance was directly affected by negotiations with state planning agencies over its prices, costs, supplies, capital investment, credit and taxation' rather than by its business operations (Walder, 1986: 28). The enterprise was thus constrained by its resources rather than demand: whatever it produced would be distributed by the state. Second, the enterprise was a mini-society. It administered on behalf of the state its labour insurance and social security provisions, and supplied a wide range of public goods and services to its employees. These welfare obligations ranged from housing, cultural and recreational facilities such as schools and cinemas, to barber shops and bathhouses (Ishihara, 1993: 28). Third, the enterprise was also a political institution which had to perform a variety of socio-political services for its employees, such as providing permission to travel or get married and handling residency permits.

This type of ownership gave the state 'the legal authority to reallocate the control rights over and residual claims' from SOEs, even if the rights had been delegated to lower levels of government (Qian and Weingast, 1997: 258). While state ownership enabled the government to pursue its heavy-industry oriented development strategy, SOEs, as the foundation of the planned economy, became the favoured recipient of government support, and were heavily subsidized and staunchly protected by the state. As a result, there were few budget constraints for SOEs (see for example, Kornai, 1986; Naughton, 1996; Warner, 1996b). This level of protection encouraged the development of problems such as overstaffing and low efficiency.

When ownership reform started in the 1980s, it aimed to reform the existing ownership structure and state ownership *per se* (Dong, 1992). The reform of the ownership structure resulted in an upsurge and the flourishing of non-state enterprises with various types of ownership, which in turn created intense competition between state and non-state enterprises. The 1984 *Provisional Regulations on Further Extending the Decision-making Power of the State Industrial Enterprises* offered SOEs more autonomy and due rights in their business operations. In 1992, the government decided to steer SOEs further into the market, holding them responsible for their own profits and losses, even in the face of bankruptcy. After the 14th Party Congress in 1992, the term 'state-owned enterprises' formally replaced 'state-run enterprises', indicating the government's intention to withdraw from enterprise management.

In spite of the reform of SOEs, they still carried burdensome social mandates and restrictions and required huge state subsidies, with many remaining inefficient. In the early 1990s, the labour productivity of foreign-invested and private-owned enterprises was over three times that of SOEs (Yabuki,

1995: 49). Although the number of SOEs has been declining and the non-state sector has grown rapidly, ownership reform in SOEs is still regarded as critical because public ownership (including state and collective) has always been emphasized by the Party and government as a dominant form of ownership and regarded as 'the key characteristic distinguishing the socialist market economy' proposed in China (Liew, 1997: 87). New SOE reform initiatives introduced in 1994 emphasized two major tasks: the introduction of a modern enterprise system through corporatization and shareholding, and the restructuring of SOEs. While the former aimed to transplant the Western public enterprise model into China to enhance internal efficiency, the latter tried to reduce their debt burden, shed their surplus labour, divest them of their obligations to provide community services, and allow the state to withdraw from the ownership of competitive industries.

The progressive reform of SOEs has profound implications for their HR practices as discussed in Chapter 2. Although SOEs, especially large and medium-sized ones, usually 'have the full stereotypical apparatus of Chinese labour-management relations with a consistent set of personnel practices' (Zhao, 1994: 7), 'one of the core problems of SOEs is their poor personnel management' (Mai and Perkins, 1997: 17). Also, the concept of Western HRM is not found in Chinese enterprises, particularly SOEs (Child, 1995). However, some researchers (e.g. Warner, 1999, 2000; Whiteley *et al.*, 2000) have observed that HR practices in SOEs are gradually moving away from the traditional personnel and labour administration activities, even though current practices are still 'more operational (wage, social welfare calculations) than strategic' (Benson *et al.*, 1998: 13). The TeleCo case study is used to illustrate how employees were managed in an SOE before and after the commencement of reforms.

DATA COLLECTION METHODS

Methodological triangulation was adopted in each case study. Documentation included TeleCo's position descriptions within each department, internal newsletters and paperwork on the factory's history. Direct observation was made during the one-week field study at TeleCo, where the author was shown around the factory and given free access to workshops to talk with managers and employees. The researcher also attended one department meeting on the fulfilment of production plans. The interviews were conducted entirely on the factory's premises, and 21 people were interviewed (see Table 4.1). The Director/Party Secretary of TeleCo had been appointed by the Municipal Post Bureau only eight months prior to the study of this case, so he was only interviewed once. The Deputy Director in charge of the factory's administrative management joined TeleCo

Table 4.1 Interviewees – TeleCo case study

- Director/Party Secretary
- Deputy Director (production)
- Deputy Director (administrative management) (3 interviews)
- Deputy Director and Chairman of the trade union of TeleCo (trade union)
- Manager of Party Committee Office (Party and personnel affairs) (2 interviews)
- Manager of Administration Office (labour and wage) (2 interviews)
- Manager (Quality Control Department)
- Manager (Research and Development Department)
- Manager (Production Department)
- Line Manager (Workshop 1)
- Line Manager (Workshop 2)
- Supervisors (4, interviewed in two groups, each of 2)
- Production workers (6, interviewed in two groups, each of 3)

when it was established 25 years ago and had worked there since. He was therefore interviewed three times, supplying and later assessing detailed information on TeleCo's past and current situation.

CASE ENTERPRISE – TELECO

Enterprise history and ownership

In late 1969 as the result of the Cultural Revolution, the Municipal Post and Telecommunication Bureau (hereinafter referred to the Post Bureau) merged its three small factories to form TeleCo. During that turbulent period, thousands of cadres and intellectuals were sent to factories or countries to undertake manual labour. This practice was reinforced by Mao's speech on 7 May 1969 that cadres should take manual work regularly to better serve the people. To follow Mao's teaching, many 'May 7' cadre schools (*wuqi ganxiao*, mainly in the country) and 'May 7' factories (*wuqi gongchang*, mainly in the city) were set up for cadres, including intellectuals, to participate in manual work. The Post Bureau was no exception. It established TeleCo as a 'May 7' factory for its cadres, including managerial and technical staff.

TeleCo was the Post Bureau's only manufacturing subsidiary. When the factory was set up, politically unreliable cadres and some workers from the Post Bureau were transferred there and some relatives of the Bureau's staff were employed as TeleCo's permanent employees. In early 1970, the municipal government allocated 60 demobilized soldiers and about 40 middle school students to the factory (between the late 1960s and the mid-1970s, millions of young people were sent to rural areas, and some were assigned to factories to be 're-educated' by farmers and workers). At that time the factory had about 200 permanent employees in addition to cadres from the Post Bureau engaged in manufacturing cables and other equipment and devices for telecommunications.

Before the reforms, TeleCo, like other SOEs, strictly adhered to state plans without worrying about inputs and outputs so long as production quotas were fulfilled. However, during the transition period of the economic system, TeleCo found it hard to compete in the market because of various problems. First, the factory was constrained by its financial resources. The factory was not only owned but also operated by the Post Bureau, and the profits it had made were all submitted to the Bureau. TeleCo's total fixed assets in 1993 were only 10,000 yuan per employee on average, and this value was probably an overestimate as the depreciation rate was fixed at a very low level by the state. Although their equipment was 15 to 20 years out of date, the factory could not purchase new equipment because the Post Bureau feared a poor return on the investment. Second, the number of non-production employees was excessive and human resources were of low quality. The ratio of production to non-production employees should normally be 100:14–17, but it was 1:1 in TeleCo. As well, many workers allocated in the 1970s had not received a proper education because of the Cultural Revolution. In addition, the factory had never conducted regular training programmes to update the knowledge of its employees.

Third (and the most important issue in the eyes of the Director), SOEs could not compete equally with non-state enterprises because many state-imposed restrictions led to heavy burdens and rigid structures. For example, the factory supplied various welfare services to its current and retired employees, such as housing, health care and pensions. In 1993 the factory paid out more than half a million yuan in medical expenses for over 100 of its retired employees. In addition, dismissal of employees was not permitted unless criminal offences had been committed. The factory was also not allowed to offer commissions to the purchasing agents of its products to facilitate sales, while non-state enterprises commonly employed this practice. Finally, the factory had suffered from the frequent change of directors – four within a three-year period (1991–3). One was demoted because of embezzlement, one was transferred to another firm because of poor performance, one died and one was appointed at the end of 1993.

The factory operated at a loss continuously from 1990 to 1993. The loss in 1993 was 6.5 million yuan, while the accumulated debt by the end of 1993 was 12 million yuan. As the factory's total fixed assets were worth only 4 million yuan, it was theoretically bankrupt. However, with the Post Bureau's protection, TeleCo was given a 'policy loan' (loan without interests) to pay its employees, and was exempted from paying tax on revenue in 1993 and 1994.

Organizational size and structure

In 1994 TeleCo employed 438 staff and workers and had 112 retired employees on its payroll. This meant that every four current employees supported one retiree. Among 438 employees, 98.6 per cent were permanent and the rest were on contract. The factory's total production output value in 1993 was 10 million yuan, or just over 22,000 yuan per head annually. However, the figure for the output value per head in 1993 should only be used for reference, because up to 1994 the contract management responsibility system (CMRS) was still in existence and contracts used in the CMRS were negotiated individually between the enterprise and its supervisory agency. The system encouraged enterprises to negotiate lower output quotas and tax rates to ease their budget position (see Chai and Docwra, 1997; Wong *et al.*, 1995). This would also help SOEs to gain institutional rent if they could sell their output above the quotas negotiated with the state at the market price.

The factory had two offices, nine departments and three workshops as shown in Figure 4.1. The Administration Office, also called the Director's Office, was responsible for two major tasks: to assist the Director and Deputy Directors in their administration work, and to manage labour and wages, including annual HR planning, workers' transfer or employment, wage reform and training. It was also in charge of the workers' personal files (*dang'an*). If a worker wanted to transfer to another enterprise (except for foreign-invested enterprises, which could recruit employees without their personal files), he/she had to obtain permission from the factory to have the personal file transferred as well.

The Party Committee Office reported to the factory Party Committee and was in charge of the administration of cadres, both technical and managerial, Party and non-Party. This office was responsible for each cadre's appointment, transfer, assessment and training. It also kept all cadres' personal files. Each office had a manager who reported directly to the Director and Party Secretary of the factory. Factory director and Party secretary had been two separate positions before the 1990s but was one position when the case study was conducted.

A Deputy Director (administrative management) was in charge of six departments. The Administration Department managed logistical affairs such as the infrastructure and facilities, while the Planning and Accounting Department was responsible for accounting and finance, and determined

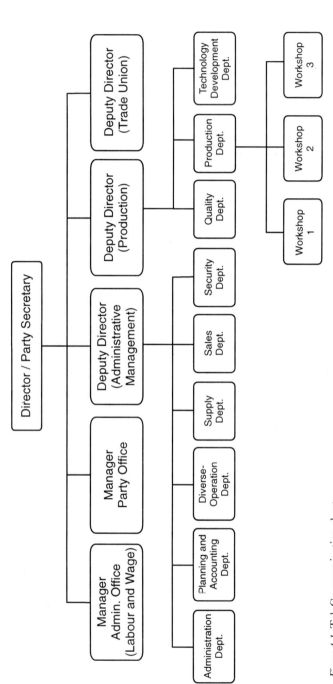

Figure 4.1 TeleCo organization chart

the allocation of funds to each department. The Diverse-Operation Department focused on the development of diversified businesses, mainly in the service industry, so as to create more jobs for redundant employees of the factory and to increase TeleCo's total revenue. The Supply Department was in charge of obtaining all material inputs for production, while the Sales Department marketed the enterprise's products. The Security Department had a range of responsibilities, such as ensuring factory's security, creating production safety devices and rules, and vehicle maintenance.

Another Deputy Director (production) was responsible for all production-related work, including production, quality control and technology development. There were three workshops in the Production Department with 150 production workers. Each workshop was led by a Line Manager and an Assistant Manager. In each workshop there were several production lines or working groups, each of which had a supervisor. The third Deputy Director was the chairman of TeleCo's trade union, and was responsible for all union work. By state regulation, the head of the trade union in this type of enterprises is automatically a deputy director.

Business strategy and the emerging role of the HRM function

TeleCo's mission was 'to be guided by the market and to seek survival by producing quality products'. Its business strategy since early 1994 was 'to face the market, adopt marketing techniques, reinforce management, and change the loss-making status'. As the Director explained, the factory had to ascertain the market demand and organize its production accordingly. The factory's main product was telecommunication cable, for which the market was very competitive, with over 3000 cable manufacturers in China in 1994. The establishment of a joint venture between the Post Bureau and an Australian company to manufacture the same products further intensified such competition (see Chapter 7 about this joint venture). In order to survive, the factory had to develop new products and diversify its service industry business whenever opportunities emerged.

In addition, TeleCo had to use direct marketing techniques to increase its sales rather than waiting passively for Post Bureau to distribute its products. Before 1990, all the cable produced by TeleCo was purchased by the local telephone company, another subsidiary of the Post Bureau, regardless of price or quality. However, with the reforms, the Telephone Company became financially independent and began to select better quality products at lower prices. TeleCo was forced to compete in the market, and thus marketing skills and strategies to find suitable markets became crucial. The

Director stressed that personal connections and networking were important in marketing (he had brought a lot of customers to TeleCo) and he encouraged employees to develop a similar network for promoting TeleCo's products.

Furthermore, TeleCo had to reinforce its management by adopting management by objectives, linking bonuses more closely to each employee's performance and creating competition within the factory. The factory would draw up detailed production objectives to be completed by every department, production line and work team. Bonuses would then be distributed according to the objectives achieved. With an excessive number of non-production employees, the factory planned to abolish redundant positions and let employees compete for the remaining positions. Only the most competent employees would keep their positions, the rest had to be relocated.

To implement the strategy, the factory tried to foster its own enterprise culture, expressed in the slogan: 'to work hard together, to be innovative and enterprising, to feel happiness at TeleCo's prosperity, and to feel shame at TeleCo's decline'. The factory's senior managers pointed out that the acceptance of this culture by employees depended on the effective management of human resources. During Mao's regime, the personnel and labour administration was heavily dependent on ideological education and egalitarian distribution. In order to survive in a market-oriented economy, the factory required not only new products, but quality products at a low cost. Boosting employee motivation to work hard and efficiently and aligning their interests with the enterprise's had become challenging issues for managers, especially those in the HR area. Managers interviewed for this study all believed that the traditional HR practices had to be further reformed to effectively differentiate between high and low performers in order to offer employees better incentives and to help nurture the enterprise culture.

While managers admitted that TeleCo needed better HR practices, the factory did not have an independent department to manage its human resources. From 1983 to 1992, all human resources (cadres and workers) were managed by the Administration Office. In 1993, the factory's 120 technical and managerial cadres were placed under the control of the Party Committee's Office. By separating the administration of cadres from that of the workers TeleCo hoped for better control of the quota for cadres as well as of their appointment, promotion and performance appraisal.

HR activities at TeleCo

As TeleCo had been in operation since 1968, it, like many other SOEs, had experienced centralized control of its human resource. By 1994 when this case study was conducted, it had experienced 15 years of operations under the reforms. This history of TeleCo allows a number of issues to be considered. First, are SOE employees now managed in a way that is quite different from the old practices because of reforms? Second, does state ownership still have a great impact on HR practices? Third, what is the future development in HRM likely to be? This section addresses these issues by describing and analysing practices in TeleCo before and during the reforms with respect to six HR activities, that is, HR planning, recruitment and selection, performance appraisal, compensation, training and development, and labour relations.

Human resource planning

Under the command economy, the government at different levels conducted HR planning and then allocated labourers to enterprises. TeleCo itself therefore had not handled this function before the reforms. Yet, when this case study was conducted in 1994, 15 years after the commencement of reforms, TeleCo was still not engaged in formal HR planning. Instead, quotas for its employees were specified by the Post Bureau. The factory was allowed no more than 120 cadres, including five senior managers (e.g. Director and Party Secretary, and deputy directors), five senior engineers and 25 engineers. The rest were managerial and technical staff. Those graduates with tertiary education were all cadres; technical school graduates could be cadres or workers, depending on their job position and the availability of cadre quotas. While the quota for cadres was strictly and directly controlled by the Post Bureau, the total wage bill for workers was fixed by the Municipal Labour Bureau. The factory could alter the number of employees as long as the total wage bill was not exceeded. Only when the governing authority assigned new employees to the factory could the total wage bill be increased.

Within the limits of these quotas, the factory had its own annual plans for retirement and replacement. State regulations specified that cadres should retire at 55 for women and 60 for men, while workers retire at 50 for women and 55 for men. New recruits had to be selected to replace the retirees and any workers who left. As the factory was not running profitably, the bonuses offered were limited, which led some experienced and skilled employees either to resign and join other companies or to transfer to the Post Bureau's foreign-invested enterprise, CableCo (see Chapter 7), for better pay. In 1991, 70 managers and workers transferred to CableCo.

Though TeleCo suffered from overstaffing, it lacked specialized technical people in the area of cable manufacturing. This deficit was caused by several factors, including: the lack of a long-term business strategy and HR planning due to frequent change of directors; the short-term emphasis on replacing retired or resigned employees rather than selecting new recruits to meet production development needs; and TeleCo's lack of power to dismiss surplus or incompetent workers and recruit more qualified ones. In 1994 the factory still had to submit an application specifying the type of technical people to be recruited to the Post Bureau one year in advance for approval. The factory's needs could not always be satisfied because of the constraints on quotas. However, the new Director stressed in the interview that both the Administration Office and Party Committee Office had been required to formulate a three-year human resource plan by the end of 1994 to clarify the type and number of employees to be recruited, kept or relocated based on the factory's business plan and job analysis details.

As part of its HR planning, personnel and labour managers, production engineers and managers at TeleCo were to jointly conduct a job analysis project in late 1994 to specify the duties, responsibilities and workload involved for each job position and the employee characteristics required. The factory only had brief job descriptions for each department as a whole and a description for some production positions. The absence of job descriptions for individual positions, especially non-production positions, has partly contributed to the problem of overstaffing and low efficiency. Once job analysis details become available, the factory could identify and abolish redundant positions and introduce internal competition for each position. The senior managers expected that this competition could keep the best employees at their positions and thus increase productivity. Meanwhile, the factory encouraged surplus employees to set up their own businesses, offering them assistance to obtain business registration, paying them basic wages before their own business started up, allowing them to keep welfare packages, and even investing small amounts of money to help them get started. In return, these self-employed workers or staff had to pay one per cent of their sales revenue to the factory as sort of compensation. In 1994, more than 60 employees owned individual businesses, each earning 20 per cent more than TeleCo's average wage. Those who could neither keep their positions nor develop their own business would remain on the factory's payroll, but only received the basic pay without any bonuses. It was the factory's responsibility to deploy rather than sack them.

Recruitment and selection

Like HR planning, the function of recruitment and selection did not exist before the reform process. In fact, the factory itself had never recruited anyone from external sources before 1985. New employees either were allocated by government authorities such as the Post Bureau and the Municipal Personnel and Labour Bureau, or, as close relatives (sons and daughters) of those who had retired, inherited a position ('occupational inheritance', also called *dingti*). From 1970 to 1975, four groups of demobilized soldiers, high school leavers and graduates were assigned to the factory by government authorities. In 1978, a group of sons and daughters of retired employees was recruited to 'inherit' the positions from their parents.

Since mid-1985, when the government loosened its control over labour allocation, the Post Bureau granted autonomy to the factory to select its own employees from local school leavers and job-seekers recommended by the Labour Bureau, although the number of new recruits was still controlled by the Post Bureau. If the factory wanted to recruit an employee from another city, the Post Bureau handled the appointment. The factory first incorporated written tests into the selection process in 1986.

Since 1990 the factory has been given more freedom to recruit university graduates according to its needs. However, recruitment was still restricted by the quotas set by the Post Bureau. If a university graduate was the child of a TeleCo employee, and held a degree relevant to telecommunication, permission to recruit that person could always be obtained from the Bureau, as it was the only way for the child to return to his/her parent place from another city where he/she studied. Normally, the factory's personnel manager would visit universities to find appropriate candidates. The personnel manager would check their academic records and conduct interviews. A decision regarding employment was usually made after the interview. For each graduate recruited, the factory had to pay the university 4,000 yuan (the 1993 price for SOEs) as an education fee. The manager in charge of personnel complained that 'centralized labour allocation was free of charge but enterprises did not have the right to select, now enterprises could select but had to pay'.

TeleCo used to have more graduates from technical schools because they could be employed without an education fee, and they were not restricted by the cadre quota, as they could be classified as either cadres or workers. Usually they were assigned to production lines and became workers. After 15 years of work experience, they could apply for promotion to technicians (with similar status as engineers). In contrast, university graduates were automatically classified as cadres by state regulation and would normally be promoted to engineers after working for 5 years. The factory normally had to obtain quotas for both cadres and engineers in order to recruit and promote university graduates.

Since 1993 the control of quotas for cadres started to loosen in a number of ways. The cadre quota no longer applied to new university graduates, which meant TeleCo could recruit university graduates while maintaining its current number of cadres. Furthermore, cadres were no longer guaranteed tenured positions and could be appointed as workers if a cadre position was not available or if they were judged to be incompetent for the cadre job. Cadre numbers thus became flexible and the factory had more freedom to take on university graduates if necessary. In the selection of managerial cadres, different processes applied to different levels of management. The factory director was appointed directly by the Post Bureau; senior managers were recommended jointly by the director and the Party Committee Office and approved by the Post Bureau; middle-level managers were selected by the Party Committee Office and appointed by the director. The selection criteria for managerial cadres focused on political reliability, technical competence, previous working performance and education qualifications.

Performance appraisal

During Mao's regime, TeleCo's performance appraisal was conducted annually only for managerial and technical cadres. There were no specific criteria for appraisal. Each cadre was required to submit a self-evaluation of the previous year's work, usually including details regarding one's political attitude and work results. Each individual's narrative would be commented on by his/her direct superior and then the head of department. The main purpose of this appraisal was for promotion or transfer. Since the reforms, performance appraisal has been emphasized and conducted for everyone with different approaches for different groups of people.

The performance of senior managers including directors and deputy directors was assessed annually by an appraisal group composed of a manager from the Post Bureau, the personnel manager from the factory's Party Committee Office, and representatives from TeleCo's Workers' Representative Congress. There were four appraisal criteria: political attitude and practice (*de*), competence at work (*neng*), working attitude and effort (*qing*), and performance record (*jie*). Between 1988 and 1992 while the CMRS was in practice, each senior manager signed an annual individual contract with the Post Bureau. The contract specified the tasks to be completed in that year, thus providing some measurable assessment criteria. The appraisal process started with a self-report on the previous year's work with respect to these four areas. The appraisal group would then comment on this report and give feedback to the relevant manager. The assessment was used to decide whether the individual should retain managerial position. If the manager performed badly because of incompetence or poor interpersonal relationships with employees, he/she would probably be transferred to another position at the same or lower level in another organization of the Post Bureau. A senior manager could be dismissed only if he/she had committed a crime.

The performance of middle-level managers was assessed annually by the Party Committee Office. Each manager was also required to compile a self-report on the previous year's work, focusing on work attitude, ability, achievement and potential area for further improvement. This report would be sent to senior managers for their comments, which would often be returned to the appraisee. The purpose of appraisal was to decide on the continuation of appointment. However, middle-level managers would either retain or lose their positions rather than be transferred to other places.

Technical cadres (including engineers and technicians) were assessed every three years by a Technical Assessment Committee. The Committee had assessment criteria with standardized marks for each criterion. The criteria focused on the research conducted, application of research results, improvements made in production or productivity, and research papers published. The first step in appraisal also required an individual to report on his/her work over the previous three years, including the work completed within this period, problems identified in the work and a plan for the future. Based on individual reports and the Committee members' knowledge of the appraisee's performance, the Committee would then assess each person's performance and give marks accordingly. At the end of 1993, 113 cadres were assessed, with four achieving the result of 'excellent', 105 'good' and four 'average'.

This assessment served two purposes, that is, appointment and promotion. In 1994 the appointment of technical people was still limited by the overall quota. This meant a technical cadre could have the title of engineer without being appointed to the engineer's position. When the case study was conducted, the factory was allowed to have only five senior engineers and 25 engineers. If a replacement was needed because of retirement or resignation, or if the Post Bureau decided to increase the quota, then assessment results would be used to determine appointments or promotions.

Staff working in the non-production departments, including technical and managerial employees, were assessed by the head of each department on a monthly basis. As there were no job descriptions for individual positions, only brief descriptions for each department as a whole, the appraisal criteria were quite vague, with an emphasis on work attitude, cooperation with colleagues and ability to complete the task. Usually the staff wrote a monthly work summary and gave it to the department manager for appraisal. The monthly bonus would not be affected if one had completed the assigned task. As few objective standards were used and the appraisal was conducted in an informal way, there was little feedback for appraisees except for the occasional chat with the department manager when problems occurred in their work. The appraisal became a routine practice and was used only for the purpose of distribution of bonuses.

The assessment of workers' performance, unlike that of departmental staff members, was based solely on their production quantity and quality, and performance results were openly posted in the workshop. Employees working in the production department said they had 'hard' assessment criteria (i.e. quantifiable and measurable), while staff members only had 'soft' ones (i.e. subjective and non-measurable). This was the major reason for differentiation of bonuses between production and non-production employees. Performance appraisal for workers was conducted by their supervisor, who would then send a copy of the assessment to the line manager for record-keeping. The assessment was ostensibly used to link monthly bonuses to individual performance.

Compensation and welfare

Until 1993 a centrally fixed wage system operated at TeleCo; then a number of revisions were introduced. Wage increases became linked to each enterprise's total performance and economic results rather than relying on unified national wage increases. Local government agencies such as the Post Bureau were given more autonomy in deciding the time and conditions of wage increases. One type of wage increase was an adjustment to keep up with inflation and was universal. The other type was wage promotion, which was usually limited by conditions specified by the Post Bureau, such as the quotas for promotion and length of service.

The basic wage before 1993 depended heavily upon one's wage level and seniority. In mid-1993, TeleCo began to use the position-and-skill wage system, under which each person's wage was split into two parts: position wage and skill wage. The former was linked to the responsibility assumed and the latter to skills required. Based on the four aspects of each job (i.e. the knowledge and skills required, workloads involved, labour intensity and working conditions), the Ministry of Post and Telecommunications broadly classified job positions in the telecommunications industry and specified different levels within each position. The ranges for different levels of position wage and skill wage were stipulated by the Ministry and recommended to its enterprises. TeleCo then determined a wage package for each position and its related levels within the factory. For example, workers' jobs were categorized under eight broad positions, with four levels within each position, which were determined on the basis of knowledge, skills and responsibilities involved. This meant employees with the same qualification and similar experience but different work positions received the same skill wage but could receive a different position wage.

Under this wage system, workers were required to sit a technical test to determine their skill levels. Technical staff applying for titles as engineer or senior engineer had to sit a test prepared by the Post Bureau. Employees applying for titles as assistant engineer or technician were tested by TeleCo's own senior technical staff. The tests were offered once a year. If an employee passed a higher level skill test without changing job position, his/her skill wage would be increased. Certain conditions applied to increasing an employee's position wage. The factory Director could exercise autonomy to offer special promotion to two per cent of the employees annually. Employees who were promoted in this way could have their wages increased (both position and skill wages). Some positions, such as engineers and senior engineers, had quotas controlled by the Post Bureau. The factory could only promote someone to a higher position within the limits of this quota.

The new wage system offered incentives to employees who held higher positions with more responsibilities, and also encouraged people to gain more skills. However, two major issues undermined the effectiveness of the new wage system. One was the meagre differentiation between wage levels, for example, the difference between junior, middle and senior levels engineers was only two to three per cent which translates to 15–20 yuan per month between levels at an average monthly wage of 600 yuan. The other was vague classification of positions and levels as the factory had not conducted job analyses and lacked job descriptions.

Before trying different wage packages, the bonus system abolished during the ten-year chaos was restored with the intention of offering employees some incentives. However, bonuses were distributed equally among employees until 1983 and failed to serve as a motivational tool. In 1984 the factory adopted a 'two-level bonus distribution' method, aimed at linking bonuses to the performance of the department, workshop and employees. The two levels were the department and the employee. Each month the factory would determine the amount of bonus offered to each department based on the objectives it had achieved. The department would then distribute bonuses to a lower level. In the Production Department, bonuses were distributed to each workshop according to the quality and quantity of tasks completed, and then the bonuses would be similarly allocated from the workshop to each production line or work group. Employees working in the same production line or group usually received the same amount of bonus except for those with a very poor work record. If the workers were dissatisfied with their bonus, they could seek help from the trade union.

In TeleCo, the ratio of bonuses distributed to the production and non-production departments was 10:6–6.5. The distinction existed to encourage employees to work in production lines and to acknowledge workers' efforts, as they all had 'hard' assessment criteria for their work. Such a bonus system did offer greater incentive to production workers, but was less effective for other groups of employees, especially technical staff and managers. In

TeleCo, bonuses accounted for 30 per cent of an employee's wage package. Although technical staff earned higher position-and-skill wages than workers, the smaller bonus they received minimized the difference between their pay and that of the workers. In addition, bonuses were usually equally distributed among technical staff without discriminating between high and low performers. Technical staff could only receive an extra bonus from the Post Bureau when they accomplished significant results that could lead to a patent. Managers were also dissatisfied with their payment. For example, the factory Director complained of having the most responsibilities, limited autonomy and yet the least benefits, because his monthly bonus was lower than what production workers received.

While the position-and-skill wage system focused on distinguishing between more and fewer responsibilities as well as higher and lower skills rather than between the titles of cadres and workers, some welfare benefits offered still differed dramatically between cadres and workers. For example, cadres at the senior level could receive 100 per cent of their wages as pension upon retirement, while retired workers were paid only 75 per cent of their previous wages. However, cadres and workers enjoyed many similar welfare items, including housing and health care. The money that the factory spent each year on collective welfare benefits, such as building dormitories and paying medical expenses, represented 11 per cent of its total payroll.

Training and development

Before 1975, training was mainly offered to newly recruited workers in the form of apprenticeship. It involved a three-year training period and the apprentice worked closely with his/her supervisor to learn all the necessary skills required for the job. At the end of the period, the apprentice could become a permanent worker at grade-one level if he/she passed a written exam and practical test. This system was abolished in 1975, and the factory had to organize training courses for new workers who were totally unskilled school leavers. This was because vocational education was not popular until the early 1980s, and students from high school had only general secondary education. In the 1980s, training programmes also covered areas such as mathematics and physics as high school education had been severely disrupted by the Cultural Revolution. This kind of training was greatly reduced from the late 1980s when more vocational and technical school graduates were assigned to the factory.

All new employees (including workers and university graduates) were offered one week of orientation and induction, which helped new employees to become familiar with TeleCo's factory history, rules and regulations, business operations, the working environment and tasks to be performed. After induction they were assigned to departments to work with a supervisor. After a one-year probationary period, university graduates could work independently without any assessment, while other trainees (usually workers) could work with little supervision if they passed both written and practical tests.

Before 1993, the training offered to workers was mainly on the job as required by the import of new machines or new technology. A few off-the-job training programmes were also conducted to help workers reduce wastage of raw materials and rejected products, and to prevent workplace accidents. If the Post Bureau required employees to undergo specific training during working time, the factory complied. Once the factory adopted the position-and-skill wage system in mid-1993, it was required by the Post Bureau to offer regular training to its employees, particularly workers, so as to advance their skills to match job demand. The Post Bureau worked out quotas for TeleCo, specifying the number of workers who should reach an education level of grade 12 each year. The Post Bureau also conducted annual assessments of the effectiveness of training offered in its subsidiaries, which formed part of the appraisal criteria of the head of each subsidiary. This exerted pressure on the director of the factory to budget money and time for training.

The factory also encouraged its employees to undertake part-time study at a university or a correspondence technical school. The factory would give workers one to two days off work per month for study and reimburse their tuition fees if they passed all the examinations. Normally, 66 per cent of tuition fees could be reimbursed for university degrees and 100 per cent of fees for technical school degrees. For workers who could not enrol in technical schools or universities, the factory offered a one-day training course every month. The training was conducted by factory technical staff with a focus on the knowledge and skills required for the job. Technical and managerial staff had more training opportunities than workers, as the Post Bureau offered programmes for them, such as new technology training for technical employees and managerial training for supervisors and line managers. It was usually compulsory for the factory to send relevant people on training programmes offered by the Post Bureau. These programs would be conducted in the evenings or take up half a day per week for several weeks. A frequently used training method was to have managerial employees watch management training programmes on TV.

In the early 1990s, TeleCo devised a training plan for technical staff to update their knowledge, but this plan was suspended because of the factory's financial losses. The personnel manager expected to reactivate it once the factory was in a better financial position. The factory Director noted that training was particularly important as TeleCo had to improve performance, update equipment and to develop more new products for the market. These objectives would not be achieved without proper training. Although the Director noted that political education (e.g. building the socialist market economy and eliminating bourgeois liberalism) should be part of employee training, all other managers interviewed believed that training should focus on current production needs and future development.

Labour relations

TeleCo was unionized, and everyone was a union member. The function of the trade union was abolished during the Cultural Revolution and restored in the early 1980s. In addition to the trade union, the factory had a Workers' Representative Congress (also called an enterprise staff-and-worker-council, and hereafter referred to as the Congress) that was re-established in 1984. According to union regulations, in a factory with fewer than 500 people, 15 per cent of employees could be elected to the Congress. TeleCo's Congress had 60 members, proportionately representing technical and managerial staff, and production workers. The Congress was the major channel for employees to participate in enterprise management because Congress members were involved in the factory's decision-making. The Congress usually held meetings twice a year to examine the factory Director's work report and the factory's production and business development plans. Only when the plan was approved by the Congress could it be implemented. The Congress also had several specific groups focusing in the areas of wage and bonus, welfare and assessment, which helped to monitor the implementation of relevant policies and decisions in the factory's plans.

The routine work of the Congress was carried out by the trade union. The chairman of the union was also a Deputy Director but solely engaged in union work. Congress members elected a chairman from a list of candidates nominated by employees. Each department and workshop had an elected union head within that unit. The union head at this level might be a cadre or a worker depending on his/her own job position. They were not given release time for union work, so it was an additional task.

The current union at TeleCo served four functions: assistant to management, caretaker, representative of employees and training programme organizer. As an assistant, the union worked with management to fulfil tasks proposed by the Director, to organize labour emulation activities (*laodong jingsai*) whenever necessary to collect employees' suggestions or recommendations for production improvement and to implement production safety rules. As a caretaker, the union was responsible for employees' welfare, such as allocating housing, visiting retired and sick employees, offering financial help to employees who had temporary family problems and organizing leisure activities for employees. Being the employees' representative, the union helped to channel employee complaints or grievances to relevant managers. For example, if a worker's bonus was reduced by a line manager without apparent justification, the worker could ask the union to talk with this manager. If the manager had justifiable reasons, the union would assist the manager to consult with this worker. If the manager was in error, the union would help to correct the decision (according to the Chairman of the union, this situation had never occurred). If the factory wanted to dismiss an employee, the Congress had to approve the decision. Finally, the union organized training programmes for union members such as workshops on machine maintenance, technical innovation and quality control. The trade union at TeleCo still played the role of the 'transmission belt' between management and employees. The union helped to reduce and even avoid conflict between managers and employees, although it had never been in the position of negotiating with managers on behalf of employees. Simply put, the major task of the union was to look after the employees' welfare.

DISCUSSION AND CONCLUSIONS

This chapter has highlighted the HR practices in a SOE, TeleCo, in terms of six major HR activities as summarized in Table 4.2. It focuses on practices since the reforms, with a brief comparison with the management of human resources during Mao's regime. Before the reforms, these HR activities rarely or only partially existed because of the state strong control over SOEs under a planned economy. The state undertook HR planning, allocated human resources and fixed wage scales for enterprises. Performance appraisal was utilized mainly for cadres and training was generally provided in the form of apprenticeship for new workers. When this case study was conducted in 1994, TeleCo had experienced a series of changes in its management through 15 years of economic reforms, though it was still in transition from having 'state-run' to enterprise-managed HR practices. Although TeleCo exercised more autonomy in its own HR practices, such as the selection of employees and establishment of wage packages, its HR activities were not conducted in the same way as in the West.

Some HR activities were only partially in existence. For example, performance appraisal was emphasized and applied to everyone at the factory. However, it was used only for administrative purpose rather than for

Table 4.2 HR activities at TeleCo

HR activities	Purposes	Features	Issues
HR planning	• did not exist before the reforms • for replacement • to hire university graduates	• constrained by quotas • short-term oriented • no planning for retrenchment	• no job analysis • lack of long-term business strategy • overstaffing but lacking specialized technical people
Recruitment and selection	• not in existence before the reforms • to meet replacement needs • to build a workforce based on the factory's needs	• need to select within given quotas • no standardized procedures • written tests for selecting workers • qualification-oriented for technical staff	• lack of job description • heavy reliance on the individual judgement of personnel manager • the nomenclature system for senior managers
Performance appraisal	• only for cadres before the reforms for promotion and transfer • for reappointment • for promotion • for bonus distribution	• self-report oriented • no formal assessment sheet • 'soft' and 'hard' appraisal criteria	• only for administration purpose • no objective measurement for non-production work
Compensation and welfare	• centrally fixed wage scales before the reforms • to link wages to responsibilities and skills • to link bonuses to performance	• position-and-skill wages since 1993 • some position wages were constrained by quotas • bonus consists 30% of wage package • higher bonus for production workers	• validity of classification of position-and-skill wages in the absence of job analysis • no substantial gap between high and low performers • no performance-linked bonus for non-production employees

Table 4.2 (cont.)

HR activities	Purposes	Features	Issues
Training and development	• to prepare new employees • to improve employees' skill levels as required by the Post Bureau	• often universal and sporadic • mainly on-the-job training • reactive to solve emergent production problems	• lack of funding • no systematic training • no training for career development
Labour relations	• management assistant and employees' caretaker • a bridge between management and employees	• unionized • focus on employees' welfare • assistant to management	• To what extent does the trade union represent workers' interests in terms of their rights and power?

performance improvement or development. Furthermore, with both 'hard' and 'soft' assessment criteria being used, the reliability and validity of performance appraisal was questionable. Similarly, compensation was beginning to link wages to individual job positions and skills, and bonuses to performance. While current practice had moved away from the traditional iron wage system and offered some incentives to employees, the lack of job analysis and objective assessment criteria meant that the links between positions and wages were weak, and the differentiation of bonuses between production and non-production employees was driven by ideology.

Although the terminology describing various HR activities was used at TeleCo, the actual HR practice often existed only nominally or with typical Chinese characteristics. HR planning, for example, was used mainly for replacing employees who left, and was rarely linked to the factory's strategy, as would be the case in the West. Recruitment and selection were conducted without formal selection criteria and procedures, and were limited by quotas. Even so the appointment and promotion of senior managers remained in the hands of the state. These problems could partly be attributed to the context in which these activities were conducted as HR practices were significantly influenced by Chinese rules, regulations and traditional practices, such as quotas specified by the governing authority, state-imposed restrictions on retrenchment, the legacy inherited from the command economy (e.g. overstaffing), and the nomenclature system used for senior managers. Furthermore, the absence of job analysis, unstable leadership, a short history of the TeleCo having its own business strategy and managerial inertia also contributed to an HRM that existed mostly in name only.

Finally, some HR activities, such as career development or collective bargaining, were totally absent from TeleCo. This absence could be the result of lack of funding, HR planning and regular training. In addition, as the factory was under pressure to keep all its redundant employees and relocate them, managers were laden with routine work instead of dealing with long-term issues. The absence of collective bargaining was common in Chinese SOEs, as the trade union was expected to be 'the transmission belt' between the state and employees, and could be regarded as an extension of management. Although the rank of the union chairperson was raised to deputy director, the trade union and the Workers' Representative Congress had little impact on the operations of the factory and never considered negotiating on behalf of workers with the state and management (see also O'Leary, 1994; Unger and Chan, 1996). Some researchers (White *et al.*, 1996) believed that as long as the pre-reform urban *danwei* system stayed basically intact, the union was irrelevant. This is an accurate description of TeleCo's situation in the mid-1990s: employees were still guaranteed employment and permanent jobs, with few on contract.

Although TeleCo's current management of human resources was far from ideal, some HR activities were being recognized as useful and placed on the agenda. For example, TeleCo planned to conduct job analyses to identify its human resource needs and define job positions for the purposes of performance assessment and compensation. This plan was welcomed by the non-production employees, as they wanted to have 'hard' appraisal criteria and more rationally distributed bonuses rather than accepting lower bonuses than production workers. The factory also realized the necessity of having a long-term (at least three years) human resource plan based on its business strategy so as to identify the type of people that needed to be recruited and retained. Furthermore, systematic training of technical staff to update their knowledge and skills was urgently needed to allow TeleCo to compete in the market with new high-quality products. The factory also planned to offer regular training to its workers to improve their skills in preparation for the upgrading of equipment. The business plans that TeleCo was going to implement indicated clear trends in its HR policies and practices, namely, to develop HR planning according to its own needs, to link compensation more closely to employees' performance and to offer substantial training to employees.

From this case study, it is clear that the impact of state ownership on TeleCo's HR practices before and during the reforms has been significant. SOEs were still controlled or affected by the use of quotas, the nomenclature system and the legacy of an 'iron rice bowl' system (to keep surplus employees on the payroll). State ownership had previously protected TeleCo from bankruptcy. However, the introduction of the modern enterprise system meant that the state's protection would be reduced, as would its control over the factory's management. As a result, the factory would face more market competition. Effective management of human resources was expected to nurture TeleCo's culture and to help it achieve its objectives. TeleCo had started to move away from the traditional form of personnel and labour administration but it still has a long way to go before it will have a robust HRM system.

5 Case study 2

HR practices in a collective-owned enterprise (COE)

The second case study was conducted at RadioCo, a collective-owned enterprise (COE), or more precisely, an urban COE under direct control of the municipal industrial bureau. The first section of this chapter presents an overview of COEs in China, including their origins and development, differences from SOEs, business operations and major HR practices before and since the reforms. The case study offers background information on RadioCo, focusing on its HR practices, and concludes with a discussion of the issues arising from the research.

COLLECTIVE-OWNED ENTERPRISES (COES)

COEs are officially defined as 'an economic form in which the means of production are collectively owned by the workers' (Tang and Ma, 1985: 615). Soon after the founding of the PRC, COEs were established by the unemployed in cities and towns, and were based on the principles of voluntary participation, joint collection of funds, group work, mutual benefit and sole responsibility for profits and losses. COEs were also set up with investment from local government or neighbourhood committees. Therefore, COEs 'represent localized socialism because a significant number of the shares are jointly owned by the local community, and while workers may hold some of the COEs' shares, these shares are not legally transferable to non-workers' (Woo, 1997: 103).

While state ownership was dominant before economic reforms, collective ownership was regarded as 'a form of transition from private ownership to ownership by the whole people' (Xue, 1981: 56). COEs were long considered 'the best method to accelerate the development of productive forces for the transformation to fully public property, the highest stage in the future, when the productive forces will be highly developed' (*Beijing Review*, 18 January 1982: 15). Driven by this ideology, urban collectives were often promoted to state ownership or quasi (i.e. local) state ownership during political movements such as the Cultural Revolution (Ishihara, 1993; Wang, 1994). As a result, in 1980, COEs had 23.5 per cent share of gross value of national industrial output (see Table 2.1) and employed 30.5 per cent of the country's total industrial population (69 per cent for SOEs; Yang, 1992: 52).

China's collective sector developed through three main phases (Lockett, 1988; Kraus, 1991): during the socialist transformation of handicraft cooperatives in the mid-1950s, during the growth of neighbourhood industry in the early 1960s and during the job creation push for urban youth in the late 1970s and early 1980s. In this third phase, over 10 million young people, who had been sent to the country to be 're-educated' by farmers during the Cultural Revolution, were returned to cities and, in addition, there were about three million new school-leavers seeking employment each year (Zhou, 1995).

COEs in urban areas were classified into two categories. Those controlled by a district government or local industrial bureau under a municipality or a county were called 'major collectives' (*dajiti*), which more closely resembled state enterprises (see for example, Kraus, 1991; Naughton, 1996), while others, affiliated with a neighbourhood under the district, were 'minor collectives' (*xiaojiti*) (Ishihara, 1993; Qian and Xu, 1993). Both major and minor collectives were usually set up in branches of production that required less capital investment than SOEs, had relatively simple technology and a short production cycle such as handicrafts and simple types of light industry. Some COEs were established simply as subsidiaries of SOEs to help 'absorb' their surplus employees or employees' spouses and children (Xu, Y.C. 1996). COEs were thus often considered less glamorous ideologically, less advanced technically and less important economically than SOEs (Battat, 1986; Lockett, 1988).

Theoretically, COEs were expected to differ from SOEs in their ownership, relations with the state and their HR practices. As COEs were owned by the workforce of the collective sector, management of these enterprises theoretically lay in the hands of the employees, who should have the autonomy and rights to decide on their business operations, such as mergers and asset transfers. Being non-state enterprises, COEs should have a distant relationship with the state, qualifying for fewer subsidies and needing to compete for market share rather than relying on state distribution (Perkins, 1996). COEs were expected to be guided by state plans rather than being bound by them. Furthermore, due to the ownership structure and loose relations with the state, decisions over HR practices, such as staffing and compensation, should also be made by the COE management rather than an external body.

Before the reform, however, these theoretical differences were blurred or even obliterated in practice. Chinese collective ownership was fictitious, as most urban collective property was quasi-state-owned property controlled by various supervising bodies, such as a local government department, rather than by enterprise personnel (Putterman, 1996). Similarly, 'property rights over collective firms were frequently exercised by the corresponding administrative authorities at the next level, to which the collective firm was subordinate' (Kraus, 1991: 116). For example, the government had the right to transfer an enterprise's resources or profits at will (*pingdiao*, Zhu and Dowling, 1994), regardless of whether the enterprise was state- or collective-owned. In effect, COEs were owned by both the collectives and the local government, though the government's dominance was less pronounced in minor collectives than in major ones.

The relationship between COEs and local government was often like the one existing between SOEs and the state. 'The older pre-reform collectives, both rural and urban, had been gradually brought under the control of the planning system, especially at the county level' (Brosseau, 1995: 25.22). Many COEs had little operational autonomy, with local government exercising real control over the management of 'collective' assets, including production plans, sale of products, distribution of profits, funding, investment and personnel. For example, essential materials were allocated almost entirely by state planning bodies according to the principle of 'SOEs first and COEs later' (Ishihara, 1993: 30). This meant COEs received 'second-class' treatment and often had to forfeit their share of materials in situations of low supply. 'By the 1970s, there was virtually not a single enterprise of collective ownership that was responsible for its own profits and losses' (Dong, 1982: 127).

In the area of HR practices such as staffing and compensation, COEs possessed minimal autonomy and were again often treated as second-class enterprises. For example, while COEs, like SOEs, were allocated workers through the state system of labour allocation, they were 'often burdened with obligations that state-owned enterprises were exempted from, such as obligatory hiring of unemployed persons, physically disabled persons and vagrants' (Ishihara, 1993: 30). In addition, COEs were seldom allocated graduate level personnel, and had no access to skilled workers or managers from state enterprises. Similarly, COEs had little power in determining their compensation packages. Wage scales were usually set by the local labour authorities, following a system similar to the eight wage grades for state enterprise workers, but generally below the levels paid in SOEs (Li, W.Y. 1991). The payment of post-tax profit as dividends to COE workers was abolished in 1967 when the Cultural Revolution started (Naughton, 1996). COE employees, particularly those in minor COEs, also received lower pay and very limited welfare or other benefits. For example, few COEs provided housing for their employees in contrast to SOEs. The allocation of low skill employees to COEs and their lower wage levels all contributed to COEs' low productivity prior to the reform.

In 1981, the Party and the State Council decided to invigorate the economy and solve urban employment problems, and local governments were urged to set up different types of collectives with investment from individuals as well as from state and collective enterprises (Sabin, 1994). To facilitate the establishment and growth of COEs, the government not only offered financial incentives through the tax reform (e.g. reduced or adjusted marginal tax rates), but also devolved more authority to collectives. Four major changes in the collective sector were sparked by the reform (Wang, 1994), that is, to let enterprises assume responsibility for profits and losses so as to reduce their dependence on the local government; to return self-autonomy and flexibility to COEs so that they could diversify operations as appropriate; to let COEs design their own wage packages and link compensation to performance and to restore the dividends system in order to offer incentives to collective owners; finally, to encourage democratic management in the collectives through employee participation and a share-holding system for employees.

The 1991 *Regulations for Urban Collectively Owned Enterprises of the PRC*, provided a broad definition of 'collective ownership' and granted collective status to any enterprise in which private individuals owned no more than 49 per cent of total assets. The Regulations give COEs the right to engage independently in production and service activities and to establish their own economic responsibility systems and compensation methods. With the acceleration of the reform, many COEs became more flexible and aggressive than state ones by competing for scarce materials and even 'poaching' SOE markets (White, 1993: 127). Changes in HR practices, especially in COEs, in terms of staffing and compensation have occurred (Cyr and Frost, 1991, Sabin, 1994), as some COE managers claimed that under their jurisdiction they could adopt performance-linked wage systems, hire whomever they wish and lay off workers with advance notification. Their autonomy to hire and fire was reflected in a significant reduction of their workforce. The percentage of people working in COEs among the total industrial population dropped from 30.5 per cent in 1980 to 20.7 per cent in 1999 (*China Labour and Social Security Yearbook*, 2000: 491). Despite the flexibility in staffing, one problem in COEs was the assignment of senior managers via the nomenclature system (Wang, 1994). Most directors or general managers were either assigned by the government or nominated by the government as candidates and then selected by employees via popular vote (*guanding minxuan*). Consequently, residual control rights and rights of alienation (the right to sell the enterprise) remained in the hands of the government.

The devolution of rights had enabled COEs to post impressive growth rates. In spite of a reduced workforce, the proportion of gross industrial output value by COEs increased from 23.5 per cent in 1980 to 38.5 per cent in 1999 (see Table 2.1), compared to a sharp reduction of SOEs' proportion

(76 per cent to only 28.5 per cent). The state's emphasis on the development of COEs has raised some questions. These include whether the flourishing of collective enterprises is partly due to their different HR practices, what changes are evident in the management of human resources in the collective sector, and whether collective ownership has any influence on HR practices. These questions are addressed in the RadioCo case study in this chapter and by the survey results presented in Chapter 8.

DATA COLLECTION METHODS

The data collection methods were the same in this case study as for the others. Documentation included pamphlets on RadioCo's history, brief job descriptions for some positions and performance assessment sheets with detailed criteria for each department or workshop, and for cadres. Direct observation took place during the one-week field study, including visiting each department and workshop, participating in a routine workshop meeting, having lunch in the factory's canteen and talking freely with workers and staff of the factory. Interviews were conducted with 22 people (see Table 5.1), either in the manager's office or in the factory meeting room.

RadioCo was nominally split into two units (Radio Firm and Radio Plant), and therefore had one senior manager who was the Chairman of the Board of Radio Firm, and concurrently Director/Party Secretary of Radio Plant. This manager was the real head of RadioCo. The General Manager was ranked number two in RadioCo, assuming responsibility for day-to-day management work of Radio Firm as well as the labour and personnel administration of the whole factory (Radio Firm and Radio Plant). The General Manager and the two managers in charge of labour and personnel administration were interviewed twice, and the final draft of this case study was checked and commented on by both the first and second heads of RadioCo.

CASE ENTERPRISE – RADIOCO

RadioCo was selected for this study because of its type of ownership, location, the industry it was in and its size. Its features made it comparable with the other three enterprises chosen for the case studies. To understand HR practices in RadioCo during Mao's regime and then the reform era, background information about this factory is presented first, covering its history and ownership, organizational size and structure, its business strategy and the emerging role of the HRM function.

Table 5.1 Interviewees – RadioCo case study

- Director/Party Secretary and Chairman of the Board
- Vice Party Secretary (in charge of the Party affairs Office)
- General Manager (2 interviews)
- Deputy General Manager (production)
- Deputy Director and Chairman of the trade union (trade union)
- Head of Department (Department of Labour, Personnel and Education)
  (2 interviews)
- Manager (Department of Labour, Personnel and Education – training)
  (2 interviews)
- Manager (Department of Labour, Personnel and Education – wage and welfare)
- Manager (Department of Research and Development)
- Manager (Department of Production)
- Line Managers (2, from Workshop 1 and 2 respectively, interviewed in one
  group)
- Line Manager (2, from Workshop 3 and 4 respectively, interviewed in one
  group)
- Supervisors (2, interviewed in one group)
- Production workers (6, interviewed in two groups, each of 3)

Enterprise history and ownership

RadioCo was established in 1958 during the Great Leap Forward when people were urged to participate in industrial production to speed up the construction of the socialist state. At the time, RadioCo was a small cooperative attached to a large state-owned radio enterprise and was run by the family members of the employees of the large enterprise. RadioCo took on the unemployed spouses and children of employees of the radio enterprise and received from it manufacturing orders for some simple radio components such as radio transformers. By 1964 the cooperative had over 100 employees. In 1964 the local district government took control of the cooperative, transforming it from a minor collective (*xiaojiti*) attached to a state enterprise to a major COE (*dajiti*) led directly by the local district government.

In the early 1970s, the district government decided to merge the radio workshop of another collective enterprise and a nursery with RadioCo, which led to an expanded and better equipped factory. Between 1966 and 1976 the factory did no recruiting itself but received employees assigned by the local government, including school-leavers, young people returning from the farms and demobilized soldiers. In 1976 the factory also took on employees' children who 'inherited' their parents' work. By the end of 1976, RadioCo had more than 400 employees.

Under the planned economy, major collectives such as RadioCo had production plans and quotas like SOEs. However, they differed from SOEs in the level of government that controlled them, the production quotas they had to meet and how resources were allocated to them. RadioCo was controlled by the local district rather than by a higher level of government. The district government formulated production plans and set quotas for the factory, which were usually lower than in SOEs (because COEs were not guaranteed supply of their inputs, as the priority was always given to SOEs). While RadioCo fulfilled the production quotas, its inputs and outputs were coordinated by the district government, which meant that the government offered assistance in obtaining scarce materials and distributing its products.

In 1980, the Municipal Radio Conglomerate (MRC), a conglomerate led jointly by the Ministry of Electronic Industry and the local municipal government, was established and gained direct control over all radio factories and companies in the city, including RadioCo though its collective ownership remained the same. Under coordination by the MRC, RadioCo started to manufacture TV components in the early 1980s. In 1985 the factory imported the first colour TV component production line from Japan and its products were sold directly to a large state-owned TV enterprise that was a key member of the MRC.

Since the mid-1980s, RadioCo has not received production plans and quotas from its governing authority. Instead, it negotiated its annual tax rate with the MRC and was responsible for its own inputs and outputs, and its profits and losses. However, RadioCo was still not completely autonomous. To receive a bank loan the factory had to obtain a government guarantee. The local government still controlled RadioCo's total wage bill and had the right to adjust wage levels. Furthermore, the factory had to accept employees allocated by the local government and was not able to retrench redundant employees.

In 1988 the municipal government replaced the senior management team because of their poor performance and the losses incurred. A new Party Secretary and a Director, both of whom came from another large SOE manufacturing radio and electronic products, were appointed. The new team emphasized the development of new products according to market demand and succeeded in obtaining subcontracts from the SOE they came from. Since the early 1990s, RadioCo has started earning profits, but must pay increased taxes to the local government.

In December 1993, RadioCo formed a so-called joint venture with a Hong Kong company and the original business was nominally split into Radio Firm and Radio Plant. The Hong Kong company contributed in name only 25 per cent of the equity that was required by the joint venture law and RadioCo remained a collective factory. To outsiders, RadioCo became two separate entities, but to insiders, it was still one factory. The General Manager explained that there were four reasons for setting up such a joint venture. First, Radio Firm, the joint venture division of RadioCo, could enjoy the tax holidays granted to joint ventures, that is, it would be exempt from tax for two years once the company started to make profits, and then it would pay half of the normal tax for another three years. Second, Radio Firm would experience less interference from the government and thus enjoy more freedom in its business operations. Third, joint ventures were not bound by the wage limits set by the labour bureau so long as they paid 20 to 50 per cent more to employees than their counterparts in the state sector. They also had more autonomy in designing their own wage packages. RadioCo expected to link compensation more tightly to performance in Radio Firm and then adopt similar arrangements in Radio Plant.

Finally, RadioCo wanted to introduce new management systems, especially in the area of HR practices, such as a merit-based selection and promotion system, and a remuneration scheme more closely based on each employee's contribution. The General Manager believed that such practices would be more easily introduced and implemented in a foreign joint venture which had a reputation as an efficient workplace, where high performers would be rewarded and low performers would be sacked, than in a conventional COE.

Organizational size and structure

In 1994 RadioCo employed 760 staff and workers and its total output in 1993 was 60 million yuan, or about 78,950 yuan per head annually. Radio Firm employed 387 people on three-year contracts and the remaining 373 employees were on the payroll list of Radio Plant. Employees hired after 1983 were on contract while those hired earlier held tenured positions (i.e. 'iron rice bowl').

Prior to February 1992 the factory had separate positions for Party Secretary and Director – each with a different work focus (see Figure 5.1). The Director was in charge of production, while the Party Secretary was responsible for the Party's work, political education and campaign, leadership of the Youth League and the trade union. In the mid-1980s, with the implementation of the 'factory director responsibility system', the Director's position was upgraded and the Party Secretary's role became less significant. After the Tiananmen Square Incident of 1989, this arrangement was criticized for weakening Party leadership and the Party Secretary was then given more extensive involvement in the factory's business operations. However, the new arrangement led to increased disagreement between the two heads. To reduce the conflict between the Director and the Party Secretary, the two positions were merged in early 1992, with the Director taking on the additional role of the Party Secretary and the Party Secretary becoming the Deputy Director and Vice Party Secretary (see Figure 5.2).

RadioCo's structure became more complicated in December 1993 when part of RadioCo formed a joint venture. Despite the split into Radio Firm and Radio Plant (see Figure 5.3), the enterprises shared one Department of Accounting and Finance and one Department of Labour, Personnel and Education, which were led jointly by the Heads of Radio Firm and Radio Plant.

The General Manager of Radio Firm assumed more responsibility for labour and personnel administration of RadioCo as a whole (e.g. human resource planning and distribution of bonuses), while the Director and Party Secretary of Radio Plant remained focused on the whole factory's business operations. However, the structure of the enterprises was not as clear-cut as it appeared. For example, the Deputy Director of Radio Plant in charge of trade union affairs looked after employees from both Radio Plant and Radio Firm. And the Department of Research and Development (Dept of R&D) provided research results or newly designed products to either Radio Firm or Radio Plant depending on their production needs. Two workshops became part of Radio Firm because their products had potential for an overseas market and RadioCo's managers believed that the foreign joint venture's name would facilitate the marketing of such products. The other two workshops remained with Radio Plant as their products mainly served the domestic market. Overall, the restructuring of RadioCo did not change its ownership or its business, but increased the number of senior managers and departments and theoretically reduced its tax liabilities.

Business strategy and the emerging role of the HRM function

The business strategy of RadioCo before the early 1990s was simply to obtain more orders or contracts from the SOEs that belonged to the MRC. In 1994 its strategy became more comprehensive and was expressed in six aspects as detailed by the Director/Party Secretary. The first is 'to face the market', which required RadioCo to determine and fill the market needs while increasing its market share. With the SOEs that RadioCo had depended on for sales being forced to manufacture more components themselves instead of subcontracting to others, RadioCo had to find new markets. The second aspect is 'to adjust product structure', indicating that the mixture of products had to be modified or restructured due to withdrawal of its old SOE clients, the rapid

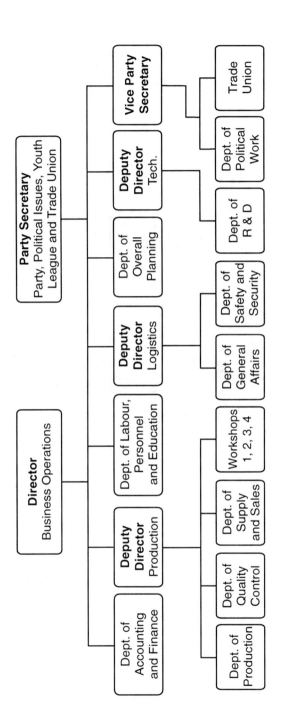

Figure 5.1 RadioCo organization chart (from October 1978 to February 1992)

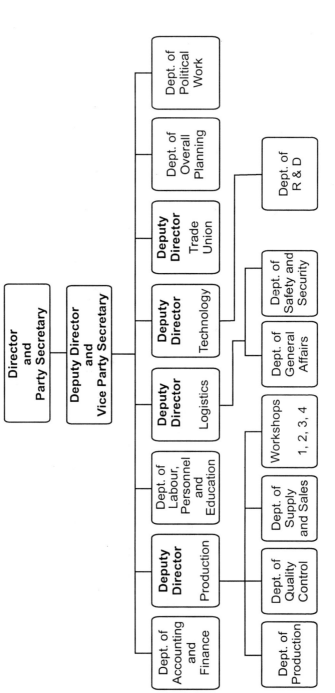

Figure 5.2 RadioCo organization chart (from March 1992 to November 1993)

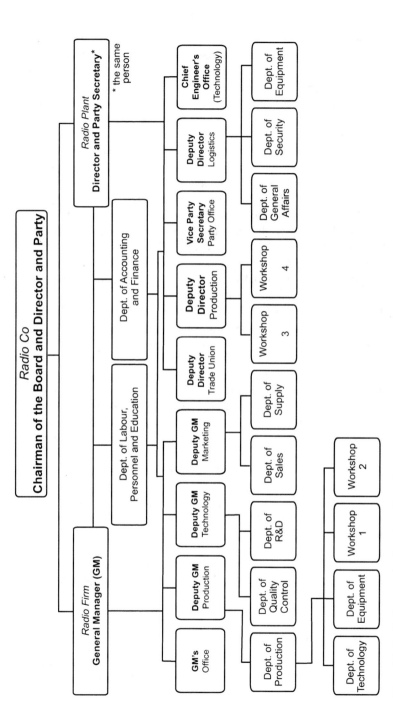

Figure 5.3 RadioCo organization chart (from December 1993) onwards)

development of technology in this industry and the pressure of market competition. The factory had to emphasize the research and development of high-tech products to increase its competitiveness. 'To develop external customers' is another aspect which required the factory to have sales in other parts of China and even overseas instead of selling only to a few SOEs. RadioCo's joint venture partner in Hong Kong would promote RadioCo's products in Hong Kong and also introduce advanced technology and products to RadioCo. The fourth aspect of the strategy was 'to deepen the reform', that is, to continue management by objective (MBO), to optimize the work teams (to be discussed later), to improve the performance appraisal system and to link compensation to performance. Another aspect is 'to accelerate development' – to put more effort into factory development. RadioCo went from making a loss to breaking even in 1990 and then to making a profit in 1991. COEs had difficulty obtaining 'soft loans', so the factory itself had to fund the purchase or importation of new equipment. Finally, 'to let the enterprise prosper' expressed RadioCo's aim to achieve better economic results.

To achieve these results, RadioCo had to rely heavily on its human resources. To attract university graduates, RadioCo supplied them with accommodation, which was the first time the factory offered such generous welfare benefits to employees. RadioCo has also placed an emphasis on education and training since 1980 when it named its HR department the Department of Labour, Personnel and Education (hereafter called the Personnel Department). This Department began to practise recruitment and selection in 1992. Its efforts resulted in an impressive increase in the education levels of RadioCo's employees. Before 1976 not a single employee at RadioCo had a tertiary education; by the end of 1993, the factory had more than 90 employees (12 per cent) with a tertiary education and more than 70 (9 per cent) with technical school certificates. All managers at middle level (head of department) and above had a tertiary education. The factory's effort to recruit qualified employees and its investment in its employees' training indicated an emerging role of the HRM function. Furthermore, one of the primary motivations for forming the 'joint venture' was to introduce Western-style HR practices, such as merit-based recruitment and selection, and performance-related compensation, first to its 'joint venture' division and then to the whole factory.

HR activities at RadioCo

In 1994, RadioCo's Personnel Department assumed responsibility for various HR activities, including human resource planning, workload assignments for job positions, recruitment and selection, wage and bonuses adjustment and distribution, training and education, internal and external transfer of employees, keeping records regarding employees' work attendance and administration of employee insurance. This section examines whether these activities existed at RadioCo during Mao's regime and then highlights the changes in these activities during the reform era. It also analyses the impact of ownership type on RadioCo's HR practices.

Human resource planning

Under the planned economy, RadioCo had neither state-formulated HR plans nor state-fixed quotas on cadres, because the state had never allocated any university graduates to the factory and the local government had assigned only a limited number of cadres, such as the factory director and the Party secretary. The factory's total payroll was controlled by the labour bureau but at the district level.

HR plans were therefore prepared on an *ad hoc* basis by the factory and were usually quite simple for two reasons. First, the history of the factory had left it without the expertise necessary to develop long-term plans. The factory had been established as a cooperative mainly run by housewives with low education levels and manufactured products that required only low technology and elementary equipment. It was self-funded and could not afford to update its equipment or invest in product development. Only school-leavers, 're-educated' young people returning to the city from the country and demobilized soldiers were allocated by the state to work there. RadioCo depended on the quantity rather than the quality of people. Second, RadioCo used to rely on SOEs for subcontracting and did not have its own business strategy. Its HR planning depended on incoming production orders and could only be short-term oriented.

The factory has improved its HR planning since the early 1980s when the factory started to produce TV components, especially after it imported a production line from Japan in 1985. The factory began to develop its own business plans and, based on business requirements, HR plans were formulated with a focus on the quality rather than quantity of employees. Since 1986, the local government had assigned both university and technical school graduates to the factory. However, it was a top-down one-way assignment: neither graduates nor the factory had the freedom to select each other. This not only caused mismatching (to be discussed later), but also interfered with RadioCo's plan to recruit suitable individuals.

In 1992 the factory was allowed to select graduates according to its own plans. In the same year the factory became profitable and was able to invest in updated equipment and facilities. It also commenced the search for new markets for its new products. The demand for product development forced the factory to select recruits carefully. In 1993, the factory's HR plan emphasized two aspects: graduates to be recruited and redundant employees to be relocated. The plan regarding graduates clarified the specializations and qualifications required and the number of each type required according to plans for product and production developments. Relocation of redundant employees occurred after the analysis of job responsibilities, workload allocations, and personnel requirements had been determined.

When this case study was conducted, RadioCo's HR plan was developed on an annual basis. The personnel manager explained that although longer term planning – three years – would be ideal, it was unrealistic because of the restrictions imposed on the factory and uncertainties caused by the economic transition. For example, in 1993 and 1994, while the factory had identified redundant employees and removed them from job positions, it was not allowed to retrench them as the government did not want to 'abandon' them while there was no social safety net and thus risk instability in society. The factory also had to follow the government's instructions on unified wage increases. In 1994, everyone was to be given a 30 per cent increase. Although the increase was mainly to compensate for high inflation, it greatly increased the factory's costs and disturbed its business plans. Furthermore, competition in the market was still not equal, as SOEs had greater access to government loans and scarce raw materials at a lower price than COEs. In the absence of full control over its own business, RadioCo could not really plan its human resources.

Recruitment and selection

Although since its establishment, RadioCo could 'freely' take on new employees within specified parameters, its governing authority, whether it be local district government, the local labour bureau or the MRC, held the real power over recruitment. RadioCo never refused to accept anyone allocated to it. Before the reforms, the low skill level required for the jobs enabled the factory to take on any job-seeker who was a permanent urban resident, had no criminal record, was not illiterate and was in good health. Between 1966 and 1991, RadioCo itself did not recruit anyone but employed only the people who were allocated by the local government or were children of its retired employees who inherited their parents' jobs (*dingti*). Thus before 1992, the activity of recruitment and selection, in its Western definition, did not exist in the factory.

In 1986, for the first time in its history, RadioCo was assigned four university graduates. Since then, the factory has been allocated technical school or university graduates nearly every year. But by the end of 1990, many of these graduates had left RadioCo for several reasons. The most common one was that COEs, compared with SOEs, had much less attractive working conditions, career opportunities, wages and welfare benefits. Whenever possible, graduates would transfer to SOEs or other companies. The second main reason was the mismatch between the graduates' knowledge and the job requirements caused by 'top-down one-way' allocation.

Starting in 1992, RadioCo was allowed 'two-way' selection: the factory could select candidates from the university or from those recommended by the government, and the candidates could select organizations. RadioCo sent representatives to careers fairs organized by the *Electronic Bureau* in Nanjing and Shanghai in 1992 and 1993. At careers fairs, graduates interested in the organization would meet recruiters to discuss the jobs, wages, working conditions and welfare benefits available. If they wanted to apply, they would hand in their curriculum vitae with academic records and a recommendation letter from their school. The recruiters would then shortlist applicants for interviews, though RadioCo did not have formal interviews as their recruiters had usually had a chat with each applicant at the stand. The area of speciality of the applicant was usually a top priority, with academic results a second major criterion. In 1992, to attract people, the factory started to offer accommodation to those recruited from other cities. Even though three new recruits had to share one dormitory room, this offer was useful. RadioCo recruited 10 graduates in 1992 and 17 in 1993.

Recruits with tertiary education, either a two-year college associate diploma (*dazhuan*) or a four-year university degree, belonged to the cadre category. This meant they did not need to sign a contract with RadioCo, as the contract system introduced to the factory in 1983 applied only to workers. However, once Radio Firm was established in late 1993, everyone working for the 'joint venture' section had to sign a three-year contract. Contract-based employees had a three-month probationary period. If both parties were satisfied, a contract, which had to be confirmed by the local labour bureau, could be offered for one to three years, or sometimes even longer. In 1994, the Municipal Labour Bureau announced that, by the end of 1995, all employees, including cadres and workers, in that city were to be employed on a contract basis. This development would blur the distinction between cadres and workers, permanent and temporary employees.

Performance appraisal

Before the reforms, RadioCo did not conduct performance appraisal for most employees. The employee who performed extremely well might be elected by co-workers or selected by management to be a model worker at the end of the year, and would be spiritually rewarded. The performance of senior managers was assessed by the local government rather than RadioCo. In 1979 the factory restored the bonus system, and performance appraisal became a regularly conducted HR activity with its major purpose being for compensation.

In the early stages of performance appraisal, workers' performance was assessed on the basis of their attendance and working hours, but non-production workers had no formal assessment and their bonuses were based on the average of the workers' bonuses. With establishment of the job responsibility system in the mid-1980s, the assessment criteria were based on job responsibilities. In the late 1980s, the criteria related to position work-loads. Since the early 1990s, the factory has been using MBO, with the over-all objectives of the factory being divided between the departments and then sub-objectives of each department being distributed to each production line or work team. Because of this system, the appraisal was formally conducted at the department level for the majority of employees and at an individual level for middle-level managers.

The performance criteria for each department were set up by the senior managers and head of each department, including the personnel manager, with each department's performance being assessed in three areas: the achievement of economic objectives, the satisfaction of quality requirements and the conduct of management activities. Taking performance criteria for the Department of Production as an example. Of the total 100 points, 40 were allocated to the achievement of economic objectives, which referred to the quantity of products produced, the materials consumed and the total cost incurred. Another 40 points were for the satisfaction of quality requirements, such as the adherence to processing procedures and standard, quality checks, and the number of rejected products. The last 20 points were assigned to the conduct of management activities, including the implementa-tion of MBO, the activity of Quality Control groups and adherence to safety rules and regulations. Within each area, there were more detailed guidelines for point allocation as well as rules for increasing or decreasing marks as reward or penalty.

The appraisal for each department was conducted monthly by the depart-ment itself first and then by the factory's Assessment Committee composed of senior managers and managers from the Personnel Department and Department of Quality Control. An assessment sheet for each department contained details for mark allocation. The marks obtained would then deter-mine the bonuses it would receive. Within each department there was no formal assessment for individual performance, which was based on assigned workload and attendance. If employees fulfilled their workload and had a full attendance, they would pass the assessment conducted verbally by their direct supervisor. The supervisor would inform the subordinate if any problems arose in their performance, which would result in the deduction of their monthly bonuses.

The formal performance appraisal of managers at and above middle-level (e.g. head of department or office director) was conducted by RadioCo's Party Office rather than by the Personnel Department. This was because over 60 per cent of them were Party members. It should be noted that even after the split of RadioCo into Radio Firm and Radio Plant, the Party Office of Radio Plant remained in charge of all the cadres of both divisions. For management appraisals, 100 points were allocated to four aspects of performance, comprising 15 points for occupational ethics or good moral practice (*de*), 15 for professional competence (*neng*), 10 for working attitudes and attendance (*qing*), and 60 for performance results (*jie*). Under each aspect, specific items were allocated marks. For example, *de* included whether instructions and decisions were followed and implemented, how cooperative the manager was and to what extent responsibilities were undertaken; *neng* referred to both technical and managerial skills; *qing* covered attendance and how well the manager set an example; and *jie* covered quantity and quality of work completed, and the contribution made to the factory. Only the assessment of performance results (*jie*) was based on the completion of the department objectives and thus had quantifiable measures. The other three aspects, except for attendance which was kept on record, were assessed as excellent, good and below average, without other specifications. RadioCo's senior managers all believed that, to 'seek truth after the fact' as advocated by Deng Xiaoping, a manager's performance should be assessed on his/her achievements. The factory allocated most marks to performance results to encourage result-oriented management.

The middle-level managers' appraisal procedure included self-assessment and then assessment by their direct supervisor and the Party Office. This appraisal was not only for bonus distribution, but for promotion as well. In regards to promotion, the Personnel Department was required to ask the relevant manager's subordinates for their opinions, which formed part of the information for decision-making.

In the performance appraisal process, the Personnel Department played three main roles: to assist in the determination of the workload for each job position, which then formed the basis of individual performance criteria; to keep records of employees' attendance as another assessment criterion; and to be involved in appraising each department's (but not an individual's) performance. According to the personnel manager, the Personnel Department was planning detailed performance criteria for each position in 1995 so as to improve the link between performance and pay. A further reform in bonus distribution, which is explained in the next section, had created an urgent need for this step.

Compensation and welfare

Before 1984, RadioCo used the eight-grade wage system fixed by the local labour bureau, which was similar to the one used in SOEs but at a lower level, that is, each grade was about 25 per cent lower in RadioCo than its counterpart in the state sector. The determinants of each person's wage grade were the job position held, seniority and government policies. By government requirements, any wage increase depended mainly on seniority. As RadioCo's total payroll was controlled by local government, any increase had to be approved by the government.

In 1984, the factory introduced a floating wage system composed of basic pay and performance pay. The basic pay – 70 per cent of total pay – depended on job position and seniority, while the performance pay (30 per cent) was determined by one's attendance and task completion based initially on defined job responsibilities and then on workloads. While the aim of adopting floating wages was to link compensation to contribution, this was not really achieved because of two flaws. First, the job responsibilities were only briefly described, especially for non-production employees. Second, the local government continued to control the total payroll, making it impossible for the factory to increase employees' wages at its own discretion (unless it could pay for them from above-quota profits). As there were restrictions on retrenchment of its redundant employees, the factory's ability to increase high performers' wages by reducing the total number of employees was also greatly limited.

In 1993, guided by government policies and regulations, RadioCo designed its own position-and-skill wage system. The new system took more job-related factors into consideration, including the qualifications obtained, workloads involved, labour intensity and working conditions. Under the new system, pay could be differentiated according to level of responsibility and qualification. It encouraged people to assume more responsibilities and to obtain higher qualifications. Nevertheless, when the 22 people interviewed for this case study were asked about their attitudes toward this new wage system, their answers were not particularly positive. Although they all believed that this system was better than the floating wage system as more relevant factors were considered in determining the wage scale, none of them was actually satisfied with the wage they received. Their complaints centred upon three issues: the government's interference in wage determination, low wage scales and the small difference between each grade. The government still had control over the total payroll and imposed a 'ceiling' on wage scales, even though the factory was supposed to make its own decisions. Despite the fact that RadioCo was making profits, its wage scale was still much lower (about 30 per cent) than the scales in the loss-making SOEs and was not remotely comparable to that of foreign-invested enterprises (often 50 per cent or more lower). Finally, the wage difference between grades was quite small, usually less than 10 per cent. The General Manager stated that these issues would be handled in Radio Firm first, as it was a 'joint venture' with much more autonomy. However, he emphasized that these changes had to be gradual so as to avoid disputes between Radio Firm and Radio Plant.

RadioCo's low wage scales were not compensated for by its bonuses, which consisted of 35 per cent of an employee's wage package in 1994 due to some problems with the bonus system. First, bonuses were distributed at department and production line or work team level, but there were no formal individual-based performance criteria or appraisal processes. People working in the same team or production line usually received the same bonus. Employees described this two-level bonus distribution system as a change from 'eating from a big rice pot' (i.e. equally distributed bonuses at the factory level) to 'eating from a small rice pot' (i.e. equally distributed bonuses at the team level). Second, when the factory assigned workloads to each position since 1990, bonuses were tied to the workloads. However, the link was much tighter for production workers, whose workloads were detailed and quantified, than for non-production employees, whose workloads were brief and vague. Workers commented that they had 'rigid and hard' targets while cadres only had 'flexible and soft' ones. As a result, the factory formulated various bonus rates for different groups of employees (that is, if the average bonus given to production workers was set at 1, the factory director would receive 1.8 times the workers' average bonus, senior managers 1.7, head of department 1.2, while managerial and other non-production employees would receive between 0.7 and 1). The use of bonus rates tried to overcome the problems caused by vaguely specified workloads for non-production employees, but it has not focused on individual performance.

In order to reduce this egalitarianism, RadioCo planned to introduce 'unpredicted bonuses' that would be deposited directly to the employees' bank account rather than being paid in cash. Unpredicted bonuses were not determined by fixed rates or equal bonuses within small work groups. Bonuses would be closely linked to each person's performance based on individual performance appraisals and big gaps could appear between bonuses received by high and low performers. To avoid jealousy and unnecessary conflicts, the bonus and wages would be credited directly to each employee's bank account. In 1994, with wages and bonuses still being paid in cash and everyone signing a big payroll sheet after receiving the payment, there was no confidentiality in the payroll system. The factory was going to use the direct payment method in 1995 for its managers first and then extend this practice to all the employees.

Being a COE, RadioCo offered welfare benefits to employees that were far less substantial than those offered by SOEs. For example, the factory only started to offer some accommodation in 1992 to attract university graduates. RadioCo did not have its own kindergarten, school or bathhouse as did SOEs, hence its employees had to pay normal rather than subsidized prices for these services. RadioCo had over 200 retired employees who were not on its payroll as the factory joined the social security system in 1987 when the system was in its experimental stage. Each year the factory paid an amount equal to 26 per cent of its total payroll to the system as pension funds while individuals paid three per cent of their wages. RadioCo also contributed 150,000 yuan per year as medical funds to this system, which would then pay the pensions and medical fees of its retirees. RadioCo had few welfare benefits, which made it easier for its retired employees to accept the social security system. This, in turn, helped RadioCo to focus on its business operations rather than having the extra burden of running a small society.

Training and development

Historically, the education level of RadioCo's employees, on average, was quite low. Some of them had only completed education up to Year 6 while a few were illiterate. Despite such deficiency in education, the education or training programmes organized by the factory before 1980 were very politically oriented, except for the apprenticeship training for new workers. Occasionally, when required by its governing authority, RadioCo offered training programmes such as the total quality control systems or sent employees to programmes organized by the government or other organizations.

The situation started to improve in 1980 when RadioCo organized comprehensive education programmes for its young employees. The programmes offered basic high school subjects, such as Chinese and mathematics. All subjects were offered outside working hours. The employees were required to pass examinations set by the local government's education department to ascertain whether they reached Year 9 or Year 12 level. All the young employees had to pass a minimum level of Year 9. By the mid-1980s, more than 400 employees were re-educated and obtained new certificates in this way.

The factory also encouraged employees to take part-time tertiary study in their speciality area to facilitate career development. Before employees sat for the tertiary entrance exams, they had to obtain permission from the Personnel Department. Only when the selected speciality matched the employee's current work or would be suitable for the factory's production needs would the Personnel Department give its permission. Subsequently, if the applicants passed the entrance exam and enrolled, they could enjoy some flexibility in their working hours during their exam period and their tuition fees were reimbursed if they passed all subjects. Some employees obtained tertiary certificates by passing all the exams offered by the State Committee of Adult Tertiary Self-Education. The Personnel Department would award such employees 300 yuan per person once they passed all exams. The policy of the factory paying tuition fees or presenting awards was revised in 1994 after the position-and-skill wage system was adopted. Employees who completed tertiary education would not receive reimbursement for tuition fees or monetary awards, but their newly obtained qualification was acknowledged and their skill wage would increase accordingly. From the early 1980s until 1994, 30 employees from the factory completed tertiary education through part-time study or self-education.

The factory also offered some training opportunities. Since the 1980s, apprenticeships for new workers had consisted of two to three years of on-the-job training, as was the situation in SOEs. For managerial staff, RadioCo organized a one-week off-the-job training programme for all supervisors and line managers as required by the industrial bureau, which supplied the training materials. The Personnel Department worked with the trade union to organize the programme and issued certificates upon completion. All the relevant staff attended the programme, as the factory required this certificate as one of the criteria for promotion. RadioCo also sent its employees, such as accountants and quality inspectors, to training programmes conducted by external organizations as required by its own business and production needs. The training for engineers or senior managers was always organized by the training department of the local electronic industrial bureau or local government.

RadioCo's efforts on training decreased in the 1990s because it could select graduates appropriate to its own needs from 1992 onwards. Employing new university graduates was free of charge in 1992, and in 1993 recruits were still free to COEs or cost less (around 1,000 yuan) than at SOEs and FIEs. These lower costs could reflect the fact that COEs were usually much less attractive than SOEs and FIEs, given their meagre welfare benefits and lower wage scales. Although RadioCo suffered from overstaffing, it had still taken on about 20 graduates each year since 1992 and planned to continue doing so. Any new production workers had to have completed technical school or Year 12. The personnel manager believed that employing these new graduates could meet production development needs much more quickly than relying on training employees, and that it was also more cost-effective. The personnel manager admitted that the factory was not constrained by a fixed budget for training as were SOEs (usually 1.5 per cent of the total payroll). But this did not mean that the factory would spend more money on training programmes – in fact the opposite was true. This was another reason to focus on recruiting more qualified employees.

RadioCo had a one-day induction programme for its newly recruited graduates. After this orientation, university graduates would rotate through a variety of job positions for six months to become familiar with the factory's products and production procedures, and then be assigned to the department of technology, quality control, or product development. Some stayed in the Department of Production and were responsible for solving technical problems. Technical school graduates were assigned to workshops after the orientation. Usually their rotation was confined to one production line or one workshop.

Before the reforms, training offered in RadioCo was based on plans and instructions determined by its governing authority. Such direction has become less common, although not extinct, since the reform. For example, the factory still had to conduct some political training programmes for its cadres to meet local government requirements. In 1994, the factory developed two principles of training. One was to organize training courses outside work time. The other was to select training courses that matched the current job. Some graduates were promoted to line manager or even department manager's positions with little training in management. They expressed concern about improving their managerial skills, but were encouraged to acquire the skills through their work.

Labour relations

RadioCo was unionized like SOEs, and everyone was a union member regardless of whether one worked in Radio Firm or Radio Plant. However, some employees were not aware that they were union members, which reflected the weak influence of the union in the factory. RadioCo established its Workers' Representative Congress (hereafter called the Congress) in 1982 which held general meetings once or twice a year to discuss the factory director's working report, new rules or regulations proposed, annual budget plans and the implementation of resolutions passed at the previous meeting. The union representatives also passed on employees' suggestions for improving production to the factory director at the Congress meetings. The principal role of the trade union, as explained by the chairman of RadioCo's trade union, was to assist managers in their work and to look after employees. The first role required listening to employees' grievances and assisting managers to solve the problems, while the second often included the organization of recreational activities and distribution of welfare benefits.

The chairman of the union in RadioCo held the position of a deputy director and he pointed out that the major task of the union was to deal with employees' welfare issues. He believed that only when employees felt they were looked after by the factory would they be willing to work hard in harmony. The fact that RadioCo had not experienced any industrial disputes or suffered any loss of working time due to conflict up to 1994 might be an indication of worker satisfaction.

DISCUSSION AND CONCLUSIONS

Table 5.2 summarizes the situation at RadioCo regarding the six major HR activities under discussion. The table indicates that the labour and personnel administration at RadioCo before the economic reform, to a large extent, was either controlled or directed by the government. This was demonstrated by the assignment of the factory director, the allocation of workers and the standardization of wage scales. During the reform era, RadioCo was granted more autonomy and was pushed to compete in the market as it received much less protection and fewer soft budget benefits from the state than SOEs. RadioCo began to practise more sophisticated HR activities, including conducting selection and offering incentives, in order to obtain quality employees.

The main features of RadioCo's HR activities observed during this study were: (1) an emphasis on the qualifications of employees; (2) the linking of performance to the achievement of business objectives; and (3) an attempt to link the compensation employees received to their contribution to the organization. The first feature was reflected in RadioCo's education programmes, HR planning and selection, and even its welfare package. The factory provided education programmes to all its young workers to raise their education level and encouraged current employees to take part-time study or self-education to obtain higher degrees. The qualifications of employees became the key issue in the factory's HR planning, while in the selection process, the major criteria were based on qualifications and academic records. Although qualifications should not be the only criterion used to judge the quality of people, the focus on qualifications at least highlighted the importance of education. RadioCo's emphasis on qualifications resulted in an increase in employees with tertiary education from zero in 1985 to over 90 (12 per cent) in 1993.

Most of the graduates made positive contributions to the technology or product development of the factory. For example, one university graduate recruited in 1992 became the Head of the Department of R&D, and developed new products that have facilitated an increase in the factory's market share. In order to attract and retain qualified employees, RadioCo even supplied them with accommodation. Senior managers believed that this welfare item was an expensive but worthwhile investment. In addition, with the contract system and the condition that employees could retain their

Table 5.2 HR activities at RadioCo

HR activities	Purposes	Features	Issues
HR planning	• to have the right people for product development • to relocate redundant employees	• focus on qualifications of people since the reform • annually planned based on workloads of a job • restricted by the state policies	• lack of measurement in job descriptions to determine workloads • short-term oriented
Recruitment and selection	• to have university and technical school graduates	• selection criteria were based on applicant's speciality and academic records • informal talks with candidates as a major selection method	• lack of job descriptions for many positions • heavy reliance on one's qualifications and recruiter's personal impression • no standardized selection methods and procedure
Performance appraisal	• for bonus distribution • for cadres' promotion	• conducted formally at department level and for some managers only • individual assessment based mainly on attendance and fulfilment of workloads • criteria were more results-oriented for production workers	• lack of detailed performance criteria, especially for non-production employees • no formal individual assessment for the majority of employees • not used for identifying training needs
Compensation and welfare	• to link wages to the responsibilities assumed and skills obtained • to relate bonuses to performance	• 65% wages and 35% bonuses • job responsibilities were not specified for non-production workers while skills were based on qualifications only	• no substantial gap between wage grades • loss of incentives because of 'eating from small rice pot' (equally distributed bonuses within each department)

Table 5.2 (cont.)

HR activities	Purposes	Features	Issues
	• to attract and maintain employees	• equally distributed bonuses within each department • started to offer accommodation to young graduates	
Training and development	• to raise employees' education level • to improve work skills	• mainly on-the-job training • passively organized • encourage further self-education and part-time study in one's own working area	• no systematic training • lack of management training for new managers • reduced training efforts because of the employment of graduates
Labour relations	• liaison between management and employees	• unionized • focus on employees' welfare • assistant to management	• to what extent does the trade union represent workers' interests in terms of their rights and power?

accommodation only while they worked for the factory, this welfare benefit was unlikely to cause further complications (in contrast to SOEs where employees could keep their accommodation regardless of their performance and sometimes even after they resigned).

The second feature – linking performance to the achievement of business objectives – was demonstrated in the performance appraisal scheme put in place for mid-level and senior managers as well as for departments. Although the government required the factory to assess its managers in four areas (moral practice, competence, attitudes and results), 60 per cent of the weight fell on performance results because they had quantified objectives. This indicated a shift from politically oriented to results-oriented assessment and followed the practice advocated by Deng Xiaoping's motto – 'to seek truth after the fact'. This feature was also evident in the assessment at department level, which placed 80 per cent of the weight on its achievement of objectives in both quantity and quality. Linking each department's performance with the achievement of objectives has led to the abolition of the factory-wide equal distribution of bonuses. However, this link had not been extended to the individual performance of the majority of employees, especially non-production workers.

Finally, RadioCo's continuous attempt to relate an individual's compensation to his/her contribution was another feature of its HR practices. The factory tried to offer employees incentives by first distributing bonuses equally within the factory, then within each department, and it now planned to introduce 'unpredicted' bonuses that would be linked to individual performance rather than being based on fixed bonus rates. Although the bonus had not proved successful in linking compensation to performance, the factory did have plans to formulate performance criteria for each job position. The implementation of the 'position-and-skill' wage system improved the connection between job responsibilities and wages, even though the new system was still constrained by government control and by aspects of historical development (i.e. a top ceiling on wages, the low wage scales and the small difference between grades). Despite the defects in its compensation system, RadioCo's endeavour to pursue performance-related pay marked a break from the compensation system existing prior to the reform, and also illustrated the practical difficulties and challenges in linking compensation to employee contribution.

Although HR activities existed in RadioCo, they were quite different from those defined in the West. For example, the lack of job analysis led to vaguely described job responsibilities, which in turn affected the establishment of full workloads and performance criteria, as well as HR planning. Furthermore, its HR plans were made only one year in advance. The factory could conduct its own recruitment and selection, but had no formal selection procedure and method. Performance appraisals were only used for bonus distribution rather than training or communication purposes as expected in the West. Compensation was partly related to an employee's skill and responsibility, yet 35 per cent of it (bonuses) was often distributed equally to each worker in the department. Furthermore, training was often passively organized to meet the requirements of the governing authority rather than actively offered as part of a systematic programme. RadioCo did not have a fixed budget for training and depended more heavily on recruiting new graduates than on training current employees. Finally, the trade union performed a totally different task – that of a welfare caretaker – compared with its counterpart in the West. These differences could be attributed to the very short history of HR practices within the factory and more significantly, to the restriction imposed on its HR practices by its ownership type.

Being a collective enterprise, RadioCo had no rights to claim the profits it made, as the tax was levied at a negotiated rate. RadioCo was also subject to some local government controls over its HR activities even in the reform era, although they were much less stringent than those during Mao's regime.

Now it had total autonomy to select its own employees without being limited by quotas on cadres and technical personnel as was the situation in the state enterprise, TeleCo (see Chapter 4). However, RadioCo could not make all the decisions – rights to retrench redundant employees and to increase the total payroll amount were retained by the local government. Furthermore, the Director of the factory was still appointed or transferred at the government's will, and this power represented the key control of the government over the factory and its HR activities. If the Director failed to obey the government's instructions, he/she could be removed by the government. The ownership type did indeed influence HR practices.

With the acceleration of reforms, RadioCo intended to further improve its HR activities, such as completing detailed job descriptions for each position. The factory was also planning to further reform its wage system by introducing 'unpredicted' bonuses. It has also experimented with, and expected to continue trials in its joint venture division (Radio Firm) of other HR activities such as contract-based employment, merit-based promotion and performance-based compensation. These features could be part of the future path of RadioCo's HRM development. However, the senior managers of RadioCo stated that improvement in their HR practices also depended heavily on the alleviation of government restrictions and establishment of a nationwide social security system.

6 Case study 3

HR practices in a private-owned enterprise (POE)

The third case study was conducted at ElectroCo, a private-owned enterprise (POE), or more precisely, a partnership POE but registered as both a collective-owned and foreign-invested enterprise. This case study adopts the same framework as the other ones. The overview of POEs in China focuses on the resurrection and upsurge of POEs following the post-Mao reforms, their major features and subsequent impact on HR practices. The data collection process for this research is in the next section, which presents background information on ElectroCo and its current HR practices. The chapter concludes with a discussion of the findings from this case study with respect to the research questions.

PRIVATE-OWNED ENTERPRISES (POES)

POEs in China did not survive beyond 1956 due to the hastily and forcefully implemented socialist transformation. Two major driving forces behind the transformation were the adoption of the heavy-industry-oriented development strategy and Mao's radical ideology. The transformation of ownership from private to public enabled the state 'to collect every bit of resources to form a huge accumulation of capital' so as to concentrate on the development of heavy and military industries (Gao and Chi, 1996: 21; also see Lin *et al.*, 1996), underpinned by the belief that the private sector of economy was 'a capitalistic mechanism of class-struggle to exploit the masses' and should thus be eliminated (Kraus, 1991:13). By the end of 1956, 99 per cent of 88,000 POEs nationwide had been transferred to the public sector (*People's Daily, Overseas Edition*, 9 April 1999: 6).

Private economy in the urban area was initially accepted only in the form of individual industrial or commercial households (*getihu*) in 1979. They were expected to fill in the gaps left by the public sector in the economy, such as in the service industry and in employment. In July 1981, the government's

Table 6.1 Recorded private businesses, 1981–97 (year-end figures)

Year	Getihu	POEs
1981	1,827,752	
1982	2,614,006	
1983	5,901,032	
1984	9,329,464	
1985	11,712,560	
1986	12,111,560	
1987	13,725,746	
1988	14,526,931	
1989	12,471,937	90,581
1990	13,281,974	98,141
1991	14,145,000	108,000
1992	15,339,200	139,600
1993	15,483,000	184,000
1997	28,500,000[a]	960,726[b]

Sources: Young, 1995: 6; a Chen and Shi, 1998: 3; b *Beijing Review*, 1 March 1999: 4.

Policy Provisions of the State Council on Urban Non-Agricultural Individual Economy recognized the existence of *getihu* 'that does not exploit the labour of others' and specified that 'employing one or two persons as helpers and two or three persons as apprentices was acceptable', but apprentices should not exceed five (Yabuki, 1995: 59). *Getihu* was thus officially defined as 'individually owned businesses employing up to eight people, including the owner, but often discounting family members' (Young, 1995: 5). The flourishing of *getihu* between 1981 and 1997 is presented in Table 6.1.

The resurrection of individual businesses provided job opportunities for young people returning to urban areas from the countryside (as a result of the Cultural Revolution) and new school-leavers, and helped to improve the service industry as well as the distribution of consumer goods. Many *getihu* soon overstepped the state-imposed limits on the number of employees. In early 1986 there were over 40,000 *getihu* that each employed more than eight employees and the number of employees grew to 16 on average by 1987 (Yuan, 1993: 30). The fast expansion of *getihu* and the vigorous development of individual businesses faced ideological opposition from leftist cadres and workers, including criticism of the wide income disparities created among employers and employees, the exploitation of workers and the restoration of capitalism. However, the central government adopted a wait-and-see stance, neither encouraging nor closing down *getihu* that had employed more than eight workers. This 'silence' was interpreted as support for individual businesses, which not only led to further growth of individual businesses, but also laid a foundation for the emergence of POEs.

A POE (*siying qiye*) is 'an individually owned enterprise with more than eight employees' (Riskin, 1995: 335). POEs were mainly engaged in the manufacturing industry and their owners were usually the managers. POEs were officially recognized and given legal status alongside individual businesses when the 1982 Constitution of the PRC was modified in April 1988. The amendments specify that

> the state approves the existence and development of private enterprise within the sphere set out in laws and regulations. The private economy is a supplement to the socialist economic system of public ownership. The state shall protect the legal rights and profits of the private economy, and will carry out guidance, supervision, and management of the private economy.
>
> (Wang, 1994: 133)

In July 1988 the state promulgated the *Provisional Regulations on Private Enterprises in the People's Republic of China* and related administrative regulations were issued in February 1989. These regulations applied to private enterprises employing more than eight people. Private enterprises were divided into three categories based on the number of investors: sole proprietor enterprise (a single investor), partnership (two or more) and limited liability company (two or more but fewer than thirty investors) (Yabuki, 1995). The regulations specified a 'ceiling' on the monthly salary for POEs' owner/managers, that is, their salary should not exceed four times that of the average wage of the workers (Gao and Chi, 1996). The regulations also addressed issues of employment and working conditions within POEs, including stipulations that the POE's labour contract should be filed through the local labour bureau and that any labour disputes in POEs be handled as in state enterprises (Young, 1995).

Private businesses were stymied and declined in 1989 by nearly 15 per cent, because they fell into 'political disfavour' for a time after the Tiananmen Square incident (Boisot and Child, 1996: 45). With the purge of ex-Premier Zhao Ziyang and his liberal supporters of reform, private businesses were accused of conducting merciless capitalist competition and exploitation, creating social chaos because of unequal distribution of income, and becoming the main source of spiritual pollution (Chan and Unger, 1990; Kraus, 1991). The state also launched a tax inspection and collection campaign, targeting the private sector in 1989, to tighten its control over *getihu* and POEs (see Young, 1995: 139–42). In spite of POEs having been granted legitimacy by the law and constitutions, owners of private business felt vulnerable due to social prejudice and ideological bias (Wong, 1996; Yuan, 1993). For example, the debate continued about whether private economy belonged to capitalism or socialism in the early 1990s. People engaged in private businesses feared being categorized as capitalists and having their assets confiscated (Yuan, 1993), so many established personal relationships with government officials and falsely registered their POEs under a different type of ownership (e.g. Boisot and Child, 1996; Pearson, 1997).

Recovery of private business occurred after Deng Xiaoping's southern tour of China in early 1992, when he stated that only three criteria, irrespective of the type of ownership, should be used to determine whether a business should be encouraged or not. The three criteria (abbreviated as *sange youliyu*) were 'whether it facilitates the development of socialist productivity, whether it favours the strengthening of the socialist country's comprehensive strengths and whether it contributes to the improvement of the people's living standards' (Gao and Chi, 1996: 40). In the CPC's 14th and 15th National Congresses, the Party further clarified the position and importance of private business. For example, the former Party General Secretary Jiang Zemin declared in his speech at the Party's 15th National Congress that

> The non-public sector is an important component part of China's socialist market economy. We should continue to encourage and guide the non-public sector comprising self-employed and private business to facilitate its sound development. This is of great importance to satisfy the diverse needs of the people and promoting the development of the national economy.
>
> (*Beijing Review*, 6 October 1997: Documents, p.19)

Deng's pragmatism initiated a new cycle of frenzied activity in private business, and the changed attitude of the Party towards private businesses from a supplementary role to an important component further encouraged the development of POEs. More importantly, this change was officially adopted by the 9th National People's Congress in 1999 and written into the constitutional amendments. Since 1992 there has been an extraordinary growth in the number of POEs. Table 6.1 shows that the number of POEs increased nearly six-fold between 1992 and 1997. Furthermore, the number of people employed by POEs increased from 1.64 million in 1989 to 13.49 million in 1997 (*Beijing Review*, 1 March 1999: 4).

Three distinct features of POEs can be observed. The first was their short-term orientation or 'mentality' (Wong, 1996:145). For example, POEs usually 'invest to gain rapid returns on their capital, emphasize liquidity and spend their returns on their personal consumption rather than investing in fixed capital' (Tan and Li, 1996: 243). The major reason for private enterprises' myopic behaviour was their persistent fears of policy changes (Murphy, 1996). Lack of confidence in government policies caused private business people to 'worry about the safety of their property and also about their future' (Gao and Chi, 1996: 118). Another reason could be the fact that China is 'a social and political environment in which *private* is still regarded with suspicion or hostility' (White *et al.*, 1996: 243). Furthermore, existing uncertainties during the period of economic transition, including the lack of clearly defined and consistently enforced property rights as well as explicit and codified information, have also contributed to this short-term mentality.

The second feature of POEs was the critical role played by kinship and nepotism in their labour relations. POEs usually employed the owners' family members, relatives or close friends as key employees. POE owners often had a 'patriarchal behaviour' management style, making all the decisions without formal rules and regulations (Gao and Chi, 1996: 118-20). The heavy reliance on kinship or connections to establish trust between employer and employees and to build up a circle of close relations reflects a legacy of the Chinese feudal society and the values of Confucianism that was severely criticised during Mao's regime (Wong, 1996).

> Patrimonial is the only word which captures adequately the themes of paternalism, hierarchy, responsibility, mutual obligation, family atmosphere, personalism and protection. Out of it (patrimonialism) flow three related themes which are in some sense expressions of it, namely: the idea that power cannot really exist unless it is connected to ownership; a distinct style of benevolently autocratic leadership; and personalistic as opposed to neutral relations.
>
> (Redding, 1993: 155)

However, nepotism may become a hindrance to the development of private business (Brosseau, 1995; Chen and Shi, 1998). POEs have to break the practice of recruiting their relations (*renren weiqin*) and seek competent employees (*renren weixian*), as competition becomes more intense for POEs.

The prevalence of the 'red hat' phenomenon among POEs was the third feature, which refers to POEs disguised as COEs by false registration.[1] Instead of red hats, some POEs had 'foreign hats' by registering their enterprises as FIEs. In exchange for permission to have such false registration, POEs pay state agency administration fees which were usually one to two per cent of output value or five to ten per cent of turnover (Young, 1991: 19). In return, POEs could 'receive protection from a benefactor in the state against public prejudice and bureaucratic harassment' (Murphy, 1996: 15). The main incentive for POEs to have red or foreign hats was to overcome their disadvantages 'with regard to financing, issuance of operating permits, pricing and taxation' (Sabin, 1994: 952), as well as access to various supplies. Such protection was especially necessary during the 1980s and early 1990s when central planning and the dual pricing system were still in operation together with negotiation-based tax rates. All of these practices favoured the public sector or FIEs. For example, newly registered COEs were granted exemption from taxes for up to three years, POEs were not (Yuan, 1993). Similarly, FIEs could enjoy tax holidays (two-year of tax free and another three-year of half tax) if they held contracts with terms of ten years or more. In contrast, POEs had to apply for tax reduction if they were in extreme financial difficulty and even then the reduction might not be granted. The red hat phenomenon indicated that the laws and regulations designed to protect and manage POEs had not been well conceived, and that social and political discrimination against POEs had not really disappeared from the socialist market economy.

These major features have had a profound impact on POEs' HR practices. POEs' profit-maximizing and short-term strategy often led them to neglect employee training and career development by offering fewer training programmes for employees than enterprises with other types of ownership as revealed by our survey results (see Chapter 8). Furthermore, POEs' heavy reliance on kinship and connections resulted in non-standardized management practices. This included informal labour contracts, arbitrary wage and welfare treatment and inadequate labour protection (Gao and Chi, 1996). Key management positions were kept mainly within the circle of close relations of the POEs' owners, a practice which could obstruct open recruitment and selection of more competent people from the outside free labour market. While a small group of employees with a close relationship with POE owners were well treated, the majority of workers in both large and small POEs, who often came from rural areas (Sabin, 1994), were paid less but worked longer hours in the 'sweatshops' under appalling conditions (O'Leary, 1994; Chan, 1996). Although workers in the private sector have not been unionized (White *et al.*, 1996), poor management of employees could lead to industrial disputes, which would accelerate the establishment of trade unions within POEs. It would also compel the unions in private businesses to be more active in working for the welfare of the workers.

Another impact on HR practices in POEs is their insecure political and social status, which reduces their ability to attract qualified employees – this was particularly true in the 1980s and early 1990s when POEs were in the early stages of development. At that time, university graduates preferred the public to the private sector, and tended to select state rather than private enterprises. Although POEs have enjoyed a better reputation since their rapid growth after the early 1990s, POEs still experienced high departure rates of qualified personnel because of career development and compensation issues. In contrast to other ownership types, POEs' compensation practices, especially the bonus distribution, were linked more to individual performance and enterprise profitability than to group performance or employee attendance (see discussion of survey results in Chapter 8).

POEs all operate under tight budget constraints and have to be self-reliant, thus they are often more efficient than state and collective enterprises (Chen and Shi, 1998). An investigation in Wenzhou (a city well known for its high number of private businesses) identified the ratio of input to output in SOEs and POEs in 1990: the ratio in SOEs was 1:1.19, and in POEs, 1:4.38 (Yuan, 1993: 128). Have HR practices in POEs made any contribution to their efficiency? The following case study conducted in ElectroCo aims to illustrate POEs' HR practices in detail.

DATA COLLECTION METHODS

The data collection methods in this case study were similar to those other case studies. However, as ElectroCo only supplied limited written information (e.g. its prospectus and product specification), the researcher spent more time on interviews and direct observation during the one-week field study. This included interviewing people at different levels, visiting each department and production lines, participating in the weekly production meeting and talking freely with workers and staff. The interviews were individually conducted on the factory's premises, with an average duration of about one and a half hours. Fifteen people were interviewed (see Table 6.2).

As ElectroCo was registered as a collective-owned and foreign-invested enterprise, it had three managers from the investors on its Board. Two were from ZC Company (Chairman and Vice Chairman/Financial Controller) and one from a Hong Kong company. Only the Deputy General Manager handling public relations and administration was sent by ZC Company and he was interviewed to gain insight into the investors' viewpoint. Day-to-day HR practices were the responsibility of the Head of General Manager's Office (called the Personnel Manager hereafter), who was also one of the two people working closely with the owner of ElectroCo in setting up the enterprise. She was interviewed three times to obtain a detailed history of the enterprise as well as its HR practices. The final draft of this case study was checked and commented on by the General Manager, the Deputy General Manager from ZC Company and the Personnel Manager.

Table 6.2 Interviewees – ElectroCo case study

- Vice Chairman of the Board of Directors/General Manager (GM) (2 interviews)
- Deputy General Manager appointed by ZC Company (public relations and administration)
- Deputy General Manager (production) (GM's son)
- Deputy General Manager (technology)
- Head of General Manager's Office (also called the Personnel Manager as she was also in charge of labour and personnel administration) (3 interviews)
- Head of Department of Marketing (GM's daughter)
- Cash manager of the Department of Accounting and Finance (GM's wife) (2 interviews)
- Head of Department (R&D)
- Manager (quality control)
- Team leader – project engineering
- Supervisors (2, interviewed individually)
- Production workers (3, interviewed individually)

CASE ENTERPRISE – ELECTROCO

ElectroCo was selected for this case study because of its similarities to the other three case enterprises with respect to the location and industry, and its relatively large size among POEs. Access to its owner was also critical because owners of POEs were generally very reluctant to release any information on the management of their business because of their vulnerability to social prejudice, ideological bias and policy changes, which was still prevalent in the mid-1990s. This section focuses on the background of ElectroCo, highlighting the context for their current HR practices.

Enterprise history and ownership

The enterprise history of ElectroCo began with its founder, owner and General Manager (called Mr. GM hereafter). Before establishing ElectroCo, Mr. GM was a senior engineer in a large state-owned electronic research institute. The institute had been fully funded by the central government under the planned economy. However, funding was gradually reduced after the economic reform began and the institute was urged to compete in the market for its survival. Hence the institute set up a company called NGT in the mid-1980s as a strategic business unit. NGT specialized in telecommunications systems. It designed, manufactured and sold its products directly to the market. NGT quickly started to earn profits because of its strengths in product design, technology development and the new niche market it was in.

Mr. GM was a senior engineer at NGT and designed some new products based on his research of market needs. However, he did not experience adequate job satisfaction because NGT maintained a pre-reform management style. He was not rewarded for his technical innovations or his design of unique products because pay and promotion were still mainly based on seniority rather than performance and the bonus distribution failed to distinguish between high and low performers. Furthermore, the profits earned by NGT were shared by other departments of the institute which still relied on government funding. Mr. GM also disapproved of his superior's leadership style that favoured blind obedience from employees. Given his own technical expertise, understanding of the market demand and an established customer network, Mr. GM decided to establish his own enterprise. Two of Mr. GM's subordinates were impressed by his entrepreneurship and capability and followed him.

In late 1992, Mr. GM and his two followers submitted their resignations, but the company only gave approval to the two staff rather than Mr. GM because of his technical expertise. Seeing that Mr. GM was determined to leave, the company made him an offer with two conditions. First, his departure would be treated as a secondment rather than a resignation, which meant NGT would hold his personal file and allow him to return at any time if he wanted to. Second, Mr. GM would not be paid by NGT but he had to pay NGT 8,000 yuan per annum (equivalent to one and half times his annual salary at that time) during his secondment to keep his accommodation supplied by NGT. Although these conditions were deliberate obstacles to prevent him from resigning, he accepted them because it was the only way he could start his own business and not risk the worst-case scenario (no job, no accommodation and no new business).

In December 1992, Mr. GM registered ElectroCo as a privately owned electronic firm with registered capital of 100,000 yuan (drawn mainly from his own savings, with some lent by friends). ElectroCo was in the same telecommunications industry as NGT. After registration, Mr. GM and his two followers started from scratch; selecting the enterprise location, acquiring the factory building, purchasing production equipment and staffing. ElectroCo was located in a high technology development zone where some preferential benefits were offered, such as exemption from import duties for the equipment brought in for production purposes. Mr. GM also persuaded some of his former colleagues at NGT to join ElectroCo by offering them much better compensation packages. ElectroCo started operation in July 1993, with key positions being filled up by the people 'poached' from NGT.

From the first day of its operation, ElectroCo paid particular attention to customers' needs and adopted a flexible operation strategy, customizing products whenever necessary. Because of its quality, flexibility and negotiable prices, ElectroCo soon operated at its maximum capacity and at the end of 1993 it made profits of up to 200,000 yuan (the return on investment in the first year was over 100 per cent). Despite ElectroCo's profitability, Mr. GM had difficulties obtaining a bank loan because private businesses were not trusted and considered 'risky'. Furthermore, he noticed that tax would be lower if ElectroCo was not a POE. Therefore, Mr. GM decided to form an alliance with partners from other sectors in order to obtain financial support to expand his operation and to change the 'private' status of his business.

In late 1993 Mr. GM found two partners for his alliance. One was a subsidiary called ZC Company under a Chinese Investment Corporation (CIC) that boasted powerful connections in China (most of its senior managers were related to high-ranking officials in the central government). CIC was based in Beijing but had subsidiaries in many countries. Its role was to channel funds into technology-related ventures and had attracted many foreign companies as its business partners. ZC Company agreed to form a partnership with ElectroCo with a total investment of 3 million yuan (51 per cent of the total equity) and would return all its profits for production expansion of ElectroCo. The other partner was a Hong Kong Import and Export Company, which would be responsible for ElectroCo's imports and exports. The Hong Kong company's investment was in the form of equipment, amounting to 15 per cent of the total equity of ElectroCo. In order for ElectroCo to become an FIE, the Hong Kong company's investment was falsely reported as 25 per cent as required by the Foreign Joint Venture Law (i.e. 10 per cent was invested by Mr. GM but put under the name of the Hong Kong company). With assistance of ZC Company, Mr. GM obtained financial support of a state bank and he invested another 1 million yuan into ElectroCo, thus achieving 24 per cent of ownership. As a result of these alliances, ElectroCo became a collective-owned and foreign-invested enterprise.[2] The change of ownership gave the enterprise a more competitive edge in terms of reduced tax and increased financial and other support from the government, such as access to some state-controlled production materials and goods with fixed low prices.

Since 1 January 1994, ElectroCo has officially been a COE and FIE, even though its day-to-day operation is the responsibility solely of Mr. GM. Both ZC Company and the Hong Kong company were satisfied with ElectroCo's performance in 1993 and had confidence in its potential for development under Mr. GM's management. In late 1994 it was estimated that the return on investment could be over 40 per cent. While ZC Company and the Hong Kong company were quite willing to increase their investment in ElectroCo, Mr. GM told the researcher during an interview that he wanted to increase his ownership from the current 24 per cent to over 65 per cent in 1995 because of the high return on investment achieved by ElectroCo, the financial support he had secured from a state bank and the management team he had formed.

Organizational size and structure

In late 1994 ElectroCo had 76 staff and workers, and 30 of them (nearly 40 per cent of total) had completed tertiary education. The total production output of ElectroCo at the end of its first year of operation (June 1994) was 15 million yuan, or more than 197,000 yuan per head. Although the size of the enterprise was small, it had a relatively complex structure, with a general manager's office, six functional departments, three production lines and three project teams (see Figure 6.1).

The Hong Kong company had one member on the Board and ZC Company held three positions in ElectroCo. However, the Chairman of the Board and the Financial Controller normally received regular information from the enterprise and came only for the Board meetings. The Deputy General Manager appointed by ZC Company was the only person from the investors to work full time in ElectroCo. His main role was to handle public relations, especially to deal with bureaucrats such as government officials and state bank staff, because ZC Company had strong connections with the government at central and local levels. He was also involved in ElectroCo's general administration work, which gave him a clear overview of the enterprise business and enabled him to offer assistance whenever necessary.

Of the other three Deputy General Managers, one was a friend of Mr. GM's who came from NGT and was responsible for ElectroCo's technology development; the other two were Mr. GM's son and son-in-law in charge of production and project engineering, respectively. Mr. GM's son was also the Head of Production Department and assumed responsibility for three production lines and nearly half of the employees (37 out of 76). ElectroCo also had three project teams in three locations (the north, south and middle part of China), helping its customers to install electronic equipment and offer timely after-sales service. The three project team leaders reported directly to Mr. GM's son-in-law (see Figure 6.1).

Among the six functional departments, two departments (Marketing and Accounting & Finance) were under Mr. GM's direct control. The heads of other departments reported to relevant Deputy General Managers. Mr. GM's daughter was the Head of Department of Marketing and his wife was the cash manager in the Department of Accounting and Finance. The Personal Assistant (PA) to Mr. GM and the Head of General

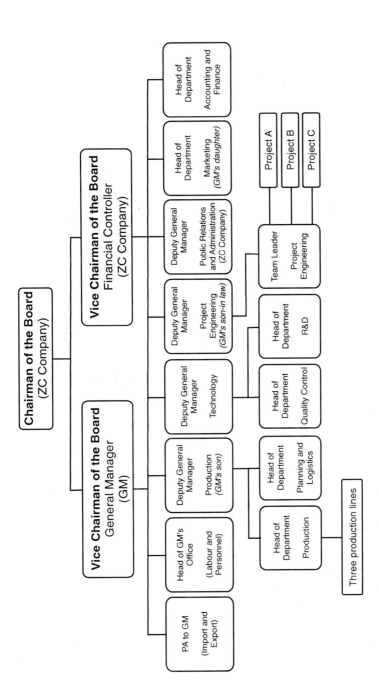

Figure 6.1 ElectroCo organizational chart

Manager's Office were the two people who had followed Mr. GM from NGT. The PA dealt with imports and exports for the enterprise, while the Head of GM's Office assumed responsibility for all HR practices. From the organization chart it is clear that ElectroCo was basically a family operated and controlled business irrespective of its registration as a private or a mixed COE and FIE.

Business strategy and the emerging role of the HRM function

The mission of ElectroCo as stated in its prospectus was 'to develop high technology in the telecommunications system, to meet the market demand by manufacturing quality products and offering first-class services, and to continuously increase market share through technical innovation and customer-oriented strategies'. The telecommunications industry, including enterprises involved in cable TV and computer networks, has developed in China since the mid-1980s. Parts of the telecommunications system in China still relied heavily on imports and ElectroCo aimed to manufacture more import substitutes and develop more suitable telecommunications systems in response to the residential and geographical situations in China.

In late 1994 ElectroCo was ranked fifth among its competitors in terms of size and market share in China. However, the enterprise was facing intense competition as more companies were entering the industry due to the high return on investment and the huge potential market. ElectroCo planned to expand production, increasing its output value from 15 million yuan in 1994 to 20 million yuan in 1995. It also intended to set up an office in the USA to keep up to date with the latest technology in the industry and to seek more business opportunities (Mr. GM's daughter, the Head of Marketing Department, would head the US office).

As the industry required advanced technology and innovation, Mr. GM emphasized that it was critical to have competent, highly motivated and loyal employees. His strategy of managing human resources was to promote the concept that ElectroCo was a big family and everyone belonged to and worked for the family. He required all managers to set examples and invest time and effort in looking after their subordinates, such as rewarding high performers, celebrating employees' birthdays and offering assistance with personal or family problems. ElectroCo's core staff, including all managers, engineers and key technical people, who comprised just over 30 per cent of the total employees (24 out of 76), were quite committed and played critical roles in ElectroCo's business operations. The following section elaborates on the management of six major HR activities at ElectroCo.

HR activities at ElectroCo

In ElectroCo, HR activities were conducted by the Head of General Manager's Office, who was also the Personnel Manager, but major decisions regarding some activities were made by Mr. GM, such as the recruitment of a manager, an increase in wages or bonuses and the budget for training. The Personnel Manager admitted that she was still learning how to manage employees because she had been involved only in routine administrative work at NGT before she joined ElectroCo. Since ElectroCo formed its business alliance, the senior manager from ZC Company passed on some HR policies and regulations from his company to the Personnel Manager. The HR activities at ElectroCo, as noted by the Personnel Manager, were still at an experimental stage with different methods being tried. The six major activities are examined below.

Human resource planning

HR planning at ElectroCo was conducted on an *ad hoc* and informal basis for two reasons. First, the prejudice and uncertainties faced by private businesses made it difficult to institute long-term business planning, let alone HR planning. Mr. GM commented in the interview that although private businesses were 'officially' protected and treated in the same way as other types of business, they were actually discriminated against by government policies. For example, the tax rate of the enterprise was determined annually by negotiation with the local government department, and POEs often paid a higher tax rate if they did not have strong connections with the government. Private businesses were also often charged excessive levies by government organizations (such as the industrial and commercial bureau, the communication and transportation bureau and even local education department) in the belief that private business people earned enormous profits and should make a higher contribution to society. Private businesses also encountered more obstacles in obtaining bank loans.

Second, the family-style management practices led to the informality in HR planning. Although managers were often invited to discuss business plans and offer their suggestions for future development, it was Mr. GM who made the final decisions and formulated short- and long-term business plans. Mr. GM also set the policy but the Personnel Manager had to get his approval regarding the steps to implement it, such as the number and type of people to be recruited for production expansion and training programmes to be offered. His paternalistic leadership style plus many uncertainties in conducting private business led to *ad hoc* HR planning.

Mr. GM noted that theoretically it was important to have both short- and long-term HR planning to ensure that any vacant job positions would be filled by competent candidates. However, he argued that it was not realistic for a newly established private business like ElectroCo to have such a plan because of the volatile environment it was in. Other senior managers agreed with Mr. GM that once the business was well established, the enterprise could adopt formal HR planning based on one- to two-year business plans. Although the enterprise did not have a formal HR plan, its job descriptions for production and managerial positions were being prepared when this case study was undertaken. The Personnel Manager had provided each department with a framework for position descriptions, which included the position's title, classification, technical (or managerial) level, major accountability, work standard required and requirement for the position holder such as qualifications, skills and experience. The managers in charge of relevant positions were to complete descriptions accordingly. The Personnel Manager believed that these position descriptions would facilitate both the establishment of a HR plan in the future and the conduct of other HR activities.

Recruitment and selection

The staffing activity in ElectroCo was conducted mainly at the level below the head of department, because all the positions at and above the department level were taken either by Mr. GM's family members or his close friends. Mr. GM personally made these appointments to be certain of their reliability and capability. His family members (i.e. his wife, son, daughter and son-in-law), who all held university qualifications, were placed at key positions to ensure the family's control over the business. His close friends, who were his former colleagues at NGT, were also regarded as trustworthy and competent. Mr. GM also preferred to employ technical experts recommended by his family members or close friends as they were seen as more reliable. The people appointed directly by Mr. GM did not sign contracts, which meant their employment was based on mutual-trust and mutual-benefits, and once the mutual-dependence ceased, employment could be terminated.

The enterprise also had an unwritten rule that recruitment of any technical staff had to be approved by Mr. GM or another Deputy General Manager. The Personnel Manager could only recruit and select production workers and general administrative staff. A production manager was normally involved in the selection of production workers to ensure that new recruits had adequate knowledge and skills. The sources of workers were local schools and labour markets. Although vocational school graduates were preferred as they had three years' education of electronic technology, they usually applied for SOEs or larger enterprises first. Hence ElectroCo often had to select normal high school graduates who lacked vocational skills. Candidates were generally considered suitable if they had completed Year 12, had some evidence to demonstrate their dexterity (such as their practical work or part-time work experience) and were willing to work on production lines. Decisions were made at the end of interviews and successful candidates would be informed of the decisions and asked to sign a one-year contract.

ElectroCo's individual contracts specified job requirements, compensation packages and other employment conditions including an initial three-month probationary period and then a nine-month apprenticeship period. Before signing the contract, workers had to pay ElectroCo 300 yuan (equivalent to two months' salary) as a bond (also called 'deposit of guarantee') to ensure that they would not resign in the first year. The bond would be retained by ElectroCo if they worked for less than a year or returned to them after one year's work. This bond was added to the contract in early 1994 when the enterprise suffered a high turnover rate and lost the money it had invested in training. At the end of the first year, a one- to three-year contract could be signed if both parties (employer and employee) were satisfied with each other.

ElectroCo also searched the local labour market for technical and managerial staff and low-skilled workers. Although many engineers and managers from NGT sought positions at ElectroCo because of its attractive pay, ElectroCo decided not to take any more staff from NGT. Mr. GM did not want to risk any deterioration in his relationship with NGT as his personal file was still held by the company. Thus when the enterprise needed new technical or managerial staff, the Personnel Manager would contact the local government employment agency for a list of suitable candidates. The basic selection criteria for technical staff were their qualifications (tertiary education), age (below 35 years old) and work experience (two years or above). When selecting technical staff, the Personnel Manager would assist Mr. GM or another Deputy General Manager by shortlisting candidates and participating in interviews. Once the decision was made, the candidates selected had to sign a one-year contract (without a bond). The contract could be renewed at the end of the first year.

For general staff and low-skilled workers, the Personnel Manager conducted selection by herself. Positions that required no or low skills and involved heavy physical work were usually filled by local rural workers who had left farming. These workers often worked harder, received lower pay than other employees and were employed on a casual basis without contract.

Performance appraisal

Performance appraisal was emphasized at ElectroCo through a pay system that offered low salaries but high bonuses to reward outstanding performance. Assessment of workers' performance was conducted monthly by the supervisor of each production line or by the project team leader. The purpose of assessment was mainly for bonus and promotion. For example, three supervisors were selected from production workers on the basis of such assessments and workers could also be promoted to higher job positions. The criteria for appraisal were based on enterprise regulations and specific requirements put forward by the relevant department.

The enterprise had unwritten regulations on labour discipline which were verbally transmitted to employees on their first day of work. Furthermore, each section had its own performance standard. The production line instituted specific job requirements for each position, including quantity, quality and allowable reject rate. The engineering project teams also had general requirements such as the timely completion of task, quality achieved and customer-oriented services. The supervisor and team leaders would assess their workers against these requirements in addition to their attendance record and cooperation with others. The assessment results would be reported to the Personnel Manager to decide the bonuses given to each worker (see next paragraph). Neither supervisors nor team leaders gave much feedback to the workers. One supervisor commented that he only alerted workers to their substandard performance when they queried the reduced bonus that they had received.

While production workers had quantified and detailed assessment criteria and regular appraisal, technical staff and managers had no job descriptions specifying responsibilities or targets to be achieved, and therefore no appraisals. They also had no fixed level of bonuses as the amount of bonuses they received was decided solely by Mr. GM and was completely confidential. During the interviews, some managers showed concern or even dissatisfaction towards bonuses distribution without any formal performance assessment. They preferred to be accountable for specified tasks and have their achievements rewarded accordingly. One senior manager remarked that Mr. GM had considered listing responsibilities for job positions so that all people below the Deputy General Manager's level could be assessed on objective performance criteria. The Personnel Manager told the researcher that she had suggested to Mr. GM to adopt a ten-point appraisal system for production workers. The ten items for appraisal included attendance, punctuality, job knowledge, quantity, quality, safety, production materials saving, cooperation, reliability and obedience of instructions. The appraisal form would be posted at the workplace so workers would be clear about their assessment criteria. A similar form, with the ten items modified appropriately, was also proposed by the Personnel Manager to be used for technical and managerial staff. Mr GM agreed to use them once all job descriptions were completed.

Compensation and welfare

ElectroCo had its own policies and wage scales for compensation and welfare and was not constrained by government regulations in matters such as the 'ceiling' pay for the owner/manager of the private enterprise. When this case study was conducted, the *Labour Law* of the PRC had just been introduced without being formally implemented. So there were no legal regulations regarding minimum pay or necessary insurance payments, such as pension and medical treatment, for the enterprise to follow.

The wage scale used in ElectroCo had 13 grades, based on position, qualification, skills and seniority. For example, a worker with a Year-9 certificate would be paid at a lower grade than one who had finished Year-12 education even though they might work in similar positions. The wage level for each grade was determined according to the local market wage ranges. Mr. GM usually selected the median of the market salary range but offered higher monthly bonuses as an incentive to employees. Wages usually accounted for 60 per cent of the compensation packages, with bonuses making up the rest. In August 1994 the enterprise raised its wage level by over 70 per cent to address two major issues. The first was the high inflation rate. The government required all SOEs to increase salary levels by 20 to 40 per cent by the end of 1994. Although this requirement was not imposed on private businesses, ElectroCo had to increase its wages to be competitive. The second issue was the high turnover rate of its skilled workers despite introducing the training bond (guarantee deposit) for newly employed workers, which only reduced the high turnover rate among new employees. Mr. GM decided to increase wages at each level to retain a skilled workforce. For example, people at grade five (technical staff with bachelor degree) were paid the same as the general manager of a COE like RadioCo (in Chapter 5), or as a head of department in a SOE like TeleCo (in Chapter 4). The wage scales at ElectroCo were also characterized by significant differentiation between grades, ranging from 20 per cent to over 50 per cent, such that a Deputy General Manager's monthly take-home pay (including wage and bonus) could be six- to eight-fold of the lowest wage level. As Mr. GM did not reveal his wage level, the wage discrepancy could be even larger than observed. Compared with wage differences between scales in enterprises with other types of ownership, ElectroCo had the largest gap between the highest and lowest wage level and between each level.

ElectroCo distributed bonuses every month. An average bonus level for blue-collar workers was announced each month. Workers with excellent assessment results would be recommended by their supervisors or team leaders to receive above average bonuses, which had to be approved by the Personnel Manager. Those who had poor results on the performance assessment might have their bonuses reduced. The bonuses for managerial and technical staff were confidential although they were also distributed each month with wages. As the Cash Manager, Mr. GM's wife was the person solely responsible for the distribution of wages and bonuses, even managers at a senior level might not know the amount of bonuses distributed to others.

In addition to its competitive compensation packages, ElectroCo also offered its core group of employees welfare benefits, including a pension (which would guarantee a reasonable retirement payment), life insurance and medical insurance. Individually they could receive free medical treatment worth up to 3,000 yuan by contributing only 10 yuan per month. For any amount above that, ElectroCo would pay 85 per cent to a nominated hospital or 70 per cent to an individually selected hospital. They also received 20 yuan per month from the firm for other individually selected commercial insurance.

In contrast, the welfare benefits for other employees were almost non-existent except for the lunch allowance. The Personnel Manager explained that the high technology development zone where ElectroCo was located did not require the enterprise to purchase insurance for employees, so this cost could be avoided. In addition, the high turnover rate once suffered by the enterprise made management feel there was little value in providing such benefits. However, the lack of welfare benefits seemed to be a significant factor for some skilled employees leaving the enterprise. One interviewee revealed that although ElectroCo seemed to offer a better compensation package, it was not attractive in the long term, especially if one needed accommodation, which was often supplied by state enterprises. With implementation of the *Labour Law* of the PRC on 1 January 1995, ElectroCo was required to offer some welfare benefits, such as insurance for a pension, unemployment and medical treatment. This would inevitably increase ElectroCo's expenditure on employees' welfare benefits, but as it did not supply any housing allowances or accommodation to its employees, ElectroCo still spent far less on such benefits than did other types of enterprises, especially state- and collective-owned enterprises.

Training and development

ElectroCo did not have any plans for training, let alone any plans for employee career development. New workers were usually given two to three months of on-the-job training to enable them to operate with minimal supervision. For some skilled positions, on-the-job training could last six months. The enterprise also encouraged employees to obtain further skills or knowledge through part-time study. Achievement of a higher level certificate or degree would lead to a salary increase. For example, a worker who had completed Year-9 education would be promoted to a higher wage scale if he/she obtained a Year-12 certificate through part-time study. However, the enterprise would not reimburse tuition fees for employees whether they passed examinations or not and would not give them any leave time for study.

In 1994, after experiencing a high turnover rate in the previous year, with many workers resigning after they had completed on-the-job training ElectroCo introduced a bond payable by newly employed workers to ensure that the enterprise received a fair return on its training investment. However, the enterprise did not introduce any plans or programmes for further training or career development for its current workforce. The Personnel Manager was concerned about the managerial skills of supervisors and managers including herself and expressed a strong desire for further training to improve the managers' skills. However, with Mr. GM's attention focused on the development of new products and on increasing ElectroCo's market share, training and development were not a priority. As the Personnel Manager did not have any autonomy over the budget for training, she could not take initiatives in this matter, but had to wait for Mr. GM to make a decision.

Labour relations

Private enterprises were not required by the government to set up trade unions and so ElectroCo had no trade union. ElectroCo was able to avoid providing welfare benefits to its ordinary workers who were obviously discriminated against when compared to the core group of employees. Apart from this injustice, workers also lacked the opportunity to participate in enterprise management. Some workers interviewed pointed out that they were never invited to management meetings or encouraged to be involved in any decision-making as supervisors often emphasized that workers should just follow instructions and complete their tasks. The workers also noted that although the enterprise was small, it was hierarchical, and workers seldom had the opportunity to talk to senior managers. Workers could only make complaints to the Personnel Manager after they had decided to resign. Mr. GM claimed that it was unnecessary to have trade unions, as he believed that managers, especially the Personnel Manager, would be able to look after the employees. In the absence of trade unions, discrimination against workers could continue unchecked.

DISCUSSION AND CONCLUSIONS

The case study of ElectroCo conducted in this chapter has provided details that support some previous research on POEs. Previous research has described the distinctive features of POEs, the type and behaviour of owner-managers of POEs (Siu, 1995) and the impact of private ownership on its HR practices. This section first discusses how these findings have been substantiated by the ElectroCo case. It then summarizes the current HR practices at ElectroCo, explores the impact of ownership on such practices and examines a probable path of HRM development in ElectroCo.

This case study has highlighted how ElectroCo managed its business on a short-term basis (no more than one year), how it established a core group of employees based on kinship or friendship with its general manager (Mr. GM), how decision-making was controlled by Mr. GM and how the enterprise was privately operated while registered under the name of a collective and foreign-invested enterprise. Its history and current situation illustrates the major features of POEs as observed by many researchers (e.g. Chen and Shi, 1998; Gao and Chi, 1996; Yuan, 1993), that is, its short-term orientation, heavy reliance on kinship or nepotism in staffing, family-style management and the red hat phenomenon.

While ElectroCo possessed the major features of a POE, its owner-manager, Mr. GM demonstrated the attributes and behaviour of private entrepreneurs. Mr. GM belonged to a group of private entrepreneurs who started their own ventures because of dissatisfaction in their previous jobs plus their greater technical skill and strong networking capability. This type of owner-manager would use certain practices to break the 'iron rice bowl' expected by Chinese workers, in an attempt to motivate them to do better work. These private entrepreneurs would also actively

> solicit customers' comments in evaluating the product, and make changes accordingly. They identify unique selling points for their products and build up distinctive advantages or competence of their own companies in order to compete better with state-owned enterprises.
>
> (Siu, 1995: 59)

Mr. GM, through his business strategy, has followed such a path: he left NGT to set up his own company, he emphasizes customized products and guaranteed after-sale service, and he established policies of low salaries with high bonuses to link individual workers' performance to their compensation. Mr. GM's strategy helped him to compete successfully in the market.

The typical features of POEs and their owner-managers have a profound impact on the HR activities in POEs. POEs tend to neglect employee training and career development, have non-standard practices in managing employees, appoint family members and close friends to key management positions and discriminate against blue-collar workers with respect to welfare provision. To be more specific, the HR practices offered at POEs are usually characterized by less extensive career development and promotion procedures, except for family members; less reliance on formal performance appraisal and feedback; a more authoritarian management style; lower levels of staff training; low levels of explicit job analysis; a strong emphasis on the management of extrinsic rewards; lower levels of welfare and fringe benefits; and lack of emphasis on formal industrial relations procedures, which are also identified by other researchers (Shaw *et al.*, 1993).

These HR practices, typical in the private sector, are well illustrated by the ElectroCo case. For example, ElectroCo only supplied on-the-job training to prepare new employees for work and not to improve existing employees' technical or managerial skills. Furthermore, the HR practices that applied to its core group of employees differed from those for blue-collar workers: examples include Mr. GM's personal appointment of key employees versus the Personnel Manager's recruitment and selection of low-skilled employees, and bonuses based on monthly performance appraisals for workers while arbitrarily determined by Mr. GM for managers. ElectroCo's heavy reliance on Mr. GM's family members and his close friends in the management team also demonstrated one of the features of private business: *renren weiqin* (staffing based on kinship and nepotism).

The HR activities at ElectroCo are summarized in Table 6.3. The table indicates, firstly, that ElectroCo employees were not allocated by the state or local labour bureau as was the case in other types of enterprises. Rather, it recruited and selected some of its employees although the procedure was informal and lacked detailed selection criteria and structured interviews. Second, the enterprise set up some quantifiable criteria to assess workers' performance rather than relying merely on their attendance and working hours. Third, it used performance-related bonuses instead of distributing rewards equally among blue-collar workers. However, these activities were only performed partially and were either non-standardized or only applied to some employees.

Table 6.3 HR activities at ElectroCo

HR activities	Purposes	Features	Issues
HR planning	• to satisfy the production needs	• *ad hoc* and informal • based on the General Manager's (GM's) decision	• lack of long-term business plans due to the uncertainty and insecurity surrounding private businesses • lack of formal plans because of family-style management practices
Recruitment and selection	• to have reliable and competent employees • to ensure family's control over the business	• GM's personal appointment to key positions • informal selection procedures • contract-based employment for blue-collar workers	• lack of job description for many positions • informality • kinship and nepotism based
Performance appraisal	• for workers' bonus distribution • for workers' promotion	• quantified criteria for workers • only conducted for workers • no feedback	• no performance appraisal for white-collar employees • little feedback to appraisees • not used for identifying training needs
Compensation and welfare	• to link individual performance to compensation	• low wages, high bonuses • GM determined confidential bonuses for key employees • welfare benefits only for core group of employees	• no welfare benefits for non-core group of employees • substantial gaps between high and low performers

Table 6.3 (cont.)

HR activities	Purposes	Features	Issues
Training and development	• to prepare new employees	• only on-the-job training	• no training for supervisors and managers • no career development for employees
Labour relations	• to work in harmony, like a big family	• no trade unions	• employees did not have any power to negotiate with management and their rights were not protected

Table 6.3 also reveals that some HR activities were lacking at ElectroCo. It neither conducted HR planning as is expected in Western enterprises, nor did it make any investment in its employees' career development except for on-the-job training for new workers. It did not have trade unions to deal with problems in labour relations and failed to protect workers' rights such as their right to labour insurance and involvement in management decision-making. HR activities such as recruitment and selection and performance appraisal were non-existent for employees holding key positions because they were either Mr. GM's family members or close friends. From a long-term perspective, this family-style management would be likely to prevent the enterprise from hiring more competent employees and could thus reduce its competitiveness (Chen and Shi, 1998; Zhao, 1998).

What is the probable path of HRM development in ElectroCo? The case study revealed that managers, including Mr. GM, considered working towards longer-term HR plans once ElectroCo's business was firmly established and had expanded further. ElectroCo was preparing detailed job descriptions for each position, including technical and managerial jobs, with the intention of establishing more detailed selection and performance assessment criteria for white-collar employees in the near future. Furthermore, two appraisal forms, each with ten assessment items, were proposed for blue-and white-collar workers, which would not only standardize this HR activity but also link pay to performance for a greater number of employees. The intention to embark on more HR practices indicates that HRM was perceived favourably by managers in this POE and this trend is supported by the survey results in Chapter 8.

However, the vulnerability of private businesses to the external environment has demonstrated that the development of HRM in POEs will ultimately be influenced by government policies and regulations as well as by changed social attitudes towards the private sector. Only with the removal of discrimination against the private business sector can POEs have confidence in their businesses and thus prepare longer term planning in both their production and human resources areas. The official change in the status of private businesses, from being supplementary to becoming an important component in the Chinese economy, should increase the use of HR activities, which should, in turn, increase POEs' effectiveness and efficiency.

7 Case study 4

HR practices in a foreign-invested enterprise (FIE)

The fourth and final case study was conducted at CableCo, a foreign-invested enterprise (FIE), or more specifically, a Sino–foreign joint venture. With the same objectives as in the previous three chapters, this chapter first presents a brief overview of FIEs in China, and then explains the data collection methods employed in this case. The case study begins with background information on CableCo, then focuses on its current HR activities and discusses the findings.

FOREIGN-INVESTED ENTERPRISES (FIES)

The open-door policy announced in late 1978 marked a sharp turn-around in China's attitude: China moved from having an inward-looking and closed economy to having one that rapidly opened up to foreign investment and has since then actively participated in the world economy, especially after accession to the WTO. China has thus witnessed a tremendous upsurge in the inflow of foreign direct investment (FDI). Of particular interest is the enthusiasm for establishing FIEs, including Sino–foreign joint ventures and wholly foreign-owned ventures (FIE is commonly used as the umbrella term to describe FDI in China). The FIE structure has been strongly fostered by the government because it has offered Chinese enterprises access to foreign capital, advanced technology, management know-how and better quality products for export. FDI has tended to take the form of an international joint venture with an SOE as its local partner, or as a fully owned subsidiary. To a certain extent, foreign ownership is instrumental in protecting FIEs from the various pressures of localization (Lu and Bjorkman, 1997). However, many FIEs in China are either under-performing or failing, and many of their problems are attributable to pitfalls in human resource management (e.g. Fung, 1995; Glover and Siu, 2000; Schuler, 2001). Some of these issues are highlighted in the following paragraphs.

A major issue has evolved around the development of effective HRM strategy by foreign companies to improve the productivity of their workforce in China. Although China is under transition from a command economy to a market economy, 'the shift from the older practices has only been partial, especially in larger enterprises, whether state-owned enterprises or even Sino-foreign joint ventures' (Warner, 1997: 40). Large foreign companies, especially multinational enterprises, often have a stronger association with government partners in China than in other developing countries, and can be locked into retaining management practices that are a legacy of the pre-reform days (Beamish, 1993). For example, in some FIEs, the egalitarian pay system is still in practice even though the eight-grade wage structure has been abandoned (Goodall and Warner, 1997). As Chinese HR policies and practices are quite different from those used in developed and market-economy developing countries, careful consideration of local idiosyncratic practices is required to operate successfully (e.g. Ding *et al.*, 1997; Paik *et al.*, 1996). Knowledge of how employees have been managed in the past may help foreign companies to understand local managers' difficulty or reluctance in accepting non-traditional or Western-style HR practices, which is a precondition to formulating effective HRM strategy in FIEs.

A second issue lies in the extent to which foreign companies can transfer their own HR practices to their joint ventures or subsidiaries in China. With the transfer of technology from a foreign firm to an FIE in China, it is generally thought that transfer of management techniques, of which HRM is an important component, is also required. However, foreign managers cannot necessarily assume that identical HR practices can be applied to their Chinese enterprises, and Western-style HR practices can usually be introduced only when a Chinese perspective with respect to Chinese values and methods has been incorporated (e.g. Fung, 1995; Gamble, 2000).

Another major issue concerns the way HRM is developing in China. Many HR practices commonly used in the West have been introduced through the operation of FIEs with some now being employed in China, and 'both Western and Chinese management find HRM appropriate as a non-adversarial and consensual management style that succeeds in co-opting the workforce' (Chan, 1995: 48). However, a particular term may carry a different connotation or orientation in the specific cultural context. Training in China, for example, is more focused on improving current performance deficiencies than on career development. The absence of career development plans plus a heavy emphasis on material incentives have contributed to the problems of high turnover and 'disloyalty' observed in many enterprises, including FIEs (Tomlinson, 1997).

While developing and retaining quality staff has become a critical factor in resolving future HRM issues, compensation also plays an important role. China has traditionally been a collective-oriented society, but its employees now prefer reward differentials 'determined primarily according to individual contributions' (Zhao, Y. 1995: 127) and there is greater acceptance of wider reward disparities based on individual performance (Ding *et al.*, 1997). With future reforms inevitable in China, a compensation system based on individual performance will become more common and more entrenched.

In addition, finding local managers with strong managerial skills in the areas such as problem-solving, decision-making and management of human resources could also be difficult as more foreign multinationals seek local management after expanding into China (Gamble, 2000; Melvin and Sylvester, 1997). In spite of these issues, increasing numbers of FIEs in China have adopted new operating styles and Western management practices, and foreign investors continue to call for a greater role of HRM in FIEs. The rest of this chapter draws on the case study of CableCo, a Sino-Australian joint venture, to illustrate how HR practices are conducted in an FIE and to explore the impact of this type of ownership on HR activities.

DATA COLLECTION METHODS

Three data collection strategies are adopted as in the previous case studies. A range of written materials on the company was reviewed, including company brochures, the employee handbook specifying the company's work regulations and employee regulations, the labour contract, the interview evaluation form, the performance appraisal form and internal documents such as a manager's work report and in-house newsletters. The interviews were conducted entirely on the company's premises and 20 employees of the company were interviewed (see Table 7.1). In addition, one senior manager from CableCo's Australian parent company (AuzCo) was interviewed in Melbourne as he was heavily involved in negotiations with the Chinese party for the establishment of CableCo and its business operation. This manager supplied background information on AuzCo, its general HR practices in Australia, and the establishment of CableCo. During the one-week field study, the author was given tours of the company and free access to conduct free and informal conversations with employees and to attend the company's routine weekly meeting.

CASE ENTERPRISE – CABLECO

Before examining major HR practices in CableCo, a brief introduction to the company is presented, including its history and ownership, organizational size and structure, business strategy and the emerging role of the HRM function in the company.

Table 7.1 Interviewees – CableCo case study

- Executive Manager (2 interviews)
- Personnel Manager (Deputy Head of Personnel and Administration Department, 2 interviews)
- Production Manager
- Finance/Accounting Controller (Head of Finance and Accounting Department, concurrently Head of Personnel and Administration Department, an Expatriate and Australian Chinese)
- Finance/Accounting Manager
- Material Manager
- Quality Manager
- Line Managers/Process Engineers (3 of them, interviewed in one group)
- Supervisors (4, interviewed in two groups, each of 2)
- Production workers (6, interviewed in two groups, each of 3)

Enterprise history and ownership

CableCo is a joint venture between an Australian corporation, AuzCo, and two Chinese organizations: the municipal Post and Telecommunication Bureau (the Post Bureau as mentioned in Chapter 4) and a subsidiary company of China National Postal and Telecommunications Appliances Corporation (PTA). Both organizations are located in Tianjin, a well-developed industrial city that is directly under the control of the central government. The main products of the joint venture are telecommunication cables and various other kinds of communication cables. The registered capital of CableCo was $US8.57 million, of which 70 per cent was invested by AuzCo and the remaining 30 per cent was contributed by the Post Bureau and PTA.

AuzCo is a multinational corporation and one of the top fifty companies in Australia. It has a long trading history with China and was among the first Australian companies to set up joint ventures in China. The Cable Group of AuzCo possesses the latest technology in cable production together with a 50-year history of successful cable manufacturing. Both the Post Bureau and PTA are state-owned organizations with over 40 years of experience in operating and administrating telecommunications in China. The cooperation between the Chinese and Australian parties from an early stage laid a solid foundation for the establishment and future development of the venture.

It took less than six months for CableCo to be established in late November 1990 after the signing of the first contact. The company began factory construction along with selection and purchasing of equipment in January 1991, and produced its first telecommunication cable in March 1992. The site was located in an Economics and Technology Development Zone, 47 kilometres from Tianjin. Before the establishment of CableCo, preparation work was the responsibility of a senior manager from AuzCo and six Chinese managerial and technical staff from TeleCo, a SOE under both the Post Bureau and PTA (see Chapter 4 about this enterprise). Among the six Chinese was the Deputy Director in charge of technical work at TeleCo who later became the Executive Manager of CableCo. The other five were from TeleCo's various departments, and all became senior managers in CableCo.

Organizational size and structure

CableCo's total output in 1993 was 75 million yuan and it had a total of 184 employees by the end of 1994. The annual output per head in 1993 was about 410,000 yuan. Since AuzCo contributed 70 per cent of the total investment, it maintained four directors on the Board of CableCo while the Chinese party had two members. The Chairman of the Board was an Australian from AuzCo while the Vice-Chairman was a Chinese from the Post Bureau. To encourage localization of the management team in China, AuzCo sent only two 'long-term' expatriates (the general manager and finance/accounting manager) to work in China on a full-time basis. Other expatriates, such as production and quality control engineers, came to work only on a short-term basis.

The General Manager of CableCo was also the general manager of AuzCo's other cable joint venture in China. Because of his commitment to the other joint venture, the General Manager could only visit CableCo once a month for a few days. During his short stay, he inspected the work completed and dealt with problems or issues unresolved by the Executive Manager. The General Manager was an overseas Chinese from Taiwan selected by AuzCo, as one of AuzCo's expatriate selection criteria specified bilingual skills. The Executive Manager had day-to-day managerial responsibility for the whole company. When CableCo was set up, it had five departments: Production, Finance and Accounting (abbreviated as F/A in Figure 7.1), Personnel and Administration (P/A), Marketing (Mktg) and the Technical Department (Tech). With the initiation of production in March 1994, the company set up three new departments: Quality Control (QC), Materials (Mat) and Import and Export (I/E).

The 1994 organizational chart is depicted in Figure 7.1. The Production Department was the largest and also the most important functional unit in the company, claiming more than 60 per cent of the employees (113 out of 184). In this department, the position of Head of Department (HOD) was vacant, thus the Deputy HOD (D. HOD in Figure 7.1) was responsible for all the work, with assistance from the Executive Manager when necessary. This

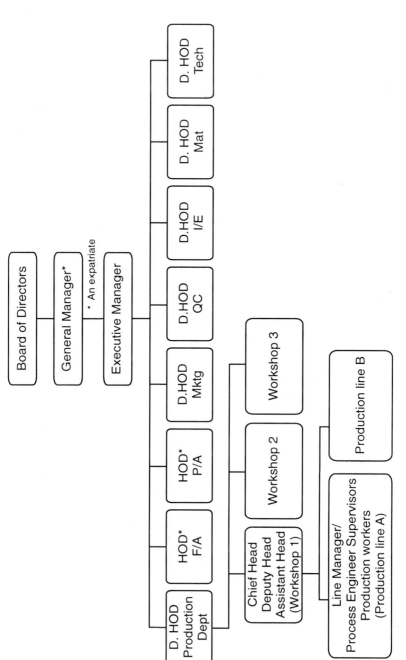

Figure 7.1 CableCo organization chart

department had three workshops (represented by 1, 2, 3 in Figure 7.1) and each workshop had its own Chief Head, Deputy Head and Assistant Head. Within each workshop there were two to three production lines (shown as A, B in Figure 7.1). The line managers who were also process engineers were in charge of both the management and technical aspects of production. Each production line had two or three groups of 7–9 employees, and each group had one supervisor.

The HOD of the Finance and Accounting Department was an expatriate sent by AuzCo, who was an Australian Chinese and could speak fluent Mandarin. This manager was concurrently the HOD of the Personnel and Administration Department because it was felt that a foreigner could deal better with difficult personnel management issues in China. For example, Chinese managers often found it hard to reject a candidate who did not satisfy the job requirement but was introduced or strongly recommended by friends, relatives or superiors. Nepotism is criticized but still widely practised in China. In contrast, a foreigner would feel much less obligated in this regard and could refuse to accept this connection-based practice. Due to the small size of the other departments including Marketing, Technology, Quality Control, Materials and Import and Export, each of these departments had only one Deputy HOD and a small number of staff. A senior manager from AuzCo who had been responsible for preparation work prior to the establishment of the venture often came to the joint venture to help coordinate contact between AuzCo and CableCo.

Following his appointment, the Executive Manager was given the power to form a management team composed of his colleagues who had been involved in the establishment of CableCo. The management team preferred to recruit employees for the joint venture from the open labour market rather than from the Chinese partner's enterprise, TeleCo, because of the concern that employees from SOEs were used to egalitarian pay regardless of performance. However, the joint venture law required that selection priority should be given to employees from the Chinese partner, and the contract signed by both parties stipulated that 60 per cent of CableCo's employees should be recommended by the Chinese partner. Therefore, of the staff initially employed in the joint venture, 60 per cent came from TeleCo while the rest were recruited from the general community through open advertisement.

Among the 70 managerial and production workers who left TeleCo and joined CableCo, 21 later returned to TeleCo. Their reasons for leaving CableCo were various, including personal reasons, difficulties in meeting the requirements of efficiency and work intensity in the joint venture and dissatisfaction with the pay system. However, the remainder became key employees of the joint venture, performing roles such as supervisors, line managers or heads of departments. Employees were classified into two groups, managerial or non-managerial, rather than cadres or workers as in SOEs. The former included managers and administrative staff while the latter mainly referred to production workers. This distinction was based entirely on their current job position.

Business strategy and the emerging role of the HRM function

As a modern enterprise in the cable industry, CableCo was equipped with the most advanced machinery and technology and a team of highly qualified employees. Using the trademark of AuzCo's Cable Group, CableCo soon attained a high reputation for its quality products and prompt service within domestic and international markets. The company's mission was 'to produce quality products, provide first class service to customers and guarantee reliable delivery'. The business strategy was to continuously develop new products, improve the quality of goods, reduce costs, manage its human resources efficiently and strengthen management control. Implementation of the company strategy depended heavily on effective employee performance and management control. This was strongly influenced by three factors. First, the production of communication cables requires a large quantity of raw materials and any wastage greatly increases production costs. Second, being an information transmission medium, quality was a critical issue as cables were usually laid underground and quality problems would cause maintenance difficulties. Third, AuzCo's standards in terms of production, cost control and quality were used as a benchmark. Therefore, throughout the entire production process, from the selection of raw materials through to the finished products, efficient utilization of materials and output of quality products were always emphasized.

Since the reforms, the telecommunication sector in China has undergone rapid development. For example, the total number of telephones has increased from 3.69 million in 1978 to 38.02 million in 1994, or 0.43 telephones per 100 people in 1978 to 3.2 per 100 people in 1994. As a consequence, the cable industry has attracted investors from domestic and overseas markets and the supply of cables has outstripped demand. With increased competition from domestic and international cable manufacturers, the CableCo management team realized that improvements in efficiency and effectiveness had to be achieved through better utilization of its human resources. This insight was clearly reflected in the comments made by the Executive Manager during the interview:

People are the most important thing in an enterprise when other conditions, that is, technology, market and government policies, are more or less the same as in other companies in the same industry. How to manage our employees so they remain loyal to the company and become more efficient in their work is a challenge we face now.

The management of human resources at CableCo has thus become the major task for the Personnel and Administration Department (hereafter referred to as the Personnel Department) which has 26 full time staff (14 per cent of total employees) without its own budget. This department also fulfils miscellaneous functions that are beyond the control of other departments, such as public relations, employees' grievance and welfare, and even sometimes assists trade unions in conducting recreational activities. The daily work of the department was managed by two Chinese Deputy HODs while the HOD, an expatriate sent by AuzCo who was also the HOD of Finance and Accounting Department, acted mainly as a figurehead to assist Chinese managers to tackle subtle personal relationship issues whenever necessary. Apart from the administrative work, the Personnel Department became involved in developing the company's business strategy and in various other HR activities such as HR planning and compensation including wage packages and welfare. This was somewhat unusual, as wage administration is normally controlled by the department of finance and accounting in Chinese enterprises. CableCo followed the Chinese system for one year before integrating this function into its Personnel Department.

HR activities at CableCo

Before discussing HRM at CableCo, HRM at AuzCo's Cable Group needs to be addressed briefly as the Group assisted the joint venture in establishing its HRM system. AuzCo had a well-established HRM system with a HR director at corporate level, a general manager (HR) at group level and a HR manager at company level. The Cable Group practised major HR activities as defined in the West (Schuler *et al.*, 1992). The company executed HR planning, which was used with merit-based recruitment, and selection and training. It also had job analysis to clarify job responsibilities and authorities, to establish individual performance standards, and to manage performance, compensation and employment planning. Managers conducted performance appraisal interviews with their staff members mainly for performance feedback but sometimes for promotion and transfer. The Group also offered on- and off-the-job training programmes to its employees to update their knowledge and skills. However, the Cable Group did not include a bonus system in its HR practices and had insufficient employee career management as it did not offer any formal career counselling. In addition, performance appraisal was conducted mainly for white-collar rather than blue-collar employees. The concepts of HRM used in the Cable Group were introduced to CableCo and some practices such as merit-based recruitment and selection and performance appraisal were transferred to the joint venture as well. The following account will describe and analyse the six major HR activities conducted at CableCo.

Human resource planning

HR planning was conducted annually at CableCo under the control of the General Manager. The focus of planning was on the overall control of employee numbers. The demand for employees was generally based on production needs, which was greatly influenced by AuzCo because the Australian practice was used as a standard. Within the limit of a planned total number of employees, each department could put forward its staffing needs according to its production plans and number of positions available. The Personnel Department would either employ or transfer employees to meet staffing needs. Planning was mainly regulated by top management and the role played by the Personnel Department was primarily coordination and administration. The planning was mainly short-term oriented, and the reason behind this, according to the Executive Manager, was that both parties held different ideas and approaches to business development. The Chinese party strongly recommended investment in the project for producing optical fibre cable because they believed in the potential of a huge domestic market for such a product. Accordingly, they selected and employed some graduates for preliminary work on this project. However, their suggestion was ignored by AuzCo, as the Australian party did not want to further expand its business prior to the identification of a market in China. When a long-term business strategy could not be accepted by both parties, the joint venture had difficulty making long-term HR plans, thus the Personnel Department recruited staff for the short-term or sometimes on an *ad hoc* basis.

HR planning was affected not only by the company's business strategy but also by the employee turnover rate. The turnover rate was closely related to employee background and commitment. At CableCo, employees from the Chinese partner's company, TeleCo, showed more loyalty and commitment to the joint venture and had a much lower turnover rate than new employees recruited from local rural areas. The employees from TeleCo all resided in the accommodation in the downtown area supplied by TeleCo. They were all older than 35 years with about 10 years of working experience with TeleCo. Being a SOE, TeleCo offered lifetime employment to its employees even after they joined CableCo. This meant they could return to TeleCo if they resigned from the joint venture. With regard to accommodation, the joint venture paid the housing allowance (20 per cent of employees' average salary) in two different ways. One was to pay the allowance individually to those who supplied their own accommodation. The other was to pay collectively to TeleCo as compensation for the dormitories it supplied to those employees working at CableCo. Therefore, the joint venture employees from TeleCo could still live in their original dormitories and remain on a waiting list with other TeleCo's employees for housing adjustment (to move into a larger flat). This was one of the major reasons that employees from TeleCo felt obligated to the joint venture. They showed more willingness to devote themselves to the development of CableCo and most of them became committed and key employees of the company.

By contrast, the turnover rate of locally recruited employees was much higher for two reasons: the nature of their job and availability of employment opportunities in the local area. As CableCo did not supply accommodation to its employees like many other foreign joint ventures, its employees, except those from TeleCo, were primarily recruited from the local area. CableCo was located in a recently developed coastal region, which had previously been rural farmland. Between 1984, when the Economics and Technology Development Zone was set up, and 1994, over 2000 enterprises with different types of ownership had been established in the area. The local farmers had many employment opportunities even though they had less education than workers from the city. As these employees were usually offered low-skill jobs with money being their highest priority, they showed little commitment to the company and were always ready to leave for a better paid job elsewhere.

In order to keep a stable workforce, CableCo had to consider issues such as the source of employees and turnover rate in its HR planning. In dealing with these issues, as the Executive Manager noted, the supply of accommodation was a critical factor. In the mid-1990s, it was impossible for employees to purchase their own accommodation. The Executive Manager believed that the provision of accommodation to employees would attract more people from wider sources and retain them. Nevertheless, AuzCo refused to supply accommodation to Chinese employees, as they had never done so in Australia. Furthermore, AuzCo refused to increase the housing allowance (currently 20 per cent of its wage bill), thus making it impossible for CableCo to supply any kind of accommodation (see the following discussion). This prevented CableCo from recruiting employees from outside the local area unless the employees could find accommodation for themselves. With so many new companies in the area, the local labour market became competitive and the turnover rate became quite unpredictable, making HR planning even more difficult.

Apart from the accommodation issue, the lack of participation by managers, especially line managers, also affected HR planning. CableCo's line managers and other managerial staff such as supervisors were involved chiefly in the implementation of the plan rather than in the planning itself. This was partly due to the direct control exerted on the overall HR planning by the General Manager and partly because the managerial staff lacked an understanding of HR planning as the legacy of the centrally planned economy.

Recruitment and selection

The process for recruitment and selection at CableCo comprised four steps. First, the department with a staffing need would submit an application to the Personnel Department detailing both the overall quotas of employees fixed by the company each year and the departmental production needs. Each application included a brief job description and candidate specifications to enable the Personnel Department to start recruitment. Then the Personnel Department would recruit candidates according to the department's specifications through three channels. The first channel was to rent a stand in the local labour market, where the personnel staff could place job advertisements and hand out application forms. This was the cheapest way to recruit candidates (usually 300 yuan per day per stand in 1994[1]) and was mainly used for employing workers and technicians. The second was to advertise the job in local or national newspapers. This was used for recruiting experienced, middle to senior level managers or highly skilled professionals. It could cost thousands of yuan – one advertisement in the *Economic Daily* (*Jingji Ribao*, a widely circulated Chinese national newspaper) would cost 5,000 to 8,000 yuan per day. The last method was to recruit new graduates from universities. This required a payment of 10,000 yuan (1994 price) by CableCo to the relevant university for each new graduate employed by the company (in the mid-1990s, university education was nearly free to students, with the state paying most of the cost).

The third step was for the Personnel Department and the department that submitted the application to shortlist and select candidates. The Personnel Department would conduct general checks first, including the verification of applicant's qualifications, previous performance in political and professional areas, family background and social connections. After this stage, the applicant's file would be sent to the relevant department for further examination, especially in the technical area. The department would set written tests and/or conduct interviews by managers and professional staff. Candidates applying for managerial work were interviewed by the Personnel Manager and a manager from the relevant department. The Personnel Department designed a standardized interview assessment sheet for all departments that included items such as general impression (e.g. manner, attitude and appearance); verbal skills (e.g. logical thinking, synthesis of ideas, clarity of expression); understanding of the company and the knowledge required; the match between applicant's experience and job requirement; determination shown by the applicant to work in the company; and proficiency in English. The interviewee was evaluated on a five-point scale 'from excellent, through good, average and pass, to poor', and the total score was one determinant in the final decision.

Finally, after a candidate was chosen, the Personnel Department would make an offer to the applicant, who could refuse the offer without any negative consequences. However, the company had not received any rejections of employment offers. Once the applicant accepted the offer, the Personnel Department would be responsible for all the administrative work, including the signing of a probationary labour contract, creating a personal profile and conducting a brief orientation session to present the employee handbook and brief information on the company. The Personnel Department kept a record of unsuccessful applicants with the intention of setting up a databank in the future. However, by 1994 the Personnel Department was still not computerized and many records, including personal profiles, were still handwritten.

CableCo's approach to staffing offered each department an opportunity to select recruits according to its own specifications, which was particularly important as formal job descriptions were not available for many positions within the company. CableCo had written job descriptions only for production workers; these specified the nature of the job, operation process and requirements for product quality and quantity. The descriptions set up the criteria for selection and also enabled workers to follow production instructions and perform self-monitoring. No other positions in CableCo had such formal descriptions. Supervisors in charge of these positions were required to verbally explain the work to new employees, covering details such as the type of work involved and the method used to complete the work. The verbal descriptions heavily depended on the supervisor's understanding of the job and his/her interpersonal communication skills. In addition, the transfer of a supervisor could result in inconsistency in verbal descriptions. Thus the involvement of relevant department or line managers in the selection process helped to match candidates with the job and to reduce the dismissal rate.

CableCo had dismissed only five employees during their probationary period on grounds of incompetence in a period of more than two years.

Nevertheless, this selection method had its shortcomings because of its heavy reliance upon individual leaders in each department. It could result in a lack of consistent and objective standards within the company or poor adherence to the company's business strategy due to an individual manager's ignorance or negligence. For example, the company planned to computerize the whole management system including accounting and finance in late 1994, but the accountants employed in 1993 were not computer literate. Errors of this kind could be avoided if the selection criteria were tied to the company's strategy for development and HR planning, and if the Personnel Department offered active guidance to departments rather than merely administrative assistance.

Generally, new employees had a six-month probationary period. During this period, the company could discontinue an employee's contract at any time if the person was found to be unsuitable for the job. Similarly, during this period the employee was free to resign without any legal obligation. After this period, employees would be given a formal labour contract. The contract system applied to everyone in the company and the duration of the contract was generally two years. If both parties were satisfied, the contract could be renewed for another two years. Employees who undertook training overseas and graduates who cost the company more than 10,000 yuan per head to employ had to sign five-year contracts. Anyone who resigned during the contractual period had to compensate the company for the training fee or for costs incurred in the duration of employment.

If any department wanted to dismiss an employee for incompetence, it had to submit a report to the Personnel Department, which then sent staff to talk with the recruit involved. Instead of immediate dismissal, the personnel staff usually encouraged the individual to resign to save face and minimize the negative impact on the morale of remaining employees. Only when someone had seriously violated the company's regulations or contract would the Personnel Department support immediate dismissal of the person concerned.

Performance appraisal

CableCo formally adopted a performance appraisal system in June 1993 with the intention of linking performance with compensation to break the 'iron rice bowl' practice. Based on the appraisal form used in AuzCo, CableCo's Personnel Department designed its own assessment form with the same criteria for both managerial and non-managerial employees. However, the weighting given to each criterion varied between different groups. For example, items related more to managerial skills would be weighted more heavily for managerial employees while items related to technical competencies would be weighted more heavily for production workers. There were ten major criteria in conducting appraisals: knowledge of the job, quality and quantity of work completed, supervisory potential, reliability, awareness of cost reduction, occupational safety, adaptability, cooperation and communication. Each criterion had a brief definition, for example, knowledge of the job was defined as 'the degree to which the employee has learned and understood the objectives and procedures of the job'.

Each criterion was assessed on a five-grade scale ranging from 'outstanding' to 'marginal'. According to different job positions, any quantifiable standards were incorporated into each grade. For example, the five grades for 'quality of work' were classified as:

1   Work often below standard: seldom meets normal standards, and excessive amount needs to be redone;
2   Work frequently below standard: inclined to be careless, and small amount of work needs to be redone;
3   A careful worker: a small amount of work needs to be redone, corrections made in reasonable time, and usually meets average standards;
4   Work sometimes superior but usually accurate: negligible amount needs to be redone and work regularly meets standards;
5   Exceptionally high quality: consistently accurate, precise, quick to detect errors in the work.

The appraisal at CableCo was conducted annually from the top to the bottom, which meant the Executive Manager evaluated the performance of department managers, while department managers assessed line managers, and line managers assumed responsibility for evaluating supervisors and production workers. The appraisal was conducted without the appraisees' knowledge and the rating was totally dependent upon the appraiser's daily observation and individual judgement. The appraisal ratings were kept confidential from appraisees as required by the Personnel Department. After appraisers at each level completed the evaluations, the appraisal forms were handed over to the Personnel Department. The personnel staff would then check each employee's personal records to see whether he/she received any rewards or penalties during the year, as these results would also be incorporated into the final assessment. The final score of the appraisal was calculated by the Personnel Department and would be used to determine a wage increase or reduction as the company had not set up a bonus system by late 1994.

The managers at CableCo valued this kind of appraisal, as they believed it was a time-effective method of encouraging people to work harder. They were also in favour of keeping the appraisal results confidential to avoid possible conflicts with employees. However, the confidentiality of the appraisal form aroused strong dissatisfaction among many employees. During the interviews, production workers expressed their concerns at the way the appraisal was conducted. First, they were denied access to the appraisal form and thus ignorant of the contents and criteria of assessment. Second, they questioned the appraiser's ability to make a fair and unbiased judgement of subordinates and raised doubts about the influence of personal relationship on assessment results. Finally, they were concerned about the consistency and reliability of the appraisal results that were heavily dependent upon individual judgement.

In spite of the company's intention to break traditional egalitarian practices by linking performance to individual pay, defects in the appraisal system reduced its effectiveness. First, without the knowledge of appraisal criteria and their measurement, employees were denied the opportunity to clearly understand and fulfil the company's requirements for high performance. Second, the confidentiality of appraisal results distanced managers from employees because of distrust resulting from this privately conducted assessment, which also failed to achieve other appraisal purposes such as communication and development. Without feedback regarding the assessment, employees had difficulty identifying deficiencies in their work and could not improve their performance for future appraisals. Furthermore, the lack of participation by managers and employees in formulating appraisal criteria diminished initiatives and reduced enthusiasm towards such an appraisal.

In addition to performance appraisal, the company had penalty policies. The Personnel Department issued a list of prohibited behaviours and their corresponding penalties, including verbal or written warnings, suspension from work and dismissal. Any kind of penalty would result in a one-off fine or a reduction of wage scale. However, the company did not have a policy for rewarding or encouraging positive behaviour. Those who performed well were rated higher in the performance appraisal and might receive a wage increase after the annually conducted performance assessment.

Compensation and welfare

The compensation and welfare system at CableCo was quite unique for the unpredictability and confidentiality of its wage packages. From the first day of its operation, CableCo eliminated the fixed wage scale that had been used for over four decades in China, especially in the public sector. The initial wage package for different job positions was determined by factors such as the relevant wage level in both local and domestic markets, wage levels in other FIEs and the inflation rate. While the government required that the wage scale in FIEs should be at least 20 per cent higher than in SOEs, the company kept its wage level more than 50 per cent higher than SOEs, and managers at CableCo were paid at an even higher level than their counterparts at TeleCo. Given the intense competition in the local labour market, CableCo kept its wage scale in the upper middle range among local FIEs to retain its key employees.

After employees started work, wages would be adjusted solely on the basis of performance or changes in position, rather than on seniority. Therefore, the wage package for each individual became relatively unpredictable because it was no longer fixed by the job position or length of service. Employees who achieved high scores in the annual performance appraisal would have their wages increased. Although the validity and reliability of performance appraisal were questioned by employees, it still helped to link pay to performance. Each individual's wage package was kept confidential as required by company regulation. The Employee Handbook stated that employees were not allowed to reveal their own wage scales or enquire about others' wage packages. Otherwise, they would either be warned or penalized. The reason for the confidentiality of wage packages was to abolish the old fixed wage system while avoiding unnecessary jealousy or dissatisfaction among employees. The Personnel Manager further noted that although employees favoured performance-linked pay, many people still had difficulty accepting the fact that high performers would earn more than low performers regardless of their age, position and length of service.

During the interviews conducted by the author, the interviewees were asked about their attitudes towards the company's unpredictable and confidential wage packages. The managers interviewed generally responded positively, because most of them were satisfied with the pay they received and the way it was distributed. This wage system gave them incentives to perform well and also avoided unnecessary envy or resentment from their less well paid colleagues or subordinates. However, the managers showed strong dissatisfaction towards the absence of a bonus system within the company, as they all believed that annual wage increases could not offer timely rewards to employees. Similarly, production workers interviewed considered this wage system to be acceptable except for the uncertainty of the criteria for wage increases and the absence of a bonus system. The first issue could be addressed by reforming the conduct of performance appraisal, while the second issue needed to be considered by the company. Although both managers and workers believed that a bonus system could further differentiate high and low performers and link reward more closely to individual performance, their opinion was not supported by the company.

The company had no bonus system because of concerns from both partners. From the Australian parent company's point of view, bonuses could not be considered until the joint venture had repaid all its loans and started to make profits. The Chinese partner thought the bonus system should not be established until other supporting activities were satisfactorily conducted, such as job analysis and performance appraisal. Since the bonus system was restored in 1979, it has become a significant part of wage packages in Chinese enterprises, with an aim to offer incentives to employees. However, a bonus was often equally distributed among employees to avoid potential disputes or conflicts and thus lost its function as a motivational tool. In the absence of an effective way to closely link bonuses to performance, the company preferred not to set up a bonus system. However, after more than two years of operation, managers and employees, especially those in the production and marketing departments, expressed a strong desire for a bonus system. They maintained that a bonus system would better link performance with compensation and allow CableCo to remain competitive in a tight labour market.

Although the company used performance appraisal results to help adjust wages, this method had its limitations. CableCo's managers pointed out that the wage adjustment normally occurred only once a year and hence often delayed the company's recognition of outstanding performance by employees and their contribution to the enterprise. It was also inappropriate to substantially enlarge wage differences between high and low performers working in the same position as wage scales were usually set up for long-term purposes. Furthermore, a person's wage level was not easy to reduce, as employees in China were accustomed to wage increases. By contrast, bonuses would be flexible and easily adjusted, rewarded at the appropriate time, and the gap between high and low level bonuses could be broadened to further encourage high performers. Finally, a bonus could be more closely linked to the company's total performance. As CableCo did not have a profit-share plan, managers and workers felt that a bonus system was an adequate substitute for the time being.

In mid-1994, 11 production workers resigned from CableCo and returned to their positions at TeleCo. The Executive Manager used this example to explain how a bonus system could have prevented their resignations. The 11 people were all experienced and key workers in production lines and were all high performers at CableCo. However, because of the significantly higher requirements at CableCo in terms of product quantity and quality, work intensity and a stronger management control, they had to work much harder at CableCo than at TeleCo. In addition, they spent over two extra hours in daily travel time because CableCo was nearly 50 km away from their residences. Although their wages were over 50 per cent higher at

CableCo than at TeleCo, they did not feel that their efforts were adequately compensated. Two of the workers who resigned told the author that CableCo's wage system without bonuses did not really differentiate between high and low performers as wage differences were small (some workers said that they knew their close friends' wages, and usually people working at the same position could find out this 'secret' through 'gossip'). When the company suddenly lost these 11 workers, the production lines almost collapsed and it took nearly two months to train new workers to work independently on the lines.

In late 1994, the Executive Manager submitted a report to the General Manager regarding the establishment of a bonus system. He suggested that monthly bonuses should be adopted to encourage the achievement of production or sales objectives and a reduction in material wastage. He provided detailed calculations on the amount of bonus and recommended a method of bonus distribution. During the interview, the Executive Manager emphasized that the bonus system should be used in conjunction with performance appraisal. However, he agreed that the appraisal system should be revised first to enable employee participation in criteria-setting and establish a more objective measure of employee performance. However, when this case study was completed, the company was still waiting for approval from the General Manager to alter the appraisal system and establish a bonus system.

Apart from compensation in the form of wages, the company also made efforts to meet the welfare needs of its employees. The company offered transportation for employees to travel between home and work, and supplied free meals during working time. It also purchased health and social insurance for employees' medical treatment and superannuating purposes. However, CableCo did not supply its employees with any accommodation, which was one of the major welfare items offered by many Chinese enterprises. In the mid-1990s, few employees were able to buy their own apartments or flats due to low wages. Although banks started to offer home loans to individuals who had the guarantee of the company, they had to pay 30 per cent of the purchase price as a deposit, which could be equivalent to half a year's salary for a manager for a two-bedroom apartment. That was an impossible sum for most ordinary wage earners. The accommodation problem limited CableCo's sources of labour. The Executive Manager was very concerned, especially as the situation was bound to worsen once production expanded further and more modern technology was introduced. However, the Australian partner showed little sympathy towards this issue.

Training and development

> Qualified people are the essence of manufacturing quality product; therefore, the company has placed heavy emphasis on staff training in production technical and managerial areas. Staff are encouraged to undertake advanced studies and every opportunity will be given to staff to go overseas to attend training programmes provided by equipment suppliers or cable manufacturers, in order to keep up with the latest developments in technology.
>
> (Company brochure)

As a specialized cable company, CableCo was equipped with world-class machinery and technology, which in turn required a highly skilled workforce. The managers at CableCo all believed that training was critical in maintaining a competent workforce to survive the rapid development in technology and the intense market competition. Each year the company used one per cent of its total payroll for training purposes as required by the government. The Personnel Department organized training programmes according to production needs. The target groups for training included new recruits in three categories: production workers, technical professionals and managerial staff. The training programme for new production workers included introduction to the company's rules and regulations, and provision of detailed information on operation processes, production quality requirements and control of production materials. Training for technical professionals involved familiarizing them with the technical standards of products, technological processes and technical skills used in production. Some training programmes were also organized to improve employees' analytical ability and English skills. The emphasis in managerial training was on the relevant skills needed to perform particular roles in the job, such as job analysis and conducting an interview. Most of these training programmes were offered either during employee orientation or on the job. Sometimes technical or managerial staff attended short training courses organized by external organizations.

Although training was emphasized by the company, there were no systematic training plans to assist individual career development. The personnel manager admitted that the training programmes were often designed according to emerging issues in production, such as new skills required or new employees recruited. The reactive nature of the training programme could be due to two main factors. First, as the company's HR planning was short-term oriented, it was difficult to have a proactive training plan. While the company was concentrating on the current year's production and sales, the Personnel Department organized training programmes only when required by other functional departments. Second, although particular deficiencies in training might be noted during performance appraisals, this information was not used by the Personnel Department in its planning of training programmes. Performance appraisals were used primarily to determine wage levels, not as information sources for feedback, development or planning. The *ad hoc* nature of training and the lack of integration of the various HR activities further reduced the effectiveness of training.

Some key technical staff who were promoted to management positions also commented on the training in management. One newly appointed department manager talked about his difficulties with management work as he was employed based on his technical competence rather his managerial experience. Similarly, some university graduates who had undertaken both technical and managerial work as process engineers and line managers were particularly interested in management training as few had studied management subjects at university. However, the company did not have a programme to meet those individual needs and managerial staff often relied on self-education through work. Furthermore, the company neglected to collect feedback from training programmes offered. Without such feedback on the training's purpose, contents and approaches, it was difficult to evaluate the effectiveness of training and to make any improvements.

Labour relations

No industrial dispute has occurred since the establishment of CableCo and this could be attributed to the active role played by its trade union. CableCo's trade union was set up in December 1993, after a vote by ballot. All Chinese employees and managers became union members. A Committee of three was elected by the members. The Chairperson was the Deputy Head of Personnel and the other two committee members were the Deputy Head of Production and a line manager. The union was divided into 11 groups and each group had a head elected by group members.

The trade union at CableCo played its traditional role, namely a bridge between management and employees or 'a transmission belt'. It was both the workers' representative and the management's assistant. The former role was to look after workers in terms of their personal interests and their welfare, such as payment, accommodation and family issues. The latter role was to assist management to implement the company's decisions and to achieve the company's objectives. When the company called a top management meeting to discuss business strategy, production plans and wage increases, the chairperson of the union was present in the capacity of both the union representative and Deputy Head of the Personnel Department. The Chair-person's unique position of representing both management and labour enabled her to easily collect employee opinions, suggestions or complaints, which would then be discussed at management meetings or with relevant managers.

Being the workers' representative, the union negotiated with the com-pany on behalf of employees and helped to improve their welfare and work-ing conditions. For example, the union obtained lunch allowances from the company to offer employees free meals during working time, and a 'hot weather allowance' to purchase more soft drinks to prevent heatstroke. The Chinese managers admitted that the union was more adept in conducting negotiations with Australian expatriate managers when dealing with extra welfare for employees as the Australian partner may be more likely to refuse the Chinese manager's suggestions than those raised by the trade union. As management's assistant, the union helped management to achieve the com-pany's objectives. For example, in September 1994, the company was under pressure to export large quantities of various products. To meet this demand, the union organized a labour emulation activity under the slogan 'the com-pany is in my heart and quality is in my hands'. The union drew up a tracking plan, detailing the quantity and quality required, the deadline for each depart-ment and the prize to be rewarded for achievement of the goal. Motivated by the union, employees worked hard continuously for four weeks. Only because the union organized the work program did they manage to achieve the targets, allowing the company to successfully complete its export task.

Furthermore, the union was responsible for arranging recreational activi-ties for all employees. Usually once or twice a year the union would organize free trips to tourist attractions. It was believed that such activities could help enhance team spirit, facilitate interpersonal communication among employ-ees and increase cohesiveness within the company. During the interviews conducted by the researcher, the employees all indicated their appreciation for what the union had done for them and revealed their trust and sense of belonging towards the union.

DISCUSSION AND CONCLUSIONS

This chapter has outlined how human resources were managed in an FIE, CableCo, with respect to the six HR activities. All the major HR activities defined by Schuler *et al.* (1992) were in existence in this joint venture (see Table 7.2). However, some terms had a connotation or ori-entation in China that differs from the West. The most obvious example is regarding performance appraisal. The format of the appraisal practice

Table 7.2 HR activities at CableCo

HR activities	Purposes	Features	Issues
HR planning	• overall control of employee numbers	• short-term oriented • top management-decided	• lack of long-term business strategy • high turnover rate of local employees
Recruitment and selection	• to meet staffing needs • to have the right people	• have a standardized procedure • merit-based selection • formal selection methods, e.g. test and interviews • contract-based employment	• lack of job description for many positions • limited to the local area due to accommodation problems • heavy reliance on knowledge and quality of key individuals
Performance appraisal	• for wage administration	• have formal assessment sheet • conducted confidentially • no feedback	• reluctant to give feedback • not used for identifying training needs • reliability of assessment questionable
Compensation and welfare	• to link performance to the wage package	• unpredictable wage scales • kept confidential • no bonus	• no timely reward • no substantial gap between high and low performers
Training and development	• to prepare new employees	• mainly on-the-job training • passively organized • reactive to solve emerging production problems	• not proactive • lack of training for managers • lack of career development for employees
Labour relations	• transmission belt between management and employees • to negotiate between Chinese and foreign partners regarding employees' welfare	• Chinese employees are all union members • focus on employees' welfare • assistant to management	• To what extent does the trade union represent workers' interests in terms of their rights and power?

transferred from AuzCo was characterized by job-related criteria for assessment instead of the politically oriented criteria traditionally used in China. However, the assessment was conducted solely by the employees' superiors in confidence and was used only for wage determination. It thus failed to achieve the objectives that would be expected in the West, such as an increase in communication between appraiser and appraisee, and the identification of training needs for performance improvement and career development. In addition, the legacy of traditional HR practices can be observed in CableCo, such as its reactive and passively conducted training programme.

Some HR activities at CableCo have shown a tendency to converge with those practised in the West. This includes merit-based recruitment and selection, formal selection methods such as tests and interviews, and compensation with a focus on individual performance. Similarity in practices between CableCo and AuzCo could be partly attributed to its ownership, because the ownership of FIE had offered CableCo access to Western management practices. This type of ownership often requires the transfer of technology and management practices, at least in concept, from foreign companies to subsidiaries in China. In CableCo's case, the joint venture was required to use AuzCo's standards as its benchmark in production and quality control, which in turn has demanded more effective management of its human resources. Furthermore, the autonomy granted to FIEs, the recently emerged free labour markets and the development of a market-driven economy have all influenced CableCo to adopt or experiment with new HR practices in order to achieve the company's objectives. Nevertheless, this type of ownership also prevents the adoption of certain practices that provoke conflicting positions from the two parties. This is evident in the refusal of AuzCo to provide accommodation for CableCo employees, thus hampering CableCo's ability to make long-term plans in regard to human resources.

Some HR practices had unique Chinese characteristics, such as the role of the trade union, and non-confrontational labour relations between management and employees. This situation, however, could change if a conflict arose between the foreign and Chinese partners, where the trade union could act as a negotiator for the Chinese party including both Chinese workers and managers as occurred in CableCo. This phenomenon has been observed by other researchers (Chan, 1995; Warner, 1995, 2000). For example, Nyaw (1991: 115) has noted that 'one unique aspect of the trade unions of joint ventures in China is that they deal directly with foreign partners or their representatives with regard to labour disputes or grievances' rather than the joint ventures *per se*, because the joint ventures are owned partly by the state and the unions are not supposed to negotiate with the state.

CableCo already had plans to develop HR practices, as indicated in the case study. The company was going to replace its verbal job descriptions with written descriptions to facilitate the establishment of objective selection criteria. The conduct of performance appraisal was also going to be altered to offer feedback to appraisees and to help identify training needs. A bonus system was most probably to be established, with the aim of linking compensation more closely, both in time and quality, to individual performance. Training in management skills and other technical aspects was strongly called for by employees and managers, and was listed on the agenda of the Personnel Department. This evolution of HR practices could be indicative of future HRM trends in FIEs in China. Although the findings from one case cannot be generalized across all FIEs, this case study has offered field examination of HR activities in one FIE, which, together with the results from the survey questionnaire, can be used to draw some broader conclusions (see Chapter 8).

8 Surveys of HR practices in Chinese industrial enterprises

This chapter addresses research questions that are more quantitative in nature than those in the case study chapters. It aims to: (1) investigate the status quo of the HR department and the existence of HR activities in the industrial enterprises; (2) examine the extent to which HR activities are currently conducted and are expected to be conducted in the future, and respondents' perceived effectiveness of some HR practices; (3) explore the impact that ownership types have on HR practices; and (4) analyse probable paths of HRM development in the future. The survey was used in 1994–5 to provide a wider context for the case studies and a follow-up survey was conducted in 2001–2 to update the information about HR practices used and the development of trends in HRM in China. The survey questionnaire was divided into three major parts: the background of the enterprises and respondents surveyed; the enterprise's HR department including its structure, the HR manager, the activities conducted and the department's perceived importance; and the existence, practices and perceived effectiveness of seven major HR activities.

BACKGROUND OF ENTERPRISES AND RESPONDENTS

Questionnaires were distributed to 850 managers and employees in the Chinese industrial sector (including manufacturing and services industries) with four major types of ownership in 1994–5 and then to 900 respondents in similar industries in 2001–2. The number of usable questionnaires received was 440 in 1994–5 and 447 in 2001–2 (the response rate was about 52 per cent and 50 per cent, respectively). Responses from enterprises under the same type of ownership were grouped together in the analysis of the impact of ownership on HR practices.

Enterprises

The majority of enterprises surveyed were in the manufacturing and services industries (98 per cent in 1994–5 and 85 per cent in 2001–2), with the rest being government organizations or educational institutions. The enterprises had been in operation, on average, for approximately 44 years in the first survey and 32 years in the second one for SOEs, 24 and 13 years in 1994–5 and 2001–2, respectively, for COEs, 5 and 12 years for POEs, and 4 and 10 years for FIEs. The longer history of SOEs/COEs and the shorter period of operation of POEs/FIEs in the first survey indicate the strong dominance of the public sector before the post-Mao reforms as well as the changes in ownership structure since the reforms. The SOEs and COEs surveyed in 2001–2 had a shorter operational period by average than those surveyed in 1994–5. Take the percentage of surveyed enterprises that were established after 1978 as an example. In the first survey, 11 per cent of the SOEs and 40 per cent of COEs surveyed were set up after 1978 with the remaining established before 1978. The figure in the second survey was 52 per cent for the SOEs and 85 per cent for COEs surveyed, indicating more enterprises surveyed in 2001–2 had shorter history than those surveyed in 1994–5.

As for the size (number of employees) of the enterprises surveyed, there were some salient changes. In the 1994–5 survey there were, on average, 1,331 employees for SOEs, 538 for COEs, 221 for POEs and 328 for FIEs, which reveals the dominant position of SOEs in Chinese industry. In the 2001–2 survey SOEs were still the largest, with, on average, 2,797 employees; COEs had 476, POEs had 780 and FIEs 1,310. The doubling in size of the SOEs shows they still played an important role but may also indicate the overstaffing problem that was prevalent in the state sector. The considerable increase of the size of POEs and FIEs reflects a rapid development of private enterprises in the late 1990s.

The production output value per head in both surveys indicates a similar pattern, that is, the private sector appears to be more productive than the public sector. In the 1994–5 survey the output value per head was approximately 68,000 yuan in SOEs, 88,220 yuan in COEs, 151,500 yuan in POEs and 219,200 yuan in FIEs. These data correlate with those revealed in the four case studies where the SOE, TeleCo (Chapter 4), had the lowest output value per head and the FIE, CableCo (Chapter 7), had the highest. Such data from the mid-1990s should be used only for reference because, at that time, many enterprises still had dual accounting statements to take advantage of the dual pricing system and individually negotiated production targets and tax rates. In the second survey, the output value per head was 333,000 yuan for SOEs, 225,000 yuan for COEs, 532,000 yuan for POEs and 796,000 yuan for FIEs. All enterprises appeared to have achieved better productivity in the second survey than in the first, but the private enterprises again seemed to perform better than the public enterprises, indicating that the ownership form does have an impact on the company's performance.

In the survey each respondent was required to indicate to what extent his/her enterprise was facing certain situations in the business environment as outlined in the questionnaire (see Table 8.1). The responses were based on a five-point Likert-type scale ranging from 1 'very false' to 5 'very true'. A multivariate analysis-of-variance (MANOVA) was employed to ascertain whether the responses to the external environment varied across ownership forms, and one-way ANOVA tests were then conducted to ascertain which of these situations varied across types of ownership. For responses that show statistically significant differences across four types of ownership, a *post hoc* test (Tukey) was implemented to reveal where the differences existed.

Table 8.1 indicates that there were significant differences across the four types of ownership for 'increased market place competition' (item 1), 'changing business environment' (item 2) and 'changing government regulations' (item 3) in the 1994–5 survey, and for items 1, 2 again and 'supply of skilled people' (item 5) in 2001–2. Compared with other items in both surveys, item 1 has the highest means across the four types of ownership. This provides evidence that the transition from a planned to a market economy and further integration of China's economy into the global market (in particular, China's accession to the WTO) have resulted in more competition in both domestic and international markets for Chinese enterprises. COEs had the lowest means in both surveys and the Tukey results indicate that the differences were significant between COEs and SOEs in 1994–5 and then between COEs and FIEs in 2001–2. COEs, though in the public sector, traditionally received less government support than SOEs, often obtained contracts from SOEs and mainly served the domestic market, which could partly explain why they felt less pressure from market competition than SOEs/FIEs.

In regards to items 2 and 3, important changes occurred between the two surveys. In 1994–5, businesses in the state sector experienced stronger changes in the environment than those in the non-state sector. The differences between SOEs and COEs/POEs, and between SOEs and FIEs were significant, and indicate that in the mid-1990s, the public sector, especially SOEs, was at the centre of economic reform. However, the results of these two items changed dramatically in the second survey. The private sector demonstrated higher means than the public sector in regards to the changing business environment, with the only significant difference being between COEs and FIEs. Furthermore, the significant differences among the four types of enterprises with respect to rapidly changing government regulations disappeared in 2001–2 (although the private sector revealed higher mean

Table 8.1 The business environment faced by enterprises

Variables	1994–5 survey					2001–2 survey				
	SOEs m (s.d.)	COEs m (s.d.)	POEs m (s.d.)	FIEs m (s.d.)	p	SOEs m (s.d.)	COEs m (s.d.)	POEs m (s.d.)	FIEs m (s.d.)	p
1 Market place competition has increased dramatically.	4.5 (0.6)	4.3 (0.7)	4.4 (0.6)	4.5 (0.7)	0.05	4.4 (0.7)	4.2 (1.0)	4.4 (0.7)	4.6 (0.5)	0.05
2 Conditions in our business environment are rapidly changing.	4.1 (0.7)	3.7 (0.9)	3.4 (0.9)	3.6 (0.8)	0.001	4.0 (0.7)	3.7 (0.8)	4.1 (0.6)	4.2 (0.6)	0.05
3 Government regulations are rapidly changing.	4.0 (0.7)	3.6 (0.7)	3.1 (0.9)	3.4 (0.9)	0.001	3.9 (0.8)	3.7 (0.8)	4.0 (0.6)	4.1 (0.7)	—
4 The technology in our product/services is complex.	3.5 (0.8)	3.3 (0.9)	3.2 (0.9)	3.3 (0.8)	—	3.5 (0.8)	3.4 (0.6)	3.5 (0.9)	3.7 (0.9)	—
5 Abundant supply of skilled people	2.9 (0.9)	3.0 (0.9)	3.2 (0.9)	3.0 (0.9)	—	3.2 (0.9)	3.4 (0.9)	3.5 (0.8)	3.6 (0.9)	0.05

m = mean; s.d. = standard deviation

values than the public sector), indicating that a more market-oriented economy exists.

The responses to 'complex technology' (item 4) and 'supply of skilled people' (item 5) show that in the first survey, POEs had the lowest mean for item 4 but the highest for item 5. Although these differences are statistically non-significant, they do suggest that despite the relatively low technology in POEs, they enjoyed more flexible hiring practices because of their full autonomy. These situations changed in 2001–2, when COEs had the lowest mean for item 4 (again the differences are non-significant). With respect to item 5, SOEs demonstrated a lower mean than the non-state firms and the difference between SOEs and FIEs was significant. This indicates that SOEs have not fully resolved their overstaffing problem while FIEs appear the most attractive for employees among the four types of enterprises. The changes revealed in the second survey indicate a healthy development of the private sector business in terms of its technology and access to the free labour market for skilled employees.

Respondents

The profile of respondents from both surveys, including their age, gender, occupation, education, types of firms they worked for and the duration in the current job and with the current enterprise, is set out in Table 8.2. In regards to gender and occupation, the proportions of the two groups of respondents were similar, about two-thirds of respondents were male and 60 per cent were at managerial level. The educational backgrounds of the respondents were much higher than in the general population, with 73 per cent in 1994–5 and 86 per cent in 2001–2 of all respondents having tertiary qualifications (cf. 2.1 per cent of general population in 1995 based on the one per cent of the national population census, see *China Statistical Yearbook*, 1996). The high educational level of respondents is due to the fact that the survey was conducted in four major well-industrialized and developed cities where the educational level is much higher than in other areas. However, a significant number of respondents had received only a two-year tertiary diploma in the first survey (43 per cent), a consequence of the break in their education during the Cultural Revolution and the government's promotion of education in the diploma (*dazhuan*) once the reform programme started in the late 1970s. This education situation had improved by the time of the second survey and the percentage of those with a tertiary diploma dropped while the percentage with tertiary degrees and postgraduate qualifications increased. Furthermore, respondents in the second survey were younger and had higher qualifications.

Table 8.2 Sample characteristics of the 1994–5 survey and the 2001–2 survey respondents in the four types of enterprises

Variables	1994–5 survey (%)					2001–2 survey (%)				
	SOEs	COEs	POEs	FIEs	p	SOEs	COEs	POEs	FIEs	p
Age					0.001					0.001
• Less than 30	9	27	32	39		23	15	44	45	
• 30–9	39	34	32	35		27	32	26	36	
• 40–9	39	30	21	21		33	38	20	10	
• 50–9	13	8	10	4		17	15	9	9	
• 60 and over	0	1	5	1		0	0	0	0	
Gender					—					—
• Female	26	40	26	41		36	32	30	42	
• Male	74	60	74	59		64	68	70	58	
Highest level of education completed					—					0.05
• High school certificate or less	25	33	21	26		11	32	17	14	
• Tertiary diploma (2-year university certificate, *dazhuan*)	43	46	42	43		34	38	24	27	
• Tertiary degree (4-year university Bachelor's degree, *benke*)	30	17	32	30		40	27	41	40	
• Some postgraduate education (one-year postgraduate diploma)	1	0	0	0		6	0	4	8	
• Postgraduate degree (Master degree or above)	2	4	5	2		9	3	15	11	
Duration in current job (year)	10	10	6	7	0.05	10	11	8	6	0.001
Duration with current enterprise (year)	14	9	3	4	0.001	13	9	5	5	0.001

While the percentage of respondents from SOEs changed minimally in the 2001–2 survey, the proportion of respondents working in other types of enterprises changed considerably, with a 12 per cent decrease in numbers from COEs and a 7 per cent increase from POEs/FIEs. Thus there are considerably more respondents from the private sector (POEs and FIEs) in the second survey (42 per cent) than in the first one (28 per cent). This change appears consistent with the increased size of enterprises in the private sector. The duration in the current job, but not necessarily in the same enterprise and the average length of time spent with their current enterprise were similar in both surveys.

The sample characteristics of the respondents in the four types of enterprises in 1994–5 and 2001–2 are also displayed in Table 8.2. In the 1994–5 survey, SOEs had few employees under the age of 30. Although this situation improved in the second survey, private enterprises still had much higher percentage of younger employees than the public companies, and such a difference is statistically significant. Before the establishment of a nationwide social security system, public enterprises with an older workforce were obliged to offer more social security benefits such as pension and medical expenses to their employees, whereas private enterprises could have less or evade such obligations.

The qualifications of the public workforce appear lower than those of the private sector and the difference revealed in the 2001–2 survey was statistically significant. The fact that the private sector has more qualified employees is consistent with the finding that FIEs and POEs had stronger responses in both surveys than SOEs regarding the supply of skilled people in the labour market (see Table 8.1, item 5). Compared with other types of enterprises, COEs had many fewer respondents with four-year tertiary degrees in both surveys, which might explain why COEs had the lowest mean value in terms of technology used in the second survey (see Table 8.1, item 4). The duration in current jobs and with current enterprises in both surveys displays a similar pattern, that is, the average length of time spent in the public enterprises was longer than in private ones. The differences in duration in both surveys were statistically significant and are partly because of the short history of the private sector and partly because of lifetime employment and low job mobility in the public sector before the reforms.

THE HR DEPARTMENT

The second part of the survey questionnaire examined the existence of an HR department and the competency (i.e. qualifications, experience and political background) of the HR manager. It also listed major HR activities and asked respondents to select those currently conducted by their HR department (classified into 'is now' questions) and then to indicate those they considered ideal for the future ('should be'). The respondents' perceived importance of their HR department is discussed at the end of this section.

All variables in Table 8.3 show significant differences except for 'HR manager with tertiary education' (item 3) in 1994–5 and 'HR manager with similar working experience' (item 4) in 2001–2. In relation to 'the existence of HR department' (item 1), the first question enquired whether there was a separate personnel department (or labour department or both) in control of HR activities for the enterprise. If the answer was 'yes', respondents were asked to indicate whether this department was split into two sections to manage cadres and workers separately (item 2) as was common practice during Mao's regime. In 1994–5 more SOEs/FIEs had a separate HR department than COEs/POEs. By 2001–2, more COEs/POEs had a separate HR department, although POEs still demonstrated the lowest percentage. The first survey results also indicated that SOEs preferred to manage cadres and workers separately. The emphasis placed on the categorization of workers and cadres by SOEs in the mid-1990s was significantly different from other enterprises, demonstrating the continuing strength of traditional practice in the state sector. However, this emphasis was greatly reduced in SOEs in 2001–2, with their percentage dropping from 61 to 28. Nevertheless, the percentage for SOEs/COEs in 2001–2 is still higher than POEs/FIEs, and the difference is statistically significant.

Although many enterprises surveyed had a single department to manage all employees in 1994–5, only two FIEs surveyed used the term 'human resource' (*renli ziyuan*) to label this department; others used names such as 'personnel and administration' (*renshi xingzheng*), 'personnel and labour' (*renshi laodong*) or 'labour and wages' (*laodong gongzi*). In 2001–2, many more enterprises surveyed used the term 'human resource department' (*renli ziyuan bu*), with 43 SOEs, 42 FIEs and 13 POEs having an 'HR department'. None of COEs surveyed used this new term. Though the adoption of 'human resource' by more enterprises in 2001–2 survey does not necessarily mean that traditional personnel and labour administration has been replaced by HRM, it at least shows a break from the old concept. This broader term HRM is used in this study and the author uses the title of HR for such a department.

Table 8.3 also reveals the education (item 3) and experience (item 4) of HR managers of the enterprises surveyed. The majority of them had tertiary education, reflecting a continuing emphasis by enterprises on qualifications of managers since the reform. While the difference in item 3 across the four types of ownership was not significant in 1994–5, it became significant in 2001–2 with COEs having the lowest percentage of responses. This result is

Table 8.3 Current status of HR department and competence of the HR manager

Variables	1994–5 survey (%)					2001–2 survey (%)				
	SOEs	COEs	POEs	FIEs	p	SOEs	COEs	POEs	FIEs	p
1 A separate HR Department	72	56	39	71	0.05	76	71	51	74	0.05
2 One HR Department with two sections: one for cadres, one for workers	61	25	13	6	0.001	28	26	9	10	0.001
3 HR manager who attained tertiary education	90	84	82	88	—	93	82	89	93	0.01
4 HR manager who had similar work experience	68	47	75	75	0.01	71	73	63	82	—
5 HR manager who was politically reliable	94	72	59	85	0.001	91	84	64	71	0.001

consistent with COEs having the lowest percentage of respondents with Bachelor or Master degrees (see Table 8.2), and supports the problem as discussed in the case study of RadioCo regarding the lack of qualified employees in COEs (see Chapter 5).

As for work experience (item 4), the first survey indicated that HR managers from POEs/FIEs were more experienced than those from SOEs/COEs. This result could be attributed to more flexible hiring practices or to less rigid labour allocation in non-public enterprises, especially given that private enterprises were not as bound by government restrictions on cadres or senior managers as were COEs and SOEs. However, this pattern changed in 2001–2 when the type of ownership no longer had significant influence on HR managers' work experience, indicating that all types of enterprises have placed similar emphasis on HR managers' work experience.

Moreover, POEs in both surveys paid the least attention to 'HR managers' political reliability' (item 5, i.e. membership of the Party) (though the mean value is slightly higher in 2001–2 than in 1994–5). In the 1994–5 survey, SOEs and FIEs placed high priority on this item; this similarity was not surprising because the FIEs surveyed in 1994–5 were all foreign joint ventures with partners from SOEs and their HR managers were recommended by the Chinese partners. In 2001–2, FIEs showed less emphasis on the item, which could be due to more wholly foreign-owned firms surveyed or the Chinese partners having less influence on FIEs. The differences in both surveys were statistically significant, which indicates the ownership type does have an impact on the requirement of HR managers to be politically reliable, with the public sector placing greater emphasis on the political background of their managers.

Following the questions on the HR department and manager, respondents were given a list of HR activities as presented in Table 8.4. Some of these activities were commonly practised in Western market economies (e.g. HR planning and job analysis), while some were observed in China during Mao's regime (e.g. employee welfare and the organization of political studies). Respondents were required to select those activities currently conducted by their HR department (categorized under 'is now') and then indicate those they thought to be ideal ('should be'). When comparing results across the two surveys, an increase or a drop in 'is now' for a certain activity in the second survey means increased or reduced practice of the activity in 2001–2, while an increase or a drop in 'should be' means that the activity should be used more or that there is less room for further increase in the future. The differences between the 'actual' and 'ideal' situations in two surveys may point toward the nature and direction of future change.

Table 8.4 shows the percentage of respondents who ticked 'is now' and 'should be' for each item, organized by enterprise type. In the 1994–5

Table 8.4 Activities currently ('is now') and should be conducted ('should be') by the HR department

HR activities		1994–5 survey (%)					2001–2 survey (%)				
		SOEs	COEs	POEs	FIEs	p	SOEs	COEs	POEs	FIEs	p
1 Conducting HR planning	is now	37	34	21	41	0.01	33	38	36	51	—
	should be	63	66	79	59		67	62	64	49	
2 Being responsible for HR policies	is now	60	62	47	60	0.01	62	52	53	65	—
	should be	40	38	53	40		38	48	37	35	
3 Recruitment and selection	is now	64	70	65	70	—	64	55	69	70	0.05
	should be	36	30	35	30		36	45	31	30	
4 Job analysis and evaluation	is now	52	44	35	43	0.01	45	42	66	55	—
	should be	48	56	65	57		55	58	34	45	
5 Performance appraisal	is now	42	35	39	48	—	41	55	50	55	—
	should be	58	65	61	52		59	45	50	45	
6 Wage administration	is now	65	58	57	64	0.01	70	61	55	72	0.05
	should be	35	42	43	36		30	39	45	28	
7 Training and career development	is now	47	29	14	49	0.001	40	47	21	50	0.05
	should be	53	71	86	51		60	53	79	50	
8 Record keeping	is now	69	65	66	68	0.05	74	61	63	71	—
	should be	31	35	34	32		26	39	37	29	
9 Health and safety	is now	55	53	39	65	0.05	52	50	61	49	—
	should be	45	47	61	35		48	50	39	51	

HR activities		1994–5 survey (%)					2001–2 survey (%)				
		SOEs	COEs	POEs	FIEs	p	SOEs	COEs	POEs	FIEs	p
10 Employee welfare, recreation and sports	is now	50	46	50	39	—	55	63	48	56	—
	should be	50	54	50	61		45	37	52	44	
11 Organize political studies	is now	55	50	38	51	0.05	57	46	44	48	—
	should be	45	50	62	49		43	54	56	52	
12 Contact local Labour Bureau for potential labour supply	is now	61	100	0	70	—	57	70	50	53	—
	should be	39	0	0	30		43	30	50	47	

survey, the impact of ownership was significant for all variables except items 3 (recruitment and selection), 5 (performance appraisal), 10 (employee welfare) and 12 (contact local Labour Bureau). However, such significance was observed only in items 3, 6 (wage administration) and 7 (training and career development) in 2001–2. This difference clearly indicates a reduced impact of ownership on HR practices. To be more specific, in the 1994–5 survey, a higher percentage of SOEs and FIEs appeared to conduct HR activities than COEs and POEs. POEs had the lowest percentage on most of the items, which supports the findings from the ElectroCo case study (see Chapter 6), where major HR activities were either informally conducted or missing. However, the situation changed in the 2001–2 survey, with only FIEs consistently conducting a higher percentage of those HR practices commonly observed in the West (i.e. items 1 to 7), and POEs increasingly offering some HR practices (i.e. items 1–5, and items 7 and 9) but also conducting the lowest percentage of certain HR activities typically common in China before the reform (i.e. items 10, 11 and 12).

The variance of HR activities is particularly strong in relation to training and career development (item 7) among the four types of ownership. In the 1994–5 survey, POEs/COEs offered much less training and career development to their employees than FIEs/SOEs. These differences are even more pronounced than those found in the four case studies. This situation changed somewhat in the second survey, that is, all enterprises except SOEs seemed to conduct more training and development than they had in 1994–5. However, POEs still offered the least training and career development in 2001–2. In both surveys the enterprises demonstrated a higher percentage for 'should be' than 'is now' (except FIEs in 2001–2, where the responses are the same). This indicates that a training and development activity was offered by more HR departments in 2001–2 than in 1994–5 (except SOEs: see the following discussion) and there was still a strong desire for this HR activity to be increased in the future.

In addition to training and development, increases in HR planning (item 1), job analysis (item 4) (except for SOEs) and performance appraisal (item 5) were on the agenda of the enterprises in the 1994–5 survey as they were expected to be conducted more in the future. The non-state sector met, in a large part, these expectations in 2001–2, with more POEs, FIEs and COEs conducting these three HR activities. In the 2001–2 survey, only item 1 was expected to be practised more in the future by all the enterprises except for FIEs, with items 4 and 5 having less room for further increase in the enterprises except for SOEs. In general, the differences in the 2001–2 survey in the conduct of these three HR activities across the four types of enterprises are not significant statistically indicating that these practices have been adopted to a similar level in all enterprises surveyed.

All respondents in both surveys expected less room for further involvement of the HR department in two major HR practices, that is, being responsible for HR policies (item 2) and recruitment and selection (item 3). This might indicate a decentralization of some HR policy-making to other departments and a subsequent trend to delegate some HR activities, such as recruitment and selection, to individual departments, as was observed in CableCo (see Chapter 7).

The practice of wage administration (item 6) was used by more enterprises, especially SOEs and FIEs, in 2001–2 than in 1994–5, while record keeping (item 8) was less observed in COEs/POEs than in SOEs/FIEs in 2001–2. SOEs and FIEs demonstrated the same pattern in both surveys, as they had much higher percentages than COEs and POEs in the current practice of these two items. Such movements are more comprehensible in SOEs than in FIEs because of the transition from centrally fixed wage scales to more performance-linked and unit-determined (such as department or workshop) compensation. In FIEs, it may be partly due to the influence of SOEs on their foreign partners, and partly because the relatively short history of FIEs has not allowed them sufficient time to establish a different HRM system. However, the increased involvement of the HR department in wage administration may indicate the important role of compensation in HR practices in Chinese enterprises.

The effect of private ownership on health and safety (items 9) and HR organizing political studies (item 11) was significant only in the first survey when POEs paid much less attention to such activities than other types of enterprises. However, in the second survey POEs seemed to pay more attention to the health and safety issue. Politics is always a sensitive topic in China and people often report an emphasis on political study whether they had experienced it or not. Respondents may have answered item 11 cautiously in both surveys, thereby biasing the results. With respect to the contact made with a local Labour Bureau for labour supply (item 12), only about 12 per cent of the total respondents answered it in both surveys, with no respondents from the private sector and only two respondents from COEs in 1994–5. This could be because only HR managers would have clear information about this practice. However, the results for item 12 were still valuable as they revealed the legacy of the old labour allocation system in the public sector and also in some FIEs that received assistance from the local government.

In order to measure the respondents' perception of their HR department the data regarding several facets of the department's function, practices and effectiveness were collected and presented in Table 8.5. The responses were based on a five-point Likert scale, ranging from 1 to 5 indicating minimum to maximum presence of each condition, respectively. ANOVA tests were conducted to show the impact of ownership on the perceived effectiveness of an

Table 8.5 Perceived effectiveness of HR department

Variables	1994–5 survey				2001–2 survey			
	SOEs m (s.d.)	COEs m (s.d.)	POEs m (s.d.)	FIEs m (s.d.)	p	SOEs m (s.d.)	COEs m (s.d.)	POEs m (s.d.)	FIEs m (s.d.)	p
1 It is viewed as an important department in the enterprise.	4.1 (0.6)	3.4 (0.7)	3.6 (0.8)	4.0 (0.7)	0.001	3.8 (0.8)	3.8 (0.8)	3.9 (0.9)	3.9 (0.7)	—
2 It tends to imitate the human resource practices (e.g. in hiring, pay, etc.) used by other firms in our industry.	3.5 (0.8)	3.4 (0.7)	3.3 (0.7)	3.4 (0.9)	—	3.4 (0.9)	3.4 (0.8)	3.6 (0.9)	3.5 (0.8)	—
3 It works closely with the senior management group on the key strategic issues facing the enterprise.	3.7 (0.8)	3.6 (0.8)	3.4 (0.9)	3.9 (0.7)	0.05	3.5 (0.9)	3.6 (1.1)	3.8 (0.8)	3.8 (0.9)	—
4 It is viewed as an effective department.	3.3 (0.7)	3.0 (0.9)	3.3 (0.6)	3.5 (0.7)	0.01	3.0 (0.9)	3.3 (0.8)	3.1 (1.1)	3.3 (0.9)	—

m = mean; s.d. = standard deviation

HR department. For items that show statistically significant differences among four types of ownership, a *post hoc* test (Tukey) was then conducted to indicate where the differences existed.

The mean responses for each item in Table 8.5 demonstrate a central tendency, indicating a positive attitude towards the HR department. However, it may also indicate the respondents' caution in evaluating their HR department, given that the culture in China discourages overt criticism and conflict (Weldon and Jehn, 1993). In the first survey the results showed that ownership did have a significant impact on all aspects except item 2. The difference between SOEs/FIEs and COEs/POEs for item 1 was significant, indicating that the HR department was more highly regarded in SOEs/FIEs. The difference between FIEs and POEs for item 3 (the HR department works more closely with the senior management group) is also significant, which supports the finding from the case study of a POE, ElectroCo (Chapter 6), where the management style was observed to be quite paternalistic. Another significant difference was that between SOEs/FIEs and COEs in their view of the effectiveness of the HR department. While the HR department in COEs/POEs was regarded as less important than in SOEs/FIEs, it was deemed less effective in COEs but not in POEs.

However, such significant differences were not observed in the second survey, indicating that the HR department was perceived similarly across different types of enterprises or that the ownership type did not have significant impact on perceived effectiveness of HR department. In a comparison of the results from two surveys, only in POEs did the HR department appear to receive a better perception with respect to its importance, HR practices and the involvement in senior management teams (items 1, 2 and 3) in 2001–2, even though the mean value of its perceived effectiveness dropped slightly. These results are consistent with the previous finding that more POEs had a separate HR department in 2001–2 than in 1994–5 (see Table 8.3), which also indicates that POEs have paid more attention to their HR departments during their development over the economic transitional period. In the second survey, POEs/FIEs received similar or identical mean values for the first three items in Table 8.5 and this may imply that the HR department has started to become more active in business operations in the private sector than in the public one.

MAJOR HR ACTIVITIES

This section focuses on seven HR activities, regarded as essential practices in Western HRM (Schuler *et al.*, 1992): HR planning, job analysis, hiring practices, performance appraisal, compensation and welfare, training and development and labour relations.

HR planning

The survey questions cover three aspects of HR planning, that is, what, who and why. 'What' refers to the type of HR planning adopted by the enterprise, namely, whether it is short-term (1–2 years) or long-term (2–5 years) (items 1 and 2 in Table 8.6). 'Who' covers the people involved in HR planning, including the general manager, department managers, line managers and HR manager of an enterprise (items 3 to 6 in Table 8.6). 'Why' tries to find out why the various enterprises engage HR planning, that is, whether planning is part of the business strategy, whether it is used for staffing needs, or as required by the government (items 7 to 9 in Table 8.6).

The results in the 1994–5 survey indicate that most enterprises only had short-term HR planning; by 2001–2 more companies (except among POEs) conducted long-term HR planning. The type of ownership had little impact on this item in either survey. The short-term orientation could be attributed to the continuing transformation of the economic system, which has created uncertainties for all enterprises regardless of ownership. Only 36 per cent of respondents ($n = 157$) answered this question in 1994–5 and 47 per cent ($n = 209$) in 2001–2: perhaps only those involved in planning had access to the required information.

In 1994–5, the type of ownership did have an impact on the people involved in HR planning, with the involvement of a general manager (item 3), department managers (item 4) and a HR manager (item 6) all demonstrating significant differences across the enterprises. While more general managers participated in HR planning in COEs than in other types of enterprises, more HR managers were involved in such planning in SOEs/FIEs than in COEs/POEs. The level of participation of department mangers in FIEs is significantly higher than in other enterprises, which might partly explain why the HR department in FIEs was viewed in 1994–5 as more effective than those in other types of enterprises (see Table 8.5). A common pattern observed across the enterprises surveyed in 1994–5 was that few line managers participated in the planning.

The pattern of managers' involvement in HR planning had changed in 2001–2. First, only the percentage of HR managers involved in HR planning (item 6) showed a significant difference across all the enterprises surveyed, with major difference existing between FIEs and POEs. The greater involvement of HR managers in HR planning in FIEs is consistent with the previous finding that more FIEs conducted this activity in both surveys (see Table 8.4). Second, there was a considerable decline in the department manager's participation in HR planning and an increase in the number of line managers involved. Third, in the 2001–2 survey, the percentage of HR managers

Table 8.6 HR planning

Variables	1994–5 survey (%)					2001–2 survey (%)				
	SOEs	COEs	POEs	FIEs	p	SOEs	COEs	POEs	FIEs	p
1 The HR planning is short-term based (1–2 years).	67	56	71	81	—	60	45	71	65	—
2 The HR planning is long-term based (2–5 years).	33	44	29	19	—	40	55	29	35	—
3 General Manager is involved in HR planning.	48	78	47	40	0.001	46	49	53	43	—
4 Department managers are involved in HR planning.	9	7	29	47	0.001	5	9	4	3	—
5 Line managers are involved in HR planning.	8	7	12	6	—	19	27	18	29	—
6 HR manager is involved in HR planning.	62	29	29	60	0.001	48	42	39	61	0.05
7 Planning as part of the whole enterprise's business strategy.	61	49	35	59	—	51	68	61	55	—
8 Planning for enterprise's own staffing needs.	38	51	47	51	—	44	38	41	48	—
9 Planning as required by the local government (e.g. Labour Bureau).	16	15	12	7	—	20	15	8	12	—

involved in HR planning was higher than in the first survey except for SOEs. The overall pattern in the second survey is that HR planning seems to be conducted more by HR managers and line managers, indicating a decentralization of HR practices.

HR planning was conducted principally as part of the business strategy and for staffing needs in both surveys (items 7 and 8). It appears that in the 1994–5 survey more SOEs/FIEs used HR planning for business strategy than COEs/POEs, but in the 2001–2 survey, it was COEs and POEs that had greatly increased this practice for business purposes. Although the impact of ownership on these differences is not statistically significant, over half of the enterprises surveyed in 2001–2 used HR planning as part of their business strategy, a healthy increase over the 1994–5 results. In regards to staffing needs, SOEs used HR planning much less than other enterprises in 1994–5, but had increased its use in 2001–2 while the others demonstrated a decline. The results suggest that in 1994–5, SOEs were still affected by the old labour allocation practice, but this problem seemed to have been alleviated in 2001–2. Furthermore, the results indicate that in 1994–5 FIEs, and in 2001–2 POEs, were subject to less stringent HR planning regulations by local government (item 9) than other types of enterprises, reflecting government's lingering impact on public enterprises. The increased percentage of item 9 for FIEs might reflect the impact of Chinese partners who are often from the public sector.

Job analysis

The survey questions on job analysis are divided into three parts. The first explored the existence of job analysis and involvement of the HR manager. The second part examined the factors included in job analysis. The factors include items often expected in Western HRM, such as employee's qualifications, skills, physical health and tasks to be carried out, and also some items specific to the Chinese context, such as the description of tools and equipment to be used, product standard and production quotas. The last part focused on the different uses of job analysis. The impact of ownership forms on these various aspects of job analysis was also examined. The results of the first two parts from both surveys are displayed in Table 8.7.

The impact of ownership on job analysis appears to have waned between 1994–5 (results significant for items 1, 2, 3, 9) and 2001–2 (significant only for item 1). The percentage for item 1 in the 2001–2 survey showed a remarkable increase across all types of enterprises except for SOEs and the differences between various enterprises are significant. Written job analysis thus appeared to be conducted in more companies, especially in FIEs than previously. The decrease in SOEs could be the

Table 8.7 Job analysis: existence, HR manager's involvement and factors included

Variables	*1994–5 survey (%)*					*2001–2 survey (%)*				
	SOEs	*COEs*	*POEs*	*FIEs*	*p*	*SOEs*	*COEs*	*POEs*	*FIEs*	*p*
1 Conduct written job analysis	62	27	50	57	0.001	55	65	59	73	0.01
2 **HR** manager was involved in the job analysis.	76	81	50	58	0.05	83	72	59	73	—
3 Factors to be included – employee's qualifications	65	43	47	70	0.01	78	71	60	76	—
4 Factors to be included – employee's skills	94	94	88	90	—	92	85	87	87	—
5 Factors to be included – employee's physical situation	54	49	24	45	—	45	53	42	44	—
6 Factors to be included – tasks to be carried out	75	64	88	82	—	70	65	59	69	—
7 Factors to be included – tools and equipment to be used	49	36	31	45	—	38	36	25	45	—
8 Factors to be included – product standard	63	74	44	60	—	55	68	55	52	—
9 Factors to be included – production quotas (e.g. number of products to be produced per hour/shift)	72	74	50	56	0.05	54	29	48	52	—

result of ongoing restructuring and radical reform in the state sector since the mid-1990s.

Table 8.7 also indicates that in 1994–5, more HR managers in COEs/SOEs were involved in job analysis, while in 2001–2 more HR managers in FIEs and POEs were. By 2001–2, the significant difference between SOEs/FIEs and COEs/POEs in emphasis on employee's qualifications that had existed in the 1994–5 results had disappeared, as the emphasis on qualifications had increased greatly in all enterprises surveyed (though SOEs/FIEs still had a higher percentage of qualified employees than COEs/POEs).

In 1994–5, production quotas (item 9) were more prevalent in SOEs/COEs than in POEs/FIEs. This finding is consistent with the case study of ElectroCo (see Chapter 6), where bonuses were linked to work outcomes rather than to pre-set quotas. However, the significant impact of ownership on item 9 in the 1994–5 survey was no longer evident in 2001–2, indicating a break from the traditional practice in the public sector. Furthermore, the table illustrates that in both surveys the majority of enterprises have incorporated an employee's skills (item 4) into job analysis and most of them also specified the tasks to be carried out (item 6).

How did the enterprises use their job analysis? The questionnaire listed six major uses of job analysis (see Table 8.8). The first five uses are often observed in Western HR practices, whereas the last one (for determining position salary) was typical in the Chinese setting after the position-and-skills wage system was introduced in the early 1990s. The table compares the current uses of job analysis ('is now') to its ideal use in the future ('should be'). The results are grouped under the four types of ownership.

For items 1, 4, 5 and 6 in Table 8.8, the impact of ownership was statistically significant in 1994–5 but not in 2001–2, indicating that job analysis is now used for similar purposes in all types of enterprises. Results for items 1, 4 and 5 in both surveys indicate that all types of enterprises except SOEs had increased their utilization of job analysis for the classification of responsibility and authority (item 1), performance standards (item 4) and job evaluation (item 5) in 2001–2 over 1994–5.

With respect to the use of job analysis for determining position salary (item 6), different patterns were observed in the two surveys. In 1994–5, more SOEs than the other types of enterprises used this practice, possibly as a consequence of wage reform when different kinds of wage packages were on trial. In 2001–2 all enterprises surveyed had increased their current use of job analysis for this purpose regardless of the ownership type, which indicates that salary is now more closely tied to job position and skills than it was previously.

In the 2001–2 survey the type of ownership demonstrated a significant impact only on items 2 and 3. All enterprises appeared to use job analysis more

Table 8.8 Uses of job analysis

Variables		1994–5 survey (%)					2001–2 survey (%)				
		SOEs	COEs	POEs	FIEs	p	SOEs	COEs	POEs	FIEs	p
1 Classify job responsibility and authority	is now	62	61	53	67	0.05	60	64	62	71	—
	should be	38	39	47	33		40	36	38	29	
2 For HR planning	is now	24	33	23	38	—	28	35	29	47	0.05
	should be	76	68	77	62		72	65	71	53	
3 For recruitment and selection	is now	46	55	57	52	—	49	41	62	63	0.01
	should be	54	45	43	48		51	59	38	37	
4 For performance standards	is now	49	41	41	45	0.05	47	50	61	56	—
	should be	51	59	59	55		53	50	39	44	
5 For job evaluation	is now	46	38	30	37	0.01	45	50	53	62	—
	should be	54	62	70	63		55	50	47	38	
6 For determining position salary	is now	58	40	50	48	0.01	60	64	65	61	—
	should be	42	60	50	52		40	36	35	39	

for HR planning (item 2) than they had in 1994–5, with FIEs displaying the highest percentage. The difference between FIEs and SOEs is significant, indicating that SOEs could still be deterred from using job analysis for HR planning because of further restructuring and reform in the state sector. Only HR planning among the six uses of job analysis is expected to increase in all types of enterprises. In addition, the difference between the public and private sector in their use of job analysis for recruitment and selection (item 3) is significant. Currently FIEs and POEs used the practice more frequently than SOEs and COEs, and the latter is expected to use the practice more in future.

In the 1994–5 survey, regardless of the ownership type of their enterprises, respondents felt that job analysis should be used more for most of the purposes listed in Table 8.8. This response indicates a perceived importance for job analysis, which is supported by observations from the four case studies. In each of the case enterprises, the lack of job analysis or job description was identified as a major problem that needed to be addressed by the enterprise in the near future. The respondents' expectations in the first survey were met to some extent since the second survey indicates that all types of enterprises, except for SOEs, now use job analysis more for all these purposes than they had in 1994–5.

Hiring practices

The survey questions in this section covered three aspects. The first was selection criteria and methods for hiring. Respondents indicated to what extent 13 selection criteria and methods (labelled from H1 to H13) currently influence hiring decisions (classified into 'is now' questions) and should influence such decisions in the future ('should be'). The responses were measured by a five-point Likert-type scale ranging from 1 'not at all' to 5 'to a very great extent'. The second aspect concerned the respondents' perception of the effectiveness of hiring practices in terms of employee performance, job satisfaction and organizational operation. The final aspect focused on internal and external sources of labour for different types of enterprises.

Selection criteria and methods

Factor analysis was used to identify clusters of related items among the 13 selection criteria and methods (see Zhu, 2000 for details). Two factors were uncovered: the first is termed 'job-specific information' and comprises six items labelled as H1 (a person's ability to satisfy technical requirements of the job), H2 (a personal interview), H6 (an employment test in which applicants need to demonstrate their skills), H7 (proven work

Table 8.9 Summary of the four scales associated with hiring practices (with mean and standard deviation)

Name of scale (Corresponding items)	Interpretation of high scores	Cronbach's alpha		1994–5 survey	p	2001–2 survey	p
		1994–5	2001–2	Mean/s.d		Mean/s.d	
Job-specific information (is now) H1–H2 H6–H9	Job-specific information including personal ability and skills are regarded as vital.	0.75	0.72	3.7/0.4		3.6/0.5	
Job-specific information (should be) H1–H2 H6–H9	Job-specific information including personal ability and skills should be regarded as vital.	0.85	0.88	4.0/0.4	0.001	3.9/0.6	0.05
Archival biographical data (is now) H10–H13	External sources of information including archival biographical data are often invoked.	0.70	0.65	3.1/0.6		3.4/0.7	
Archival biographical data (should be) H10–H13	External sources of information including archival biographical data should be often invoked.	0.70	0.70	3.3/0.5	0.001	3.2/0.8	0.05

experience in a similar job), H8 (a person's potential to do a good job, even if the person is not that good initially) and H9 (the person's ability to conform to the enterprise's values and ways of doing things); the second factor, 'archival biographical data', included four items, that is, H10 (future co-workers' opinions about whether the person should be hired), H11 (personal qualifications), H12 (political background) and H13 (personal file records), which all relate to external sources of information. The remaining three items were discussed separately from these two factors.

Item-averaging was employed to generate a single score for each factor. Four scales were constructed and each corresponded to the average score on the items that related to a particular factor. The estimates of inter-item reliability (i.e. the values of Cronbach's (1951) alpha that corresponds to each scale in both surveys) exceed or approximate 0.70, which is considered adequate to conclude internal consistency (Nunnally, 1978) and the reliability can be regarded as acceptable. Two paired-sample *t*-tests were conducted on the two factors to ascertain whether or not current practices ('is now') depart significantly from ideal practices ('should be').

The first *t*-test reveals a clear preference for increasing the emphasis on job-specific information from the already relatively high level. The emphasis placed on this factor indicates a move away from the traditional labour allocation practice, which was often based on political orientation rather than on merit (see Ding *et al.*, 1997). With respect to selection methods, items H2 (personal interview) and H6 (employment test) were subject to further paired-sample *t*-tests. The results indicate the same pattern in both surveys, that is, the employment test has higher means in both current and ideal situations ('is now' = 3.6 and 3.7 in 1994–5 and 2001–2, respectively, and 'should be' = 4.0 and 3.9, $p < 0.001$) than the personal interview ('is now' = 3.4 and 3.6 in 1994–5 and 2001–2, respectively, and 'should be' = 3.7 and 3.8, $p < 0.001$). This finding is consistent with some researchers' observations that employment tests in a written and/or practical form (e.g. to operate a machine) are still regarded as a more effective recruiting method than interview in China (Huo *et al.*, 1999; Zhao, 1995).

The second *t*-test revealed different patterns in the two surveys. In 1994–5 the utilization of archival biographic data was at a lower level than respondents expected in the future, while the 2001–2 survey presented an opposite situation, and the differences in both surveys are statistically significant. Since archival biographic data included information relevant to traditional hiring practices under Mao's regime, the question arises as to whether they took precedence over H10 and H11 in both surveys. What changes occurred in the second survey regarding the emphasis given to these items? In order to answer these questions, the four items in the archival data factor were analysed individually by using paired-sample *t*-tests (see Table 8.10).

Table 8.10 The extent to which external sources of information and archival biographic data influence hiring decisions

Variables		1994–5 survey			2001–2 survey		
		Is now m (s.d.)	*Should be m* (s.d.)	*p*	*Is now* m (s.d.)	*Should be m* (s.d.)	*p*
H10	Future co-workers' opinions about whether the person should be hired	2.9 (0.9)	3.2 (0.9)	0.001	2.9 (0.9)	3.3 (0.8)	0.001
H11	Personal qualifications	3.4 (0.8)	3.6 (0.7)	0.001	3.7 (0.7)	3.7 (0.8)	—
H12	Political background	2.9 (1.0)	2.9 (0.9)	—	3.1 (1.0)	2.7 (1.1)	0.001
H13	Personal file records	3.2 (0.9)	3.2 (0.9)	—	3.4 (0.9)	3.1 (1.0)	0.001

A number of differences are statistically significant. There was a clear tendency to increase the use of 'future co-workers' opinions' (H10) in future hiring practices in both surveys. 'Personal qualifications' (H11) were expected to be used more only in 1994–5, with the same level for both current and future situations in 2001–2 indicating that the respondents' expectations expressed in 1994–5 had been met. 'Political background' (H12) and 'personal file records' (H13) showed parallel changes between the surveys: both showed the same mean value in 1994–5 for both current and future practices, both were expected to be used less in 2001–2. These findings indicate that China's economic reforms have facilitated a move away from the Maoist 'politics in command' to post-reform 'economics in command' (Walder, 1995).

The items (H3, 'a person's ability to get along well with current workers'; H4, 'having the right connections', e.g. school, family, friends, region, government, etc; and H5, 'the company's belief that the person will stay with the company for five years or longer') that did not belong to either of the two factors were also investigated (see Table 8.11). Respondents showed a preference for greater priority on items H3 and H5 in the ideal situation in both surveys, and for a reduced emphasis on the use of one's connections in hiring (H4). While having the right connection (*guanxi*) is highly regarded and claimed as crucial to getting a job in China (Bian, 1994, 2002; Hanser, 2002), a decline in the mean of H4 in both surveys indicates respondents' resentment towards such a practice.

Table 8.11 The extent to which items H3, H4 and H5 influence hiring decisions

Variables		1994–5 survey			2001–2 survey		
		Is now m (s.d.)	Should be m (s.d.)	p	Is now m (s.d.)	Should be m (s.d.)	p
H3	A person's ability to get along well with current workers	3.5 (0.7)	3.8 (0.7)	0.001	3.6 (0.8)	3.9 (0.8)	0.001
H4	Having the right connections (e.g. school, family, friends, region, government, etc.)	3.4 (0.9)	3.3 (0.9)	—	3.4 (0.9)	3.2 (1.1)	0.01
H5	The company's belief that the person will stay with the company for 5 years or longer	3.2 (0.9)	3.5 (0.9)	0.001	3.3 (0.9)	3.5 (0.9)	0.001

While the survey results indicate a salient trend to increase the use of most of these selection criteria in the future, it needs to be asked whether the trend is similar in all types of enterprises. The mean scores in Table 8.12 indicate that in 1994–5 all respondents expected an increased use of selection criteria in future hiring, except for the use of archival biographical data by FIEs. A MANOVA test revealed that the type of ownership did influence the scales. A series of ANOVAs then disclosed that neither job-specific information in the 'is now' nor 'should be' situation varied with the type of ownership, but archival biographical data both at the present and in the future depended on the type of ownership. Further tests showed that SOEs/FIEs used 'political background' (H12) and 'personal file records' (H13) more than COEs/POEs, and that SOEs would continue to emphasize the use of 'personal file records' in future more than other types of ownership. The Tukey test indicates that political background would receive less emphasis in FIEs in their future practices, which explains why FIEs would use less archival biographical data than their current practice (see Table 8.12). These results demonstrate that a person's political background was still regarded as more important in SOEs than in other types of enterprises.

The pattern changed somewhat in the second survey although the MANOVA results revealed that type of ownership still influenced the scales in 2001–2. Neither job-specific information ('should be') nor archival biographical data ('should be') varied with type of ownership. In contrast, job-specific information ('is now') and archival biographical data ('is now')

Table 8.12 Impact of ownership on two major factors of hiring decisions

Variables	1994–5 survey					2001–2 survey				
	SOEs	COEs	POEs	FIEs	p	SOEs	COEs	POEs	FIEs	p
	m (s.d.)	m (s.d.)	m (s.d.)	m (s.d.)		m (s.d.)	m (s.d.)	m (s.d.)	m (s.d.)	
Job-specific information (is now)	3.6 (0.5)	3.8 (0.5)	3.8 (0.5)	3.8 (0.5)	—	3.5 (0.5)	3.7 (0.6)	3.7 (0.5)	3.7 (0.4)	0.05
Job-specific information (should be)	4.0 (0.5)	4.0 (0.5)	4.2 (0.6)	4.0 (0.5)	—	3.8 (0.8)	4.0 (0.4)	3.9 (0.6)	3.9 (0.5)	—
Archival biographical data (is now)	3.2 (0.6)	2.9 (0.6)	3.2 (0.7)	3.3 (0.7)	0.05	3.5 (0.6)	3.8 (0.8)	3.2 (0.8)	3.3 (0.8)	0.05
Archival biographical data (should be)	3.4 (0.6)	3.1 (0.8)	3.5 (0.8)	3.2 (0.6)	0.05	3.1 (0.8)	3.4 (0.7)	3.2 (0.9)	3.2 (0.8)	—

m = mean; s.d. = standard deviation

depended on the type of ownership, that is, the non-state sector currently used more job-specific information than did SOEs, and POEs and FIEs relied much less on archival biographical data than did the public sector in 2001–2. This finding may reveal a legacy of traditional hiring practices in the public sector. Further tests revealed that a significant difference in the emphasis placed on 'political background' (item H12) between SOEs and FIEs in the 'is now' situation. This could also indicate the existence of traditional legacy in the state sector and may reveal the slow pace of political reforms in China. However, all respondents except for those from POEs expected to use archival biographical data less in the future.

Effectiveness

The second aspect of this section is to examine the perceived effectiveness of hiring practices. This part of the survey consisted of three questions relating to the extent to which various hiring practices are perceived to be effective. The respondents were asked whether hiring practices: (1) help the enterprise to have high-performance employees; (2) help increase job satisfaction; and (3) make a positive contribution to the overall effectiveness of the enterprise. The three measures of

Table 8.13 Spearman rank-order correlations between the three measures of effectiveness and the four scales of hiring criteria

Variables	Increasing employees' performance		Increasing job satisfaction		Overall effectiveness of enterprise	
	1994–5	2001–2	1994–5	2001–2	1994–5	2001–2
Job-specific information (is now)	0.29**	0.49*	0.21**	0.32*	0.30**	0.42*
Job-specific information (should be)	0.11	0.16*	0.10	0.16*	0.07	0.17*
Archival bio-graphical data (is now)	0.07	0.16	0.11	0.17*	0.13	0.08
Archival bio-graphical data (should be)	0.11	0.13	0.10	0.12	0.09	0.12

* p <0.05; ** p <0.01

effectiveness were rated on a five-point Likert scale. They were then correlated with the four scales representing hiring criteria (see Table 8.13).

In the 1994–5 survey, the correlations indicate that only the current job-specific information was significantly correlated with the three measures of effectiveness. In other words, enterprises that emphasized job-specific information including personal ability and skills in their current hiring practices tended to produce high-performing, satisfied employees who made a positive contribution to the overall efficiency of their enterprises. None of the other correlations attained significance, perhaps because in the mid-1990s hiring practices were still in transition, and respondents may have been uncertain about the future. In 2001–2 the correlations between job-specific information and the three measures of effectiveness improved markedly in both current and future situations. Such improvement could be a result of enterprise reform in the 1990s, a better developed free labour market and the social security system being formally established since 2000, as these developments have enabled companies to retrench their employees and have also facilitated labour mobility.

The results in Table 8.13 are also consistent with our previous finding that external sources of information, especially archival data, receive less emphasis in selection than job-specific information. However, the limitation of this part of the survey is the lack of an objective measure of enterprise

Table 8.14 Labour sources in China's industrial enterprises

Labour sources (variables)	1994–5 survey (%)					2001–2 survey (%)				
	SOEs	COEs	POEs	FIEs	p	SOEs	COEs	POEs	FIEs	p
Local labour market	54	64	41	57	—	44	67	48	49	—
Advertising	25	38	64	75	0.001	40	47	69	73	0.001
Government allocation	64	40	32	20	0.001	37	29	7	13	0.001
Internal HR data bank	29	17	22	25	—	24	47	29	37	0.05
Internal transfer	75	72	61	85	—	70	63	69	64	—
Inheritance of jobs	24	19	17	18	—	23	9	10	19	—

performance. It is possible that a hiring practice believed to be crucial by respondents may not necessarily be truly conducive to organizational effectiveness as measured by objective criteria (Huo *et al.*, 1996).

Sources of labour

The final aspect of this section investigates internal and external sources of labour for different types of enterprises. The results presented in Table 8.14 strongly indicate that government allocation of labour to enterprises, especially to SOEs and COEs, did not come to an end even in the early 2000s. Feng (1996) noted that centralized labour allocation was still in practice after more than a decade of enterprise reforms, and his claim is not out of date after over two decades of reform. Another finding worth noting is that, while the literature indicates that the practice of inheritance of jobs (*dingti*) has been phased out since the introduction of employment tests and labour contracts (Warner, 1996a; Zhao, 1995), our survey results have shown that such a practice still existed in the four types of enterprises, though in considerable decline in COEs/POEs in 2001–2.

Summary

This section has examined three aspects of hiring practices in industrial enterprises after Mao's regime. The survey results indicate that with the acceleration of economic reforms, hiring practices are gradually changing from a politicized and highly centralized labour allocation process to an economy-focused and market-directed recruitment and selection process. The research reveals that in 2001–2: enterprises place greater emphasis on personal competency as a major selection criterion than on political background and personal file information; greater weight is given to employment tests than to personal interviews as a selection tool; and more enterprises are using the external labour market and other recruitment methods such as advertising and an internal HR data bank.

With respect to the impact of ownership on hiring practices, the research reveals that compared with other types of ownership, SOEs have continued with more traditional employment practices, such as the attention placed on political background in their selection process. In addition, the government's influence on recruitment and selection has not vanished, but its span of control has gradually diminished. Enterprises, especially FIEs and POEs, have more autonomy to select their own employees and they receive fewer government-allocated employees. Job-specific information as part of selection criteria correlates more strongly to employees' performance and the overall effectiveness of enterprises.

Performance appraisal

The analysis of the survey results on the practice of performance appraisal in the industrial enterprises is divided into three parts. The first examines whether the enterprise has standardized criteria and methods for appraisal, how frequently it is conducted, who conducts the appraisal and what methods are used. The second part focuses on the purposes for which performance appraisal is currently being used ('is now') and ought to be used ('should be') by the enterprise. Finally, the respondents were asked to indicate how they perceived the effectiveness of performance appraisal in terms of employee performance, job satisfaction, and organizational operation.

Criteria and methods

In the first survey, FIEs/SOEs used more formal types of appraisal (item 1) than COEs/POEs (see Table 8.15). For SOEs, this reflects the emphasis placed on performance appraisal by the state and the level of central government's control over SOEs. For FIEs, it could reflect the influence of state and foreign companies. By 2001–2, COEs had considerably increased the use of this practice. The differences in item 1 across the four types of enterprises are statistically significant in both surveys,

Table 8.15 Performance appraisal

Variables	1994–5 survey (%)					2001–2 survey (%)				
	SOEs	COEs	POEs	FIEs	p	SOEs	COEs	POEs	FIEs	p
1 Enterprise has standardized criteria and methods of the appraisal	67	49	56	68	0.05	65	73	57	86	0.001
2 The frequency of the appraisal:										
• Once a year	73	74	90	78		73	65	60	74	
• Twice a year	17	13	0	10		18	26	17	17	
• Monthly	10	13	10	12		9	9	23	9	
3 Who conducts the appraisal?										
• Department managers	84	71	94	84	—	82	88	79	81	—
• Line managers	37	54	24	39	—	20	27	8	13	—
• Peer group	15	12	0	9	—	15	9	10	14	—
• Individuals to be evaluated	9	3	0	4	—	6	6	4	5	—
4 Appraisal methods										
• Self-evaluation by using a standardized form	51	38	41	49	—	58	61	46	59	—
• Discussion within the work group	21	27	18	9	—	19	27	20	11	—
• Supervisor's comments	57	64	65	63	—	42	36	42	44	—

Note: Respondents may have provided more than one answer.

indicating the ownership type does have an impact on the practice of performance appraisal.

The impact of ownership forms on other items in Table 8.15 was non-significant in both surveys. For example, with regard to the frequency of performance appraisal, in 1994–5, the majority of the enterprises in this sample conducted it on a yearly basis. In 2001–2, fewer companies used yearly appraisal and more used twice-a-year appraisal. Yet, as 60 per cent or more of the enterprises still used annual appraisal, this process may not have assisted in linking compensation to performance, as bonuses are normally distributed on a more frequent basis (monthly or quarterly). It is worth noting that fewer respondents in 1994–5 ($n = 204$ in 1994–5, 289 in 2001–2) answered this question, which might be because in some enterprises employees were kept in the dark about performance appraisal, as was indicated in one of the four case studies (see Chapter 7).

Performance appraisal is primarily under the control of department managers, and supervisor's comments or top-down assessment was a more popular method in 1994–5 than in 2001–2. In general, based on the results from the two surveys, it can be said that performance of employees is now formally assessed in more enterprises with standardized forms and criteria, with department managers still holding the responsibility for carrying out this practice.

Purposes

Performance appraisal tends to be used for three major purposes within an organization: administration, development and communication (e.g. Butler *et al.*, 1991; Cleveland *et al.*, 1989; Williams, 1972). The 12 items (labelled P1–12) that relate to this aspect were therefore classified into three categories according to these purposes.

The administrative aspect may be seen in a variety of contexts. Its predominant aim is to document an audit of the workforce strengths and weaknesses to facilitate the establishment of appropriate reward systems and relate past performance to future promotability (Schuler *et al.*, 1992; Silverman, 1989). Thus the administrative purpose usually encompasses staffing, compensation, promotion, reward and punishment systems (Silverman, 1989), and is represented by five relevant items 'determine appropriate pay' (P1), 'document subordinate's performance' (P2), 'salary administration' (P4), 'determine promotability' (P11) and 'basis for bonus' (P12).

The developmental purpose aims to provide a framework to assess and evaluate past performance as well as a benchmark for future development of the individual employee (Butler *et al.*, 1991; Cardy and Dobbins, 1994). It also seeks to 'identify and develop potential for future performance, linked to

Table 8.16 Mean and standard deviation (s.d.) pertaining to each major purpose of performance appraisal

Purposes of appraisal	Corresponding items	Cronbach's alpha		1994–5 survey		2001–2 survey	
		1994–5	2001–2	Mean	s.d.	Mean	s.d.
Administration (is now)	P1, P2, P4, P11, P12	0.74	0.73	3.4	0.6	3.6	0.6
Administration (should be)	P1, P2, P4, P11, P12	0.68	0.83	4.0	0.5	3.9	0.6
Development (is now)	P3, P5, P6, P8, P9	0.82	0.86	3.2	0.7	3.3	0.7
Development (should be)	P3, P5, P6, P8, P9	0.80	0.89	3.8	0.6	3.9	0.7
Communication (is now)	P7, P10	0.77	0.82	2.9	0.8	3.0	0.9
Communication (should be)	P7, P10	0.76	0.76	3.7	0.7	3.9	0.7

All $p < 0.001$

succession ...' (Goss, 1994: 51). Accordingly, five items are grouped together: 'plan development activities' (P3), 'recognize things done well' (P5), 'specify ways to improve performance' (P6), 'evaluate goal achievement' (P8) and 'identify strengths and weaknesses' (P9). Items P5, P8 and P9 focus on the assessment of past performance, while items P3 and P6 relate to planning for future development.

In the context of performance appraisal, communication is seen as a function allowing for the development of a dialogue between appraiser and appraisee to improve the understanding of perceived goals and objectives (Schuler *et al.*, 1992). The aim is to draw appraisees into voicing ideas and suggestions for problem-solving and decision-making (Goss, 1994). Therefore, this purpose involves providing feedback to employees about behaviours and results they should continue or achieve (Butler *et al.*, 1991). The two items related to this purpose are to 'discuss subordinate's views' (P7) and 'allow subordinate to express feelings' (P10).

The three major purposes of performance appraisal are displayed in Table 8.16. After inter-item reliability had been confirmed, two paired-sample *t*-tests were conducted to examine whether current practices are significantly different from ideal practices. The *t*-test results revealed a clear trend to increase the use of performance appraisal for all three purposes from the current level, with the differences between 'is now' and 'should be' being statistically significant.

In both surveys performance appraisal was used more for administration than the other two purposes with an expected increase in future. The emphasis placed on the administration of performance-related pay, bonuses and promotion is mainly the result of the Chinese industrial enterprise reform. The survey result is consistent with the findings from the four case studies, where performance appraisal was used only for the purpose of administration (see Chapters 4 to 7).

Table 8.16 also indicates a trend to increase the use of performance appraisal for development in the future in both surveys. Traditionally, this practice was used mainly for a cadre's promotion and transfer, and decisions were based on one's past performance. Ordinary employees, under the centralized labour allocation system before the reforms, were expected to remain in one position during their lifetime employment. The introduction of the enterprise responsibility system put managers under performance-based contracts to the state. Consequently, many managers focused on short-term goals rather than adopting a long-term strategy, such as investing in employee education to further develop an employee's career (Chen, D.R. 1995; Zhao, 1995). Lack of career development, especially for ordinary employees, was identified as one of the major problems in the four case studies.

Performance appraisal is least used for the purpose of communication in both surveys, although there is a pronounced view that it should be used more for this purpose in the future. In Western market economies, the communication process in performance appraisal is thought to facilitate an open and honest discussion between appraiser and appraisee (which could include criticism), leading to a more open and interactive workplace (Chow, 1994). However, due to political constraints and cultural differences in China, people are usually cautious during such exchanges (see Easterby-Smith *et al.*, 1995; Fung, 1995). Lack of communication in performance appraisal was also identified in the case studies presented earlier. For example, little feedback was provided by appraisers to appraisees in the case of ElectroCo (Chapter 6) and CableCo (Chapter 7), where results of performance appraisal were kept confidential.

In general, the survey results in Table 8.16 manifest a trend for performance appraisal to be used more for the purposes of administration, development and communication in future. A MANOVA test was then conducted to explore the extent to which performance appraisal was used for the three major purposes in the four types of enterprises, and to examine whether the use varied across different ownership types (see Table 8.17).

The results indicate that, in 1994–5 ownership did not have significant impact on the use of performance appraisal for different purposes. Furthermore, the expectation that utilization of performance appraisal for the three major purposes would increase in the future is evident across the four types of

Table 8.17 Impact of ownership on three major purposes of performance appraisal

Variables	1994–5 survey					2001–2 survey				
	SOEs m (s.d.)	COEs m (s.d.)	POEs m (s.d.)	FIEs m (s.d.)	p	SOEs m (s.d.)	COEs m (s.d.)	POEs m (s.d.)	FIEs m (s.d.)	p
Administration (is now)	3.3 (0.5)	3.3 (0.5)	3.5 (0.8)	3.5 (0.7)	—	3.5 (0.6)	3.6 (0.6)	3.7 (0.6)	3.7 (0.6)	0.05
Administration (should be)	3.9 (0.5)	3.9 (0.4)	4.0 (0.6)	4.0 (0.4)	—	3.9 (0.6)	3.8 (0.7)	4.0 (0.6)	3.9 (0.6)	—
Development (is now)	3.1 (0.7)	3.0 (0.5)	3.3 (0.9)	3.2 (0.7)	—	3.2 (0.7)	3.5 (0.7)	3.5 (0.7)	3.6 (0.7)	0.01
Development (should be)	3.8 (0.6)	3.8 (0.5)	3.9 (0.5)	3.7 (0.6)	—	3.9 (0.7)	3.9 (0.7)	4.0 (0.7)	4.0 (0.6)	—
Communication (is now)	2.9 (0.8)	2.7 (0.7)	3.1 (0.9)	3.0 (1.0)	—	2.9 (0.9)	3.2 (0.7)	3.2 (0.9)	3.4 (1.0)	0.05
Communication (should be)	3.7 (0.7)	3.6 (0.6)	3.7 (0.5)	3.6 (0.8)	—	3.9 (0.8)	3.9 (0.7)	3.8 (0.8)	3.9 (0.7)	—

m = mean, s.d. = standard deviation

enterprises. All enterprises, regardless of ownership, used performance appraisal more for administration than for the other two purposes. Regarding administration, in the first survey POEs and FIEs had higher means in both 'is now' and 'should be' situations than SOEs and COEs. This result is consistent with one of the findings to be discussed in the next section, namely, that POEs and FIEs have placed more emphasis on performance-based compensation and therefore use performance appraisal to a greater extent for this purpose.

In the 2001–2 survey some changes can be observed. The type of ownership significantly influenced practices in performance appraisals in the 'is now' situation. FIEs demonstrated the highest means across the three purposes and a significant difference exists mainly between FIEs and SOEs. Thus, while FIEs have increased their use of performance appraisal for all three purposes as they expected in 1994–5, SOEs increased use mainly for administration without any change for communication purpose. POEs and COEs also increased their emphasis on these purposes, especially in regards to development and communication purposes. Although current practices in performance appraisal do not fulfil the ideals across all enterprises, the gap

Table 8.18 Spearman rank-order correlations between the three measures of effectiveness and the three major purposes of performance appraisal

Variables	Increasing employees' performance		Increasing job satisfaction		Overall effectiveness of enterprise	
	1994–5	*2001–2*	*1994–5*	*2001–2*	*1994–5*	*2001–2*
Administration (is now)	0.30**	0.34*	0.25**	0.39*	0.25**	0.42*
Administration (should be)	0.10	0.11	0.13*	0.17*	0.11*	0.13*
Development (is now)	0.28**	0.38*	0.31**	0.41*	0.24**	0.52*
Development (should be)	0.18**	0.09	0.24**	0.13	0.21**	0.09
Communication (is now)	0.34**	0.36*	0.34**	0.37*	0.26**	0.48*
Communication (should be)	0.10	0.04	0.15*	0.09	0.10	0.05

*P <0.05; ** $p <0.01$

between 'is now' and 'should be' situations is diminishing, especially in the non-state sector.

Effectiveness

To measure perceived effectiveness of this practice, respondents were asked whether performance appraisal practices: (1) help the enterprise to have high-performance employees; (2) help increase job satisfaction; and (3) make a positive contribution to the overall effectiveness of the enterprise. The three measures of effectiveness were rated on a five-point Likert scale and then correlated with the three major purposes served by performance appraisal.

The correlations between the three measures of effectiveness and the 'is now' practices are all higher than correlations between effectiveness and the 'should be' practices in both surveys, and they are also much stronger in 2001–2 than in 1994–5 (see Table 8.18). This indicates that currently conducted performance appraisal, regardless of the purpose(s) it served, was positively and significantly correlated to job satisfaction, high performance and overall effectiveness of the enterprise, which is more obvious in the 2001–2 survey. The positive attitudes towards this practice, particularly the increased correlation between the practice and effectiveness in 2001–2, indicate that performance appraisal has been recognized as an effective tool in individual and organizational development. The lower and, in some cases, non-significant correlations in the 'should be' situation, especially in the second survey, may be attributed to the ongoing economic reforms and transition from a planned to a market economy with its associated uncertainties.

Summary

To summarize, the practice of performance appraisal has been used by more enterprises, especially FIEs, as a means of implementing enterprise reforms: it is helping to break the 'iron rice bowl' by linking performance to compensation and placing emphasis on merit and achievements. This study has found that, in 1994–5, performance appraisal was used primarily for determining bonuses and wages, which is consistent with the findings from the four case studies (Chapters 4–7). However, our results from the 2001–2 survey indicate that performance appraisal has been used more for communication and development even though these purposes are expected to become yet more prominent in future.

Despite the controversy raised in Western market economies about performance appraisal in terms of its validity, reliability and credibility, this practice is often used on an annual basis by most Chinese enterprises regardless of their ownership. In addition to our findings that earnings of employees have started to become performance indicators and the bonus system is moving away from egalitarian distribution, the survey results reveal that performance appraisal is now and will continue to be utilized in all types of enterprises as a useful tool to help raise the effectiveness of work by linking compensation more closely with the fulfilment of various tasks and responsibilities.

Compensation and welfare

The survey questions relevant to compensation and welfare dealt with four areas: compensation practices in general; the perceived effectiveness of compensation practices; current wage packages including bonus across the four types of ownership; and welfare benefits offered across the four types of ownership.

Compensation

Respondents to the survey indicated to what extent nine practices of employee compensation (labelled from C1 to C9) are being used currently ('is now') and should be used in the future ('should be'). These were

Table 8.19 Summary of the four scales associated with compensation practices

Name of scale	*Corresponding items*	*Interpretation of high scores*	*Cronbach's alpha*	
			1994–5	*2001–2*
General Compensation (is now)	C1, C3, C4, C6, C8, C9	Compensation in general is regarded as important.	0.81	0.81
General Compensation (should be)	C1, C3, C4, C6, C8, C9	Compensation in general should be regarded as important.	0.79	0.89
Welfare (is now)	C2, C5, C7	Welfare is regarded as important in this enterprise.	0.52	<0.5
Welfare (should be)	C2, C5, C7	Welfare should be regarded as important in this enterprise.	0.64	<0.5

measured by a five-point Likert-type scale ranging from 1 ('not at all') to 5 ('to a very great extent'). In order to group related items, factor analysis was employed. Two factors were uncovered: the first, termed 'general compensation', comprised six items: 'pay incentives such as bonus or profit sharing are an important part of the compensation strategy in this enterprise' (C1); 'in this enterprise a portion of an employee's earnings is contingent on group or enterprise performance goals being achieved' (C3); 'our pay policies recognize that long-term results are more important than short-term results' (C4); 'pay incentives are designed to provide a significant amount of an employee's total earnings in this organization' (C6); 'the pay system in this enterprise has a futuristic orientation: it focuses employee's attention on long-term (two or more years) goals' (C8); and 'in this enterprise pay raises are determined mainly by an employee's job performance: there is a large pay spread between low performers and high performers in a given job' (C9). The second factor, called 'welfare', includes three items: 'the benefits are an important part of the total pay package' (C2); 'an employee's seniority does enter into pay decisions' (C5); and 'the employee benefits package is very generous compared to what it should be' (C7).

After the items were averaged, a single score for each factor was generated. Four scales were thus constructed (see Table 8.19). As the inter-item reliability associated with the welfare scales is insufficient in both surveys (Cronbach's alpha <0.7), these scales were discarded from further factor analyses. The inter-item reliability associated with the general compensation scales is high and is thus encouraging.

Table 8.20 Spearman rank-order correlations between the three measures of effectiveness and the general compensation practice

Variables	Increasing employees' performance		Increasing job satisfaction		Overall effectiveness of enterprise	
	1994–5	2001–2	1994–5	2001–2	1994–5	2001–2
General compensation (is now)	0.41**	0.52***	0.39**	0.44***	0.40**	0.55***
General compensation (should be)	0.18**	0.10	0.19**	0.16	0.18**	0.12

*P <0.05; ** p <0.01; *** p <0.001

A paired-sample *t*-test demonstrated that the current general compensation practices ('is now' mean = 3.47 and 3.43 in 1994–5 and 2001–2, respectively, standard deviation = 0.64 and 0.61) do not fulfil the ideal ('should be' mean = 4.00 and 4.04 in 1994–5 and 2001–2, respectively, standard deviation = 0.51 and 0.65) and that the differences between the current and future situations in both surveys are statistically significant (p <0.001). Significant differences between current and future practices across the six items in both surveys indicate a clear expectation of greater emphasis on each of these pay practices in the future. These results show that material incentives (C1) are emphasized by employees in both 'is now' and 'should be' situations in 1994–5 and 2001–2. The respondents also placed more weight on practices such as 'individual performance-linked pay' (C9) and 'futuristic orientation of the pay' (C8) in both surveys (the emphasis on individual performance-linked pay will be discussed later.) The attention given to long-term oriented pay in 1994–5 was consistent with some researchers' findings that it, to some extent, reflected dissatisfaction with the contract management responsibility system (CMRS) popular in enterprises, especially SOEs, from the late 1980s to mid-1990s (Liu, 1996; Xu, 1996). Contracts under CMRS usually lasted one to five years, and their short-term nature induced myopic managerial behaviour. This phenomenon could also be observed in FIEs at that time where the 'Chinese partner pressed for a high level of short-term profits and profit distribution to secure short-term returns' (Child, 1994: 277).

However, this myopic behaviour seemed to have changed little in the 2001–2 survey when 'futuristic orientation of the pay' (C8) achieved the lowest mean value compared with others and also expected to increase more in the future (3.1 for 'is now' and 4.0 for 'should be'). As the problem of short-term orientation in compensation practices has not been solved by the replacement of CMSR with the modern enterprise system, CMSR seems not to be the only reason for such behaviour. Other aspects in regards to corporate governance, such as the appointment of general manager through the nomenclature system, or the regulatory system that supports long-term or short-term behaviours should also be considered.

As the three items related to 'welfare' were excluded from the factor analysis due to insufficient inter-item reliability, paired-sample t-tests were conducted to compare the current and future practices of those items individually. Apart from 'seniority' (C5), there is a clear increase in the emphasis on employee benefits including various subsidies and allowances (means of C2 and C7 increase from 3.3 and 3.0 to 3.8 and 3.7, respectively in 1994–5, and from 3.4 and 3.2 to 3.7 and 3.6 in 2001–2, p <0.001 in all the situations). The significance of these differences indicates that benefits are perceived to be important in employee compensation. In contrast, seniority in pay decisions is expected to become less important in future (mean decreases from 3.3 to 3.2 in 1994–5, and from 3.2 to 2.9 in 2001–2, p <0.001 in 2001–2 only). This reduced emphasis on seniority is consistent with extant literature (e.g. Jackson, 1992; Nyaw, 1995). Caution should be displayed, however, when deriving conclusions from these findings as each of these analyses utilized only a single item.

Effectiveness

Three items related to the extent to which the various compensation practices are perceived to be effective. Survey respondents were asked whether compensation practices: (1) help the enterprise to have high-performing employees; (2) help increase job satisfaction; and (3) make a positive contribution to the overall effectiveness of the enterprise. The three measures of effectiveness were rated on a five-point Likert scale. Spearman rank-order correlations between effectiveness and current practices tended to be greater than for future practices, especially in the second survey (see Table 8.20), indicating that the general compensation practice is perceived positively correlated to the three measures, especially to the increase of employees' and company's general performance. The reduced correlations in the 'should be' situation in 2001–2 could be the consequence of ongoing transition along with enterprise reforms, which has brought with it more uncertainties about the future.

A MANOVA test was conducted to ascertain whether the two scales of the factor 'general compensation' varied across the four types of ownership. The results in Table 8.21 demonstrate that the type of ownership did not influence current or future practices in general compensation practice in

Table 8.21 Impact of ownership on the factor of general compensation

Variables	1994–5 survey				2001–2 survey			
	SOEs	COEs	POEs	FIEs	SOEs	COEs	POEs	FIEs
	m	m	m	m	m	m	m	m
	(s.d.)	(s.d.)	(s.d.)	(s.d.)	(s.d.)	(s.d.)	(s.d.)	(s.d.)
General compensation (is now)	3.5 (0.6)	3.5 (0.5)	3.3 (0.9)	3.4 (0.6)	3.5 (1.0)	3.6 (0.6)	3.7 (0.6)	3.6 (0.6)
General compensation (should be)	4.0 (0.5)	4.0 (0.5)	3.9 (0.5)	3.9 (0.5)	4.1 (0.7)	4.1 (0.4)	4.1 (0.6)	4.0 (0.6)

m = mean; s.d. = standard deviation

Table 8.22 Components of wage packages

Variables	1994–5 survey (%)					2001–2 survey (%)				
	SOEs	COEs	POEs	FIEs	p	SOEs	COEs	POEs	FIEs	p
Base pay	98	95	92	98	—	95	100	94	97	—
Floating wage	77	70	50	41	0.001	56	40	34	36	0.05
Positional allowances	78	54	42	44	0.001	76	70	41	41	0.001

either survey even though the mean values indicate that non-state enterprises all increased the use of this practice in 2001–2 over usage in 1994–5.

Wage packages

Table 8.22 shows that 'base pay' is part of wage packages for all enterprises without any significant differences in both surveys. However, the adoption of a floating wage (usually based on individual and/or group and enterprise performance) and positional allowances (based on qualification and skills at different positions) were more common in SOEs/COEs than in POEs/FIEs in both surveys, with an obvious reduction in the use of floating wage in 2001–2. The impact of ownership on these practices is statistically significant. While the private sector demonstrated the decline in the use of floating wage in the second survey, the public sector had the greater reduction in this aspect compared to the private one. There was also a decline in the use of positional allowances in all types of enterprises except COEs. These changes may reflect the

Table 8.23 Variables that determine the bonus distribution

Variables	1994–5 survey (%)					2001–2 survey (%)				
	SOEs	COEs	POEs	FIEs	p	SOEs	COEs	POEs	FIEs	p
Individual performance	75	72	78	71	—	74	71	86	89	0.01
Group performance	46	42	17	30	0.05	38	59	18	30	0.01
Attendance	62	59	39	49	—	32	44	14	30	0.05
Profitability	9	8	18	12	—	12	6	4	10	—
CPI	91	92	82	88	—	88	94	96	90	—

new trend of adopting an annual salary or market-based rates over a modified wage package based on old practices.

All the enterprises surveyed included bonuses in their compensation packages, though less than a third used a profit-sharing plan for their bonus system. Various items had an impact on bonus distribution. Table 8.23 indicates the consumer price index (CPI) was used by nearly all enterprises as a major determinant of bonuses in both surveys. The next strongest determinant of bonuses was 'individual performance', though, in addition, SOEs/COEs used group performance more than POEs/FIEs. The survey results indicate that the economic reform has brought radical changes to the compensation system and the private sector appeared to rely more on individual performance to determine bonuses than the public sector.

Table 8.23 also indicates that 'attendance' was used as a prominent determinant of bonus in 1994–5, but its importance was greatly reduced in 2001–2, especially in the private sector. The differences across the four types of ownership are significant only in 2001–2. This might be the consequence of the higher attention given to individual's performance in POEs or because the work pattern is more flexible. 'Profitability' received only minor consideration in both surveys. In 1994–5 this might be attributed to the fact that Chinese managers had little concern about 'the relationship between costs and revenues' under a planned economy (Davidson, 1987: 72). However, in 2001–2 bonuses could have been used to attract or retain employees rather than as a reflection of profitability.

Welfare benefits

Table 8.24 sets out the major allowances offered by enterprises and the impact of ownership on the practice of offering these welfare benefits. The results of each survey have to be discussed separately because the

Table 8.24 Welfare: pension insurance, medical and housing allowances

Variables	1994–5 survey (%)					2001–2 survey (%)				
	SOEs	COEs	POEs	FIEs	p	SOEs	COEs	POEs	FIEs	p
Pension insurance	97	87	90	84	0.01	91	84	69	91	0.01
Medical allowances	86	83	84	90	—	89	86	63	78	0.01
Housing fund	82	60	74	57	0.001	57	45	19	64	0.001

social security system was reformed in the mid-1990s. In the 1994–5 survey, 'pension insurance' was provided by most SOEs but not by all the other types of enterprises. It was predicted at that time that the significant differences would likely diminish as the pension insurance became compulsory when the *Labour Law* came into effect on 1 January 1995. 'Medical allowances' were offered by over 80 per cent of enterprises, with no significant difference between the ownership types. As for the housing allowance, it was supplied quite unequally across the enterprises. It appears that a much greater portion of SOEs than of FIEs offered it to their employees. It was argued that foreign partners of joint ventures often resisted the Chinese expectation 'that they should provide accommodation for their employees' (Child, 1994: 271). However, national regulations in the mid-1990s required enterprises, with the exception of small and private-owned enterprises, to make some provisions for housing even it was not mandated in the *Labour Law*. Due to the vague policies and conflicting regulations issued by state and local governments, foreign investors found that requirements were unclear in regards to social welfare systems. Further, practices vary greatly even within a municipality, depending on negotiations between the enterprises and local labour authorities (Stevenson-Yang, 1996).

The reform in social security reform in the late 1990s has made insurance payments for certain items compulsory, at least in theory. However, the 2001–2 survey results reveal discrepancies in the insurance coverage in different types of enterprises. Many fewer POEs than other enterprise types offered pension and medical insurance to their employees, and ownership type does have a significant impact on the supply of social security to employees. The discrepancies could be due to the fact that the new social security regime lacks an effective mechanism to enforce compliance and restrain free riding (i.e. evasion of the insurance payment) especially in the private sector.

With respect to housing fund, the 2001–2 survey results show a considerable decline, except for FIEs, and such differences are statistically significant.

With the reform of the housing system since the mid to late 1990s, fewer enterprises offer free accommodation. Instead, employees are encouraged to purchase commercialized accommodation with some subsidies offered by enterprises. Some companies, including FIEs, have started to use housing allowance as a long-term incentive to attract and retain their employees.

Summary

Enterprises under different types of ownership have fairly similar approaches to general compensation practices, such as placing emphasis on material incentives by including bonuses in pay packages and linking pay to performance rather than seniority. The findings of this study support previous research suggesting that compensation reform has started to 'introduce *economism* into workers' attitude' (Goodall and Warner, 1997: 579) and that compensation in China is undergoing a transition from state-planned egalitarianism to an enterprise-determined motivational mechanism (e.g. Liu, 1996; Warner, 1998b).

Although ownership did not have a significant impact on general compensation practices and adoption of profit-sharing plans, it did affect the choice of wage packages, the methods used to distribute bonuses and insurance coverage. When the survey was conducted in 1994–5, the floating wage system was popular, though its popularity declined after the mid-1990s when FIEs/POEs developed more simplified wage packages. Both surveys show that more companies linked bonus distribution to individual performance rather than group performance and attendance, and this trend seemed to be reinforced in 2001–2, especially in the private sector. With regard to insurance coverage, the private sector, particularly POEs, demonstrated their reluctance to offer such benefits to their employees.

The survey results clearly indicate that compensation practices in general are regarded as important and show positive correlations with enterprise effectiveness. There was also a clear preference for greater emphasis on linking individual performance and reward, performance-differentiated pay and long-term oriented pay practices. Overall, the results show that reforms in China have instigated a clear trend towards a performance-based compensation system. The findings also suggest that there is likely to be greater diversity in employee compensation in China in the future, with POEs and FIEs, in particular, placing increasing emphasis on each individual's performance.

Training and development

The analysis of the survey results related to training and development is divided into three parts: a review of the types of training programmes

Table 8.25 Types of training programmes offered with different types of ownership

Training offered	1994–5 survey (%)					2001–2 survey (%)				
	SOEs	COEs	POEs	FIEs	p	SOEs	COEs	POEs	FIEs	p
On-the-job training	92	83	80	68	0.001	86	85	79	89	—
Off-the-job training	58	27	20	40	0.001	51	41	33	49	—
Induction/ orientation	69	47	77	73	0.01	46	67	62	63	0.01
Occupational skills	85	70	71	63	0.01	75	73	68	76	—
Technical/ professional skills	81	58	64	72	0.01	78	76	70	68	—
Management development	77	44	36	47	0.001	70	73	44	65	0.01

offered by enterprises; an examination of the extent to which this practice is being used ('is now') and ought to be ('should be') used for certain purposes; and finally, a look at the respondents' perception of the effectiveness of training and development with respect to employees' performance, job satisfaction and organizational operation.

Types of training programme

In the 1994–5 survey, differences across the four types of ownership in regards to types of training programme are all statistically significant, especially for on-the-job, off-the-job and management development training. In 1994–5, SOEs offered more training programmes than the other three types of enterprises, which reflected more personnel practices including training in SOEs (Zhao, 1994) and also the high degree of state involvement in and control over training programmes. The 1994–5 survey results (Table 8.25) also indicate that compared with COEs and POEs, FIEs offered more off-the-job training, technical and professional skills training, and management development programmes. This may reflect foreign companies' recognition that in China 'training for local employees is critical to successful operations. Good training and development can make up the shortfall in skills, while also providing a company with a considerable competitive edge in the market' (Dalton and Austen, 1995: 60). POEs offered far fewer off-the-job and management training programmes for employees and this may be attributed to their informal management practices and their profit-focused, short-term strategies (Yuan, 1993), which is consistent with the findings from the case study conducted in a POE (see Chapter 6).

The training pattern observed in 1994–5 had altered by 2001–2. Owner-ship type now has a significant impact only on 'introduction/orientation' and 'management development'. While the impact of ownership has dimin-ished, the use of training programmes has increased, especially in the non-state sector. For example, COEs have greatly increased all types of training programme while POEs and FIEs have increased off-the-job training and management development. In contrast, training in SOEs appears to have contracted in all areas. This could partly reflect the problems faced by SOEs as they had less control but also less financial support from the state and they had to reduce the training programme to cut the cost. It may also indicate that as SOEs retrenched more surplus employees, they offered less training, especially the induction programmes for new employees.

Purposes

The second aspect of this section examines the extent to which certain purposes of training and development are being and should be served. In the survey, the respondents needed to indicate to what extent training and development is being ('is now') and ought to be ('should be') used for ten purposes (labelled from T1 to T10). Response options were based on a five-point Likert-type scale ranging from 1 ('not at all') to 5 ('to a very great extent'). In order to ascertain clusters of related items, factor analyses were employed again and two factors were uncovered as the consequence. The first factor, termed 'adaptation', includes five items: 'provide a reward to employees' (T1); 'improve employee's interpersonal abilities, i.e. how well they relate to others' (T3); 'build teamwork within the enterprise' (T6); 'help employees understand the business, e.g. knowledge of competitors, new technologies, etc.' (T8); and 'teach employees about the enterprise's values and ways of doing things' (T10). The second factor is called 'specific training' and is composed of: 'improve technical job abilities' (T2); 'rem-edy past poor performance' (T4); 'prepare employees for future job assign-ments' (T5); 'provide substantial training when employees first start working in the enterprise' (T7); and 'provide employees with the skills needed to do a number of different jobs, not just one particular job' (T9). After two clusters of related items for both 'is now' and 'should be' prac-tices were revealed, four scales were constructed (see Table 8.26). Two paired-sample *t*-tests, in regards to adaptation and specific training respec-tively, were then conducted to ascertain whether the current practices ('is now') are consistent with ideal practices ('should be'). The same pattern

Table 8.26 Summary of the four scales associated with purposes of training (with mean and standard deviation)

Name of scale (Corresponding items)	Interpretation of high scores	Cronbach's alpha 1994–5	Cronbach's alpha 2001–2	1994–5 survey Mean/s.d	2001–2 survey Mean/s.d
Adaptation (is now) (T1, T3, T6, T8, T10)	Adaptation to the organization is greatly assisted.	0.77	0.68	3.1/0.5	3.3/0.6
Adaptation (should be) (T1, T3, T6, T8, T10)	Adaptation to the organization should be greatly assisted.	0.76	0.87	3.8/0.5	4.0/0.7
Specific training (is now) (T2, T4, T5, T7, T9)	Training in work-related skills is often provided.	0.81	0.80	3.5/0.6	3.6/0.6
Specific training (should be) (T2, T4, T5, T7, T9)	Training in work-related skills should be provided extensively.	0.81	0.89	4.1/0.3	4.1/0.7

All p <0.001

was observed in both surveys: neither in regards to facilitating employees' adaptation to the enterprise nor training in specific job-related skills did the current practice fulfil the ideal (and the differences identified are statistically significant).

Table 8.26 indicates that current training and development is focused heavily on job-related skills and improvement of labour productivity (note the relatively higher mean values for specific training in both surveys), which is in keeping with the result that the majority of enterprises offered on-the-job training (Table 8.25). In 1994–5, this trend was consistent with the government's emphasis on vocational training and technical education, and also reflected the growing pressure at that time on enterprises, especially SOEs, to deploy redundant employees, which called for cross-skilled and multi-skilled training to increase their employability. Liu (1994) reported that by mid-1994 more than 200,000 retrenched employees in China had received cross-work training offered by their enterprises, and 80 per cent of them obtained new jobs. By 2001–2, although enterprises no longer needed to retrain redundant employees as they can be retrenched, then retrained by the local labour bureau, the concepts of the learning organization and of obtaining sustainable competitiveness had come to the attention of Chinese enterprises, and

Table 8.27 Impact of ownership on two major factors of training

Variables	1994–5 survey				2001–2 survey			
	SOEs m (s.d.)	COEs m (s.d.)	POEs m (s.d.)	FIEs m (s.d.)	SOEs m (s.d.)	COEs m (s.d.)	POEs m (s.d.)	FIEs m (s.d.)
Adaptation (is now)	3.1 (0.7)	3.0 (0.5)	3.3 (1.0)	3.1 (0.8)	3.3 (0.9)	3.6 (0.7)	3.5 (0.8)	3.5 (0.8)
Adaptation (should be)	3.7 (0.6)	3.5 (0.5)	3.9 (0.5)	3.7 (0.5)	4.0 (0.7)	4.1 (0.4)	4.0 (0.8)	4.0 (0.6)
Specific training (is now)	3.5 (0.6)	3.7 (0.4)	3.7 (0.7)	3.4 (0.7)	3.6 (0.6)	3.8 (0.6)	3.8 (0.6)	4.4 (0.7)
Specific training (should be)	4.1 (0.5)	4.1 (0.5)	4.2 (0.4)	4.0 (0.5)	4.1 (0.7)	4.2 (0.4)	4.1 (0.7)	4.1 (0.6)

m = mean; s.d. = standard deviation
All p >0.05

management was starting to recognize the need to increase the skills base of their workforce to compete in the market with both domestic and foreign companies.

In spite of the current strong emphasis on 'specific training', there is a clear preference for increasing its use in the future. Training was used at a relatively low level for increasing workforce adaptability and employee commitment in 1994–5, with somewhat higher results in 2001–2, although these aims were expected to receive increased emphasis in the future. In the mid-1990s technical training rather than behavioural training remained standard practice (Von Glinow and Teagarden, 1990). There are several explanations for this phenomenon. One is that there is a great power distance between top and middle management in China: 'Chinese top management holds nearly all the strings of decision-making in its hands, and allows very little power to lower levels' (Laaksonen, 1988: 316). This culture, plus the bureaucratic structure of management, can make the adoption of teamwork practices very difficult (Dalton and Austen, 1995), resulting in insufficient training in areas such as team-building (T6). Similarly, as 'very few enterprises [in China] have drawn up systematic programmes for the training and development of their managers and employees, based on anything like an audit of future needs and personal potential' (Child, 1994: 174), training programmes to help employees understand business (T8) and teach employees about values (T10) were seldom conducted. Further, as decisions to send employees for training were made by senior managers, and were often influenced by one's connections rather than one's merits or needs (Wang, 1993), employees did not view training as a real, non-monetary reward (as indicated in T1).

Table 8.28 Spearman rank-order correlations between the three measures of effectiveness and the four scales of training practices

Variables	Increasing employees' performance		Increasing job satisfaction		Overall effectiveness of enterprise	
	1994–5	2001–2	1994–5	2001–2	1994–5	2001–2
Adaptation (is now)	0.22**	0.42*	0.35**	0.36*	0.29**	0.37*
Adaptation (should be)	0.23**	0.57*	0.30**	0.44*	0.27**	0.54*
Specific training (is now)	0.38**	0.19*	0.35**	0.13*	0.35**	0.16*
Specific training (should be)	0.30**	0.26*	0.24**	0.21*	0.26**	0.28*

*P <0.05; ** $p <0.01$

To explore the impact of ownership on training and development, a MANOVA test was administrated (see Table 8.27). In 1994–5 all enterprises used training much less for 'adaptation' than for 'specific training'. Although both purposes were expected to be used more extensively in the future, 'specific training' would still receive more attention than 'adaptation'. In the 2001–2 survey, all types of enterprises have increased current training for both 'adaptation' and 'specific training', and placed a similar importance to both purposes in the future. Although the results show that the ownership type did not influence current or ideal practices in training and development in either survey, SOEs appeared to use training for these purposes less than other types of enterprises, which is consistent with the finding that SOEs decreased all types of training programmes offered in 2001–2 (Table 8.25).

Effectiveness

Respondents were asked whether training and development practices: (1) help the enterprise to have high-performance employees; (2) help increase job satisfaction; and (3) make a positive contribution to the overall effectiveness of the enterprise. The three measures of effectiveness were rated on a five-point Likert scale. They were then correlated with the two training purposes (see Table 8.28).

Table 8.28 reveals that all of the correlations departed significantly from zero. In the 1994–5 survey results, none of the correlations were especially impressive, but they still illustrated that both the current and ideal training in adaptation to the organization and specific skills correlated positively with effectiveness. The respondents' positive attitude towards training and development practices indicates that this HR practice was recognized as an effective tool in individual and organizational development in the first survey. In the 2001–2 survey, respondents indicated much stronger correlations between 'adaptation' and the three measures of effectiveness in both 'is now' and 'should be' situations compared with the 1994–5 results. In contrast, the correlations between 'specific training' and the three measures became weaker in most current and future situations. The second survey findings indicate that training for adaptation purposes is anticipated to be more positively related to improved performance and overall effectiveness rather than specific training, which could be the consequence of increased off-the-job and management training as indicated in the 2001–2 survey (Table 8.25) as people expect training for adaptation purposes to affect performance and effectiveness.

Summary

The first survey results revealed that the impact of ownership on the selection of training programmes was statistically significant even though it did not affect the purposes of training. Generally, COEs/POEs made less investment in their employees, especially in terms of off-the-job training and management development, than SOEs/FIEs (in keeping with item 7 in Table 8.4 in the 1994–5 survey). However, while SOEs appeared to offer more training programmes in 1994–5, it could have been that they conducted training only to fulfil training quotas set by the government or as a perfunctory task given that in the mid to late 1990s many SOEs were suffering from unacceptably low levels of productivity (Yabuki, 1995). In 1994–5, the programmes offered were more for new recruits and existing workers than for career development and they were related more to technical skills than behaviour. The positive correlations between training practices and overall effectiveness indicate that this HR practice helped enterprises to update technical knowledge and skills, and to compete in a more market-oriented environment.

In the 2001–2 survey, the impact of ownership type was observed only on two types of training programme (induction and management development, Table 8.25) and more enterprises (except for SOEs) increased their training programmes, particularly for the adaptation purpose. The implication here is that behavioural training will be further increased in future to improve the company's overall performance and sustainable competitiveness. The survey respondents all expected an increase in the use of training for both technical and behavioural purposes. The expectation has reinforced the results displayed in Table 8.4 where 'training and career development' (item

Table 8.29 The trade union: membership rate and labour contract utilization

Variable	1994–5 survey (%)				2001–2 survey (%)			
	SOEs	*COEs*	*POEs*	*FIEs*	*SOEs*	*COEs*	*POEs*	*FIEs*
1 Have employees belonging to union in your enterprise	83	55	65	70	81	72	25	65
2 Proportion of union members half and more	88	37	100	77	72	67	20	45
3 Proportion of permanent employees half and more	92	73	44	43	73	50	36	43
4 Proportion of contract employees half and more	35	46	73	88	36	65	77	57

All p <0.0

7) is expected to increase significantly in the future in both surveys. As China is at a stage of dramatic transition towards a more market-driven economy, improving workforce quality and developing managerial skills have become critical factors.

Labour relations

This section covers three major aspects of labour relations or the process by which managers and workers determine their workplace relationships. The first is the existence of trade unions in the enterprise and union-density rates. The second is the proportion of permanent and contract employees in the enterprises surveyed. Finally, the participation of employees in management and the methods of participation are discussed.

Trade unions

Table 8.29 presents results for both surveys on the presence of trade unions (item 1), union membership rates (item 2) and the utilization of labour contracts (items 3 and 4). The type of ownership has a significant impact on all the four items in both the 1994–5 and 2001–2 surveys, though the pattern revealed in each survey is different. In 1994–5, SOEs/FIEs had higher union membership rates than POEs/COEs.

SOEs used to have more permanent employees than other types of enterprises and these employees were automatically accepted and looked after by the unions (normally only permanent employees could join unions in China, see Warner, 1995). Furthermore, as the FIEs surveyed in 1994–5 all formed joint ventures with SOEs, their close association with SOEs contributed to their high representation of unions. The results for POEs in 1994–5 need to be taken cautiously as only 17 respondents from POEs answered this question. In 2001–2, many fewer private companies had trade unions, especially in POEs. Although the 1992 revision of the *Trade Union Law* made it mandatory (rather than optional, as with the 1950 law) to have trade unions, trade unions still need to be developed in the private sector to protect employees' rights and interests.

As for the union-density rates (item 2), in 1994–5 less than one-third of the respondents who addressed item 1 answered this question (102 out of 362), with only three responses from POEs. In 2001–2, 35 per cent of the respondents who replied to item 1 gave answers to item 2 (142 out of 407). The low awareness of the membership rates reflects either the lack of influence or the weak position of unions in the enterprise. However, this situation improved somewhat in the second survey.

Permanent and contract employees

The questions concerning the proportion of permanent and contract-based employees (items 3 and 4) also received fewer responses in 1994–5 (200 and 288, respectively, for items 3 and 4 compared to 362 for item 1) than in 2001–2. This might be attributed to the fact that the labour contract system was being implemented in China at the time of the first survey and people may have been confused about their status. The response rate increased to 80 per cent of respondents in 2001–2 (355 and 358, respectively, for items 3 and 4). As some respondents might not be clear about the proportion of permanent and contract employees and ticked both questions, the sum of answers to items 3 and 4 was more than 100 in both surveys. Even so, the data strongly indicate that in 1994–5 before the labour contract system became compulsory, the public sector had more permanent employees than the private one. SOEs/COEs had far fewer contract employees than the private enterprises. The results show clearly that while the private sector had always used more contract-based employees, the public sector was also moving away from the traditional lifetime employment system. In 2001–2 all enterprises used fewer permanent employees and more contract-based employees, particularly the COEs and POEs. Many fewer SOEs had workforces with half and more permanent employees (yet they still had more permanent and fewer contract employees than other types of enterprises) indicating a legacy from the lifetime employment tradition they had. Only FIEs maintained their proportion of permanent employees while greatly reducing the use of contract-based employees, which might indicate that with increased competition to attract skilled employees in a free labour market, FIEs try to select and retain qualified employees by offering more quasi-permanent positions (i.e. unfixed contract or ongoing).

Employee participation

Table 8.30 sets out the figures that show whether employees were encouraged to participate, how they participated if they could and the percentage of employees participating in management decision-making. The results for item 1 indicate that in 1994–5 employees in the public sector were more encouraged to participate in management than those in the non-public sector and the impact of the ownership type is significant. The results from the first survey seem consistent with the Maoist and socialist ideology that workers in China should be masters of enterprises and even of the society. However, the results of item 3 clearly indicate that no enterprises were particularly democratic and none offered many opportunities for employees to participate in the management process: over 70 per cent of respondents admitted that less than 30 per cent of employees were involved in management.

The type of ownership lost its significant impact on item 1 in the 2001–2 survey. More companies, especially among POEs and FIEs, encourage employees to participate, while SOEs demonstrated a decrease in this practice. This is consistent with the answers to item 3 which indicate that employees from the private sector have more opportunities to participate in the management process. When employees were given opportunities to participate in management, the most common method was to encourage them to put forward suggestions. The differences for this practice were significant in 2001–2, with many more COEs and SOEs using it. Some respondents indicated that their enterprises might also set up a suggestion box so employees could voice their opinions in a written form. However, few enterprises actually valued employee participation by accepting their suggestions and offering rewards, especially in the non-public sector in 1994–5. Managers' attitude towards suggestions and rewards appeared more positive in 2001–2, but mainly in the private sector, especially in FIEs while public sector enterprises all demonstrated a decrease.

With respect to participation in management decision-making, in 1994–5, SOEs appeared to offer reasonable opportunities to employees, with both COEs and POEs allowing much less employee participation and FIEs the

Table 8.30 Employee participation in the management process

Variables	1994–5 survey (%)					2001–2 survey (%)				
	SOEs	COEs	POEs	FIEs	p	SOEs	COEs	POEs	FIEs	p
1 Employees are encouraged to participate in the management process	81	64	50	51	0.001	65	70	62	75	—
2 Methods used for employee participation:										
• using a suggestion box	33	18	38	34	—	39	44	33	44	—
• encouraging suggestions	74	63	75	68	—	75	83	58	47	0.001
• accepting suggestions and offering rewards	49	43	38	25	0.05	45	39	42	47	—
• participating in management decisions	37	23	25	16	0.05	31	35	22	23	—
3 Percentage of employees participating in the management process:			—							
• less than 30%	81	77	70	88		85	77	72	76	
• about 50%	12	17	20	7		12	19	20	13	
• over 60%	7	6	10	5		3	4	8	11	

least, and the differences were all statistically significant. However, in 2001–2 there were no significant differences between enterprises, and COEs/FIEs increased this practice, SOEs/POEs decreased it. This situation can be understood in private enterprises, as decision-making is highly centralized in the hands of the founder-owner of POEs (Lau *et al.*, 1999; also see Chapter 6). The implication of the results in Table 8.30 is that the concept of employee participation is applied more in theory than in practice, even though the use of this practice was on the increase in the second survey. This may be due to the lack of knowledge about participation in management and may also reflect the legacy of the traditional planning system, centralized managerial style and the impact of culture, which leads to a passive attitude towards management participation among employees.

CONCLUSIONS

This chapter has presented, compared and discussed the results from the two surveys. Compared with the 1994–5 survey results, the 2001–2 survey revealed two major changes. First, there is an obvious increase in the utilization of HR practices across all types of enterprises except SOEs, which in many situations demonstrated a decline in using such practices. Some practices conducted are either moving away from the traditional model employed under the command economy or incorporating ideas and methods often practised in advanced market economies. Second, the impact of ownership type on HR practices is considerably reduced or blurred, which has produced patterns different from those in the first survey. The details of these major findings and the issues that emerge for the future are summarized and discussed in the next and last chapter.

9 The role of HRM in transition

This last chapter has two broad objectives. First, the research findings obtained from the qualitative case studies and quantitative surveys are analysed and discussed in relation to the three research questions posed in the first chapter. Second, three major implications of the research findings which relate to government regulation of enterprises, research on HRM and HR practices in China are drawn for HRM development in China's industrial enterprises. A transitional HRM model is proposed to indicate the emerging role of HRM in China even though the role is still in transition with its ongoing economic reforms.

ANALYSIS OF FINDINGS IN RELATION TO RESEARCH QUESTIONS

The primary purpose of this book was to explore the emerging role of HRM in China's industrial enterprises, which was achieved through the development of three research questions, the investigation of four major case studies and the two surveys completed (Chapters 4–8). The analysis of each case and the discussion of survey results alone are just part of the inductive theory-building process. To further strengthen the theoretical outcomes obtained from different research methods and to enable the integration of research findings, a comparative analysis across the four cases and two surveys is necessary. Therefore, the following three sections will discuss the research findings as they pertain to each of the three research questions.

Major changes in HR practices in Chinese industrial enterprises

The first research question posed in this book is 'How were human resources in Chinese industrial enterprises managed before and after the commencement of economic reform with respect to major HR activities, including: human resource planning; recruitment and selection; performance appraisal; compensation and welfare; training and development; and labour relations?' The case studies investigated HR practices before and after the commencement of economic reform, with Chapters 4 and 5 examining industrial enterprises with state and collective ownership, respectively, and Chapters 6 and 7 examining enterprises with private and joint foreign ownership, respectively. These case studies offered a snapshot of HR practices during the transition of economic system in China up to late 1994. The survey results discussed in Chapter 8 detailed the HR practices across the four types of enterprises in two time periods (i.e. 1994–5 and 2001–2), which revealed changes in HR practices during the reform from the mid-1990s to the early 2000s.

HR practices before the economic reform

Before the commencement of economic reform, some HR practices including HR planning, recruitment and selection did not exist at the enterprise level, as was illustrated by the case enterprises TeleCo (Chapter 4) and RadioCo (Chapter 5). The highly centralized planning system and various constraints imposed on enterprises by the government precluded enterprise activity. Some other HR activities were planned by the government and implemented by the enterprises, such as compensation with its centrally fixed wage scales and unified training. Such 'puppet-like' management practices (discussed in Chapter 2) were observed in TeleCo and RadioCo.

Some HR activities were practised but exhibited typical Chinese features, such as politically oriented assessment criteria, cadre-centred appraisal and the 'transmission belt' role played by trade unions. As a result, the traditional personnel and labour administration characterized by the three 'iron practices' as reviewed in the literature and observed in the case studies either deprived enterprises of their ability to conduct HR activities or made these activities redundant. For example, performance appraisal failed to play the role expected of it in the West because cadres maintained their tenure positions and workers could stay permanently with enterprises regardless of their performance. Training other than apprenticeship was often initiated and organized by the government and usually emphasized political education. These phenomena are summarized in the traditional PRC model of personnel and labour administration in Figure 2.1 and are also reflected in the case studies reported in Chapters 4 and 5.

HR practices during economic reform

Based on the HR activities investigated through qualitative and quantitative studies in 1994–5 and then the follow-up survey in 2001–2, current HR practices discussed in this chapter mainly refer to those revealed in the second survey, with discussions about the changes that occurred between the two time periods of the study. The research findings demonstrate that a much greater number of the enterprises investigated had a separate HR department in 2001–2 and many fewer HR departments managed white- and blue-collar employees (i.e. cadres and workers) separately, as this distinction had become irrelevant in many enterprises, especially in the private sector. Although the department still conducted the more operational tasks such as record keeping, recruitment and selection, and wage administration in both surveys, the use of other practices including conducting HR planning and job analysis as well as formulating HR policies were on the increase in the second survey, again mainly in the private sector.

Many HR functional activities prevalent in advanced market economies were observed in Chinese enterprises in both surveys though with different orientations. In the 1994–5 survey and case studies, the HR practices were used with more Chinese characteristics, such as labour allocation, the specification of production quotas in job analysis and administration-oriented performance appraisal. The 2001–2 survey results showed a trend of convergence to HR practices often employed in market economies even though the legacy of traditional practices was still apparent. For example, more companies used long-term based HR planning and more HR managers were involved in this process across all enterprises except SOEs in 2001–2. Although the focus of HR planning varied between the enterprises, ranging from staffing to replacement, retrenchment or production development, more enterprises, especially those in the non-state sector, used HR planning for business strategy purposes. More formal job analyses were conducted and there was a considerable increase in this practice in the non-state sector, with FIEs being the leader. In job analysis, more attention was given to employees' qualifications and it was increasingly used to assist other HR practices such as planning, selection and compensation in the second survey as is expected in market economies. The changes in the five major HR activities across the period of two surveys further indicate such a trend of convergence.

With respect to hiring practices, more emphasis has been placed on personal competency than political background and personal archives. Sources for competent employees have broadened to include free labour markets, advertising and internal HR data banks. Employment tests and personal interviews have become more commonly used as selection tools, although the former was given more weight than the latter. An increased emphasis on job applicants' potential to stay longer with the organization so as to maximize return on investment in hiring practices is a new concept in China's HR practices, because, under the traditional labour allocation system, it was impossible to improve hiring effectiveness.

Performance appraisal has been transformed from a politically oriented bureaucratic assessment mainly for cadres to a performance-based and compensation-linked practice for all employees. The majority of enterprises surveyed conducted appraisals on a yearly basis, with the intention of offering employee incentives by linking wage packages to the fulfilment of tasks and responsibilities. Furthermore, performance appraisal was used more for development and communication purposes rather than just focusing on administration purposes as revealed by both case studies and the survey conducted in 1994–5.

Compensation practices have shifted away from centrally planned wage scales to enterprise-determined wage packages that include base pay, bonuses and various welfare benefits, and there are more varieties in the choice of wage packages used, indicating the full autonomy of enterprises to make their own decisions. Compensation is linked more closely to an individual's performance, which is more prevalent in the private sector in the 2001–2 survey. This reflects the essence of the compensation reform, which is to eliminate egalitarianism by introducing material incentives and linking pay to performance. However, less coverage in social insurance in the private sector, especially POEs, indicates that employees may face less protection while working in that sector.

Training programmes were gaining popularity in all types of enterprises in 2001–2 to equip new employees with necessary skills and technical knowledge. The 1994–5 study revealed that some training programmes were offered simply to fulfil government requirements rather than to assist production needs. The managers interviewed for the case studies were reluctant to invest in training if it was not legally required. For instance, the government requirement for SOEs to invest 1.5 per cent of the total payroll in training was ignored when the enterprise experienced financial losses (see Chapter 4). In the enterprises that were not required to invest in training, only new employees were offered some training (see Chapters 4 and 6). Although the introduction of skill-related wages in the early 1990s put pressure on employees to increase their skill level, the enterprises encouraged employees to use time outside work for further training rather than offering on-the-job or off-the-job training. CableCo was the only exception in that 1 per cent of its total payroll was used for training as required by the government for all foreign-invested enterprises (see Chapter 7). The absence of a legal requirement for training or lack of enforcement of such a requirement when the case studies were conducted might partly explain the reluctance of managers to invest in employee training. With a rapidly changing business environment and increasing competition as the consequence of further reform and China's integration into the global economy, all enterprises have increased their training practices as revealed in the second survey results. Furthermore, behavioural training and management development programmes became more popular in 2001–2 although they were still used less than technical training. Training practices in general are perceived to be positively related to organizational effectiveness and such a correlation appeared stronger in 2001–2.

Labour relations in China were mainly non-confrontational because trade unions act as management assistant and employees' caretaker, with the main focus on employee welfare as reflected in the four case studies. However, compared with findings from the first survey in terms of union membership, the second survey results indicate that fewer employees were union members in the private sector in the early 2000s even though the establishment of trade unions had been legitimized and encouraged in different types of enterprises. With greater numbers of employees on contract and in the fast developing non-state sector, at least two issues need to be considered. One is whether the interests and rights of employees, especially those outside the state sector, can be protected, and the other is whether HR managers can really play the role of 'employee champion' and listen to and respond to employees' concerns as advocated by Ulrich (1997).

The research findings relevant to these HR practices indicate that the purpose of HRM to attract, retain and develop competent employees to achieve business objectives as defined in the West (Schuler *et al.*, 1992) is being gradually recognized by more enterprises in China. Although HR activities with the same or similar titles are being tried, in various formats, HRM is shifting, at a slow pace, from being merely administrative and politically/ideologically oriented to being somewhat strategic and business-related. This trend was first observed in the case enterprises in the mid-1990s when TeleCo was using HR activities to help nurture a new enterprise culture as part of the business strategy to change its loss-making status, and CableCo was using HR practices to acquire a competitive edge by retaining loyal and committed employees (see Chapters 4 and 7, respectively). The trend became more pronounced in the second survey mainly in two areas, that is, the abolition of the three iron practices and more emphasis on strategic roles rather than the political aspect of HR practices in enterprise operations.

With respect to the abolition of the three iron practices, it may still be too early to say that these have been completely eliminated. However, there is a definite trend away from these practices, with the common use of contract-based hiring, more results-oriented assessment, more individual-performance-related compensation, and especially the social security reform being implemented in China. The entrenched welfare and social security system established in the planned economy in the public sector became a serious impediment to abolishing the 'iron rice bowl' as revealed in our case studies. The government has now accepted that the development of a market-oriented social security system is a key element in both the nation's transition to a market economy and its integration into the global economy (Chen, 2001; Hussain, 2000). To reflect this idea, in March 1998 the Ministry of Labour was restructured and renamed the Ministry of Labour and Social Security. Social insurance, as part of the social security system, covers protective arrangements such as pensions, medical insurance and unemployment benefits. The private sector has been included in the pension system since 1995 and a comprehensive social insurance system in the urban area was being established in the early 2000s, even though the extent of coverage for employees still varies greatly across enterprises (Nyland *et al.*, in press). The social security reform has facilitated the replacement of the former 'iron rice bowl' with a welfare regime more oriented to a society in which market forces and worker mobility are the principal factors guiding economic activity (Zhu and Nyland, 2004).

The subsequent emergence of a free labour market has facilitated two-way selection and more competition-based appointment and employment. With the utilization of more job-related performance criteria and results-oriented assessment, together with the blurring of boundary between cadres and workers, fewer cadres/managers hold tenured positions and their promotion or demotion is based more on their performance. Similarly, wages are also more dependent on an enterprise's operation and profitability, and a greater acceptance of wider reward disparities based on individual performance indicates that the iron wage system is fading into history.

As HR practices are now selected, planned and implemented at the organizational level with different degrees of autonomy and various styles and orientations, it appears that enterprises, especially those in the private sector, experience much less interference from government in their operations. In the mid-1990s the government relaxed its control in areas such as quota limits on cadres, allocation of employees to enterprises and determination of types of wage packages or specified welfare benefits. By the early 2000s these controls had been greatly reduced or even abandoned. However, while the public sector experienced greater change in government regulations in the mid-1990s due to this withdrawal of government from the enterprise administration, the private sector experienced similar or stronger change in 2001–2 (see Table 8.1) when the government waived some concessions, such as tax holidays enjoyed by FIEs and tolerance of POEs' lower or lack of provision of social security benefits to their employees. These changes indicate that the Chinese economy is still under transition and that the business environment is still changing as it pursues a market economy consequent to its accession to the WTO.

The changes have left enterprises with more discretion to conduct HR activities according to their own needs. For instance, the political orientation in HR practices, such as the organization of political study programmes and the emphasis on political requirements in selection criteria, became weaker in the second survey. On the other hand, enterprises, especially those in the non-state sector, indicated stronger correlations between their performance and HR practices in the second than the first survey. More HR managers, particularly those in the private sector, were involved in the formulation of an organizational business strategy and participated in decision-making on key strategic issues within the senior management team in the 2001–2 survey than in the 1994–5 survey. This indicates a continuing push towards HR participation in strategic decision-making across all types of enterprises and provides some evidence of strategic roles played by HR department and HR managers as observed by other researchers (Braun and Warner, 2002; Whiteley *et al.*, 2000).

In summary, before the commencement of the reforms, human resources in Chinese industrial enterprises were managed more by the government than the enterprises, which partly explained why SOEs were called state-run (*guoying*) enterprises before 1994. The situation has changed greatly since the reforms began. However, current HR activities demonstrate the coexistence of some radical changes and the legacy of some old practices, such as job inheritance (*dingti*), government allocation of jobs and the involvement of HR managers in more administrative work. Thus, our findings in this study in regard to the first research question support the observation of Warner (1998b: 31) that 'we are witnessing the emergence of a more complex, *hybrid* management model as marketization advances and as enterprise autonomy increases'. The shift from traditional personnel and labour administration to HRM as defined in the West is only partial and in its early stages as China is still undergoing the transition towards a more market-driven economy.

Impact of ownership forms on HRM

The second research question in this book is 'What impact does ownership type have on HR practices in Chinese industrial enterprises?' The ownership type, or the corporate governance form, in the planned economy was affected by two organizational practices: the formation of larger production units with predominant public ownership (*yida ergong*) and state ownership of enterprises with government control over management (*zhengqi heyi*). These practices enabled the government to exert strong control over enterprises through its planning system and various restrictions, while ignoring the role of the market. They also had a substantial impact on enterprise management, particularly in the way that human resources were managed. With reforms in the ownership structure in the late 1970s and subsequent emergence of enterprises with non-public ownership, managers have gained increasing control of their enterprises' operations, leading to experimentation with various management practices and changes in HR practices. As the results from two surveys indicate a quite different level of impact, the first survey results are discussed before examining the impact observed in the 2001–2 survey.

Impact of ownership on HRM in the mid-1990s

The impact of ownership type on HRM is quite obvious in the study conducted in 1994–5: public enterprises (SOEs and COEs) encountered many more constraints than private ones (POEs and FIEs) in terms of government controls, political and ideological influences, and the legacy of traditional practices. Take government control as an example: the control of cadres through quotas was emphasized in TeleCo, an SOE (see Chapter 4), and the survey results in Table 8.3 indicate that far more SOEs managed cadres and workers separately to enable better control over the cadres. The nomenclature system for senior managers was in practice in both TeleCo and RadioCo, a COE (see Chapter 5). Similarly, labour allocation was observed in the case studies of TeleCo and RadioCo, and the survey results indicate that both SOEs and COEs had a higher number of government allocated employees than POEs and FIEs (see Table 8.14). Furthermore, public enterprises like TeleCo and RadioCo were still under local government control in regards to the retrenchment of redundant employees, the total amount of payroll, the wage scales and their increases. Under the planned economy, wage scales at SOEs were fixed by the government at a higher level than that in COEs regardless of the performance of the enterprise. This explains why managers and employees at RadioCo complained about their lower wage scales compared with their counterparts in SOEs. Moreover, the government continued to initiate and organize training programmes, and enterprises such as TeleCo and RadioCo still had to send people to training programmes organized by their authority even though the programmes were not necessarily appropriate for the enterprises. The first survey results also revealed that more public than non-public enterprises conducted HR planning merely because government required it (see Table 8.6).

With respect to the political and ideological influence, public enterprises were more affected than private ones. The case study of TeleCo revealed the emphasis on the political reliability of managerial cadres and the first survey results indicate that more public enterprises sought political reliability in their HR managers (see Table 8.3). In addition, SOEs emphasized the political background of job applicants not only in their current practice ('is now') but also felt it should continue in the future ('should be'). Although this phenomenon was also observed in the FIEs surveyed in 1994–5, it was because the foreign investors of these enterprises had formed joint ventures with SOEs and the positions of HR manager were held mainly by Chinese. According to the first survey results, 73 HR managers of FIEs surveyed were Chinese and 62 of them were Party members. Furthermore, some political training programmes were reported in the case studies and the first survey results reveal that more HR departments in SOEs organized political studies than those in other types of enterprises, especially POEs (see Table 8.4).

The third type of constraint on public enterprises is the legacy of traditional practices. For instance, minimal wage differentials were recognized as an obstacle to offering incentives to high performers in both TeleCo and RadioCo. The legacy of another iron practice, 'iron rice bowl' or lifetime employment, was more prevalent in public enterprises than in non-public enterprises as revealed by the survey results (see Table 8.29). This practice was not eliminated in the mid-1990s for several reasons, including the lack of autonomy of public enterprises to retrench surplus employees in the absence of a nationwide social security system and the greater number of permanent employees in the public sector due to the enterprise-supplied accommodation as part of their welfare benefits. This is evident in the case study of TeleCo as well as in the survey results, which demonstrated that more SOEs supplied a housing subsidy to employees (see Table 8.24). The traditional roles played by trade unions, as a transmission belt and caretaker, were evident in both TeleCo and RadioCo. The Party and government maintained strong control over the unions which were more prevalent in SOEs than other types of enterprises.

As SOEs used to be within the state planning system with its management conducted by the government apparatus (*zhengqi heyi*), they were under tighter control from the government at various levels and had established a more formal bureaucratic system. Although SOEs appeared to conduct more HR practices than COEs, HRM in public enterprises in general still retained many characteristics typical of traditional personnel and labour administration. Since the founding of the PRC in 1949, public enterprises, especially SOEs, had been required by the state to combine employment and welfare with little freedom to hire and fire people, which made it almost impossible for enterprises to achieve a key goal of HRM to attract, retain and develop key employees.

Another significant impact of public ownership on HRM could be the lack of incentives and training for managers to learn and adopt new and effective HR practices. This could partly be attributed to the nomenclature system and partly to other HR practices applied to cadres. Under the nomenclature system, the government appointed politically reliable senior managers who were often transferred to another enterprise if they were unsuccessful (as occurred with former directors of TeleCo). For senior managers, performance became less important than maintaining a close relationship with the government. Managers were therefore reluctant to take risks or adopt different HR policies or practices to improve performance or to radically change the traditional system. In addition, wage scales for managers in China were still not performance-related but rather, merely determined by government policy (see Chapters 4 and 5). As managers did not have the authority to allocate residual gains when the enterprise performed well, they 'had no incentives to respond to market signals' (Hughes, 1998: 69), and were discouraged from using their initiative or creativity to introduce and implement HR practices (Zhao and Ni, 1997; Zhao *et al.*, 1998). The lack of training for managers will be discussed later.

While the case studies and the 1994–5 survey results illustrated the various constraints on SOEs and COEs due to their public ownership and the consequent impact on their HR practices, non-public enterprises including POEs and FIEs were subject to a much lower level of constraint than public enterprises. This could be observed in the case studies of ElectroCo (a POE, see Chapter 6) and CableCo (an FIE, see Chapter 7) which did not have government quotas for cadres, and were free from government control over retrenchment, total payroll and wage scales adjustment. The distinction between cadres and workers had also become blurred with the actual emphasis on the individual, the job position and the responsibility that the individual assumed. This allowed more flexibility in staffing, job allocation and the management of human resources. The survey results also show that fewer POEs and FIEs than public enterprises adhered to the government requirement of a floating wage or positional allowances (Table 8.22). The government initiated and organized training programmes were not found in either ElectroCo or CableCo, where training was offered on the basis of the production needs of each enterprise. In addition, the nomenclature system was not practised in ElectroCo as its owner and General Manager had full autonomy to appoint all managers. Furthermore, private enterprises, especially POEs, also experienced fewer political and ideological constraints. In the case of ElectroCo, the selection criteria were mainly based on job-related knowledge and skills, and political reliability for new recruits was ignored.

However, POEs and FIEs were not completely exempt from government control, especially when FIEs were jointly owned by SOEs and foreign companies. The constraints they often encountered included government appointment of senior managers, as occurred in the CableCo case, and labour allocated by government, as observed in the first survey results (see Table 8.14). The survey results also reveal that political requirements existed for HR managers and political-oriented training programmes were present in POEs and FIEs (see Tables 8.3 and 8.4), although these two constraints were not observed in the case studies. The reason that FIEs were subject to more constraints than POEs could be that this type of enterprise was in transition, as explained by a foreign general manager of a joint venture in China:

> Our enterprise is undergoing a transition from a state-owned enterprise to a foreign-managed joint venture. The change is being deliberately managed at a steady pace to ensure that it is not too quick for the local people to understand. Consequently many practices and philosophies that shall be phased out are currently still in place.[1]

Consistent with this general manager's explanation, the first survey results disclose that political requirement for new recruits was only emphasized by FIEs currently ('is now') rather than in the future ('should be'). In contrast, SOEs put emphasis on political requirement both now and in the future.

As most private enterprises started their businesses during the reforms, they were less influenced by the government and had more autonomy and authority to move away from traditional HR practices. This was evident in the 1994–5 study when more employees from POEs and FIEs were employed on a contractual basis (see Table 8.29), bonuses were distributed more on the basis of individual rather than group performance (see Table 8.23) and cadres were replaced by managerial staff whose positions were determined by competency and performance (see Chapters 6 and 7). Similarly, minimal differentiation between wage scales and enterprise supplied accommodation were not observed in either the ElectroCo or the CableCo case study, as both these enterprises designed their own wage packages and made their own decisions. These two enterprises also had more contract than permanent employees, which was consistent with survey data. With regard to the traditional roles of trade unions, the findings varied. There was no trade union at ElectroCo, but the survey reveals that many non-public enterprises had unions (see Table 8.29). The case of CableCo indicated the trade unions could assist Chinese managers to protect the rights and interests of Chinese employees in addition to their traditional roles as the transmission belt and caretaker.

While moving away from the three iron practices, POEs and FIEs did not, overall, have similar HR practices. Fewer POEs than FIEs had a separate HR department (see Table 8.3 and Chapter 6) and their HR practices were often informal and non-systematic. Table 8.4 reveals that HR departments in POEs currently conducted the least number of HR activities compared with FIEs and other public enterprises. Furthermore, significant differences were observed in activities such as 'training', 'job analysis and evaluation', 'being responsible for HR policies', 'conducting HR planning' and 'wage administration' (see Table 8.4). The first survey results also indicate that POEs offered much less off-the-job training, training for technical/professional skills and management development than FIEs (see Table 8.25). At ElectroCo there was no plan at all for employee training. POEs' lower reliance on formal performance appraisal and feedback, low levels of explicit job analysis and staff training, a strong emphasis on the management of extrinsic rewards, and few welfare and fringe benefits all indicate the *ad hoc* or informal and non-systematic nature of their HR practices, which could be the consequence of their family-based business structure, paternalistic style of management, short-term oriented behaviour and their relatively short history.

Compared with POEs, FIEs conducted more HR practices as many foreign partners of joint ventures have brought in various managerial practices commonly used in market economies together with their technology, such as a close working relationship between the HR department and the senior management group on key strategic issues (see Table 8.5), and the involvement of department managers in HR planning (see Table 8.6). In CableCo, the foreign partner, AuzCo, transferred some of its HR practices including merit-based recruitment and selection and performance appraisal to the enterprise and CableCo was required to use AuzCo's standards as its benchmark in production and quality control. The connections with foreign companies have enabled FIEs to adopt a more flexible HR approach, or an HRM programme that incorporates more of the practices used in the market economies, as is evident in the first survey results. Although the extent to which Western HR practices had been transferred to China may be debated, FIEs have consistently demonstrated in both survey and case study that they conducted more HR practices than any other types of enterprise surveyed. However, in 1994–5, FIEs (or more precisely, foreign joint ventures with local SOEs) still experienced some restrictions or limitations from the government and consequently maintained some traditional HR practices. Even so, they appeared to be moving towards greater convergence with Western HR practices as indicated by this study and other researchers (Benson and

Zhu, 1999; Warner, 1998b). Part of the explanation is that FIEs did not inherit the inefficient management system of a state enterprise or the 'burden of the past' (Tsang, 1998: 25).

In summary, our comparative analysis of the impact of different types of ownership on HRM based on the findings of the 1994–5 study has partially supported Shenkar's (1994: 15) claim that 'continuing reforms may change the situation [of traditional management practices], particularly in collective, private and foreign-invested enterprises'. The study results suggest that it is most likely that HR practices would develop more rapidly in FIEs than in other types of enterprises, especially POEs.

Impact of ownership on HRM in the early 2000s

In the mid-1990s SOEs and FIEs in general had more HR practices than COEs and POEs. However, this split was much less pronounced in the 2001–2 survey, indicating that the impact of type of ownership was diminishing greatly as other types of companies increased the use of various HR practices while SOEs reduced them. Some implications can be drawn from these findings. First, the reduced impact of ownership type on HR practices indicates that in a market-driven economy, all companies have to adopt an efficient and effective corporate governance system, in which HR practices have obviously become more popular. Second, SOEs used to have more formal managerial practices even though many of them did not perform well. The radical restructuring that they are undertaking in order to compete against other types of enterprises may lead to a reduction in their conduct of HR practices. However, with respect to the protection offered to employees, such as social insurance and the establishment of trade unions, SOEs and COEs are doing better than the private business, especially POEs, which reflects a major difference in the public and private sector.

With respect to FIEs, it can be seen that in both surveys these enterprises had more senior managers involved in HR practices, and engaged in more types or more formal HR activities than COEs and POEs, such as off-the-job training, formal appraisal criteria and methods, and used performance appraisal for development and communication purposes in addition to administration. The influence of some practices from SOEs, such as the incorporation of political background in their selection criteria and organization of political studies, was greatly reduced in the 2001–2 survey. Generally, FIEs encountered much less interference from the government than did other types of enterprises. For example, they were less frequently required to conduct HR planning by the local government or to design their wage packages according to state regulations, they received much less government-allocated labour, and had many more employees on contract when the labour contract system was first introduced in the mid-1990s. Compared with other types of enterprises, FIEs linked individual performance to compensation most closely. All these factors contributed to their higher productivity and their HR departments were perceived to be more effective than those of other types of enterprises in both surveys.

Compared with SOEs and FIEs, COEs conducted fewer HR activities in 1994–5. This reflected the loose control that the government had over COEs and also the informality of their management practices. While COEs were less dependent on the state, they were still affected by government policies and regulations to a greater degree than POEs and FIEs. They accepted government-allocated labour and adopted government policies regarding compensation practices (e.g. the use of floating wages and positional allowances). However, the 2001–2 survey results indicated that COEs had significantly increased many HR practices, such as performance appraisal and both specific and adaptation training. The results show that HR departments in COEs were perceived to be much more important and effective by respondents in 2001–2 compared with 1994–5, which could be the result of the reform in the public sector.

Similar to COEs, POEs had fewer HR practices than SOEs and FIEs in the 1994–5 survey. POEs enjoyed more autonomy than COEs in their HR practices, such as the least attention paid to the political background of HR managers and job applicants, more flexibility in their hiring practices and more individual performance-related rewards. However, POEs made the least investment in employee training and development although their respondents expected a substantial increase in the future. The HR pattern identified in POEs in the 1994–5 survey changed in 2001–2, which partly contributed to the diminishing impact of ownership type on HR practices. First, like FIEs, POEs felt more changes and increased competition in their environment, which could be the reason for them adopting more HR practices, such as job analysis and performance appraisal. Furthermore, POEs had more well-educated employees, which might explain why more HR departments were set up and were perceived to be much more important than they were in 1994–5. HR managers were also working more closely with senior managers and some activities were conducted in ways similar to those used in FIEs, such as using performance appraisal more for development and communication purposes. Even so, significant differences have been identified in the second survey between POEs and other types of enterprises with respect to: the lowest penetration of trade unions, the lowest rate of payment of social insurances, many fewer training programmes offered, the most informal performance appraisal criteria and methods used, and the lowest use of job analysis for

HR planning, which may contribute to the lowest perceived effectiveness of their HR department.

In summary, the impact of ownership on HR practices reduced greatly in 2001–2 as more POEs and COEs conducted HR practices than they had in 1994–5. This not only reflects a wider adoption of the concept of HRM by more Chinese enterprises but also indicates managerial development in the non-state sector in China. Furthermore, the second survey results consistently indicate that more FIEs conducted HR practices than did other types of enterprises, which is consistent with the first survey findings. This reflects the trend for foreign companies to transfer HR practices employed in advanced market economies to their subsidiaries in China in order to improve management practices and increase productivity.

Future perspectives on HRM

The third question for this research is 'What are the possible future development paths of HRM in Chinese industrial enterprises?' In the 1994–5 case studies, the employees interviewed suggested possible changes in HR practices, while the managers indicated what their future plans were for HRM. In the surveys conducted in 1994–5 and 2001–2, respondents contrasted the extent of HR practices being used currently ('is now') to their ideal HR practices in the future ('should be'). The differences between the current and ideal practices in each survey and between the two surveys reflect the direction of change in HRM and the possible future development paths of HRM in industrial enterprises in China. The answers to the third question are thus derived mainly from the two study findings with greater focus on the 2001–2 survey results. The following paragraphs discuss the findings in terms of each HR practice investigated.

Job analysis and HR planning

All the case enterprises acknowledged that lack of job analysis had impeded or weakened other HR practices such as HR planning and selection. Therefore, they had either started a job analysis project (see Chapters 4 and 6), or were considering the revision of job descriptions for both managerial staff and production workers (see Chapters 5 and 7). The expectation of case enterprises that job analysis would be used by more enterprises was strongly supported by the 1994–5 survey respondents, but was only partially supported by the 2001–2 results: only SOEs and COEs expected such an increase, while POEs and FIEs had already greatly increased this practice (see Table 8.4). The 2001–2 survey also witnessed more non-state enterprises conducting written job analyses as compared with the situation in 1994–5 (see item 1 in Table 8.7). The use of job analyses to assist HR planning increased in 2001–2 but needs to be practised more in the future (see item 2 in Table 8.8). The use of job analyses for job evaluation was improved mainly in the non-state sector in 2001–2 and was expected to be used more in SOEs (see item 5 in Table 8.8). Given an obvious increase in the conduct of job analyses (see Tables 8.4 and 8.7) and in the uses of job analyses for other HR practices (see Table 8.8) between the 1994–5 and 2001–2 surveys, there appears to be a trend for more enterprises, especially those in the non-state sector, to conduct job analyses in the future.

With regard to HR planning, although it was conducted by the four case enterprises, their managers were not satisfied with its short-term orientation and focus on quantity control (i.e. an emphasis on the control of total number of employees). Their preference was for longer term (i.e. 3–5 years) planning, but this depended on whether the enterprise had a long-term business strategy and whether the management had real authority to lay off redundant employees. Item 1 in Table 8.4 clearly indicates a sharp increase in the intention in 1994–5 to use HR planning in the future for all enterprises, which was realized to various extents as revealed in the 2001–2 results ('is now'), except for SOEs. This could be due to the radical reforms including the merging and restructuring of SOEs. All enterprises surveyed also expected greater usage of this practice in 2001–2, except for FIEs as they had already increased the practice substantially. In addition, more line managers and HR managers were involved in HR planning in 2001–2 than in 1994–5, when it appeared that more HR and line managers rather than senior mangers, especially department managers, would participate in this practice (see Table 8.6). This might indicate a devolution of HR practices to a strategic business unit level within the enterprise.

Recruitment and selection

Both survey results indicate that recruitment and selection was conducted extensively by the HR department but with less room for increase in the future (see Table 8.4). In the case of CableCo, the selection of new employees was conducted by functional managers, with assistance from the HR manager, so as to achieve a better fit between the job and the candidates. A similar situation was observed in ElectroCo. The 2001–2 survey results indicate a similar pattern among the different types of enterprises as the 1994–5 results, except a large decline in COEs and a small increase in POEs (item 3 in Table 8.4).

The tendency for managers to select candidates for a job in their own specialized area with assistance from the HR manager/staff may represent a trend for future recruitment and selection. Decentralizing hiring to the business unit conforms to the current best practice in the West (Ulrich, 1998). There are three major reasons for such a trend in Chinese industrial enterprises. First, with incomplete or brief job descriptions and selection criteria, managers with specialized knowledge of a job are more likely to select appropriate candidates. Second, as revealed by both survey results, job-specific information including personal ability and skills presented at interview or tests was regarded as more important than archival biographical data (e.g. personal qualifications and file records) both now and in the future (see Table 8.9). Managers were in the best position to raise key questions or issues at interviews. Finally, insufficient training of HR managers in recruitment and selection has frequently contributed to their poor performance in selection. Traditionally, the most important attributes of HR managers were their political reliability and experience as administrators. With the emergence of a free labour market and the practice of 'two-way' selection, recruitment and selection can no longer be conducted just as an administrative task. HR managers need to acquire the professional skills of managing human resources.

Recruitment and selection in an enterprise were expected to be linked more closely to job analysis for relevant selection criteria, which was reflected in the four case studies (see Chapters 4–7). Recruitment and selection were also expected to rely less on one's connections (*guanxi*). These expectations were partially realized as more enterprises, especially private ones, increased the use of job analysis for selecting staff (see item 3 in Table 8.8) and an expected decrease of the role of connections (see item H4 in Table 8.11) by 2001–2. This could indicate how recruitment and selection will be conducted in the future. However, this practice seemed less relevant to some senior managers in the public sector, especially those working in large-scale state or collective enterprises, as they were often appointed by the government as indicated by one of our case studies. This has led to the question of whether the government should still rely on the nomenclature system or whether professional managers should be selected through fair competition in a free labour market. The respondents all agreed that 'market place competition has increased dramatically' in both surveys (see Table 8.1), indicating that enterprises need competent professional managers rather than government-appointed cadres in order to compete in a market-driven economy. Therefore, recruitment and selection should also be used for senior managers, even though it would create challenges for current senior managers.

Performance appraisal

Performance appraisal was observed in the four case enterprises with future improvement expected by their managers and employees. The proposed improvements include establishing objective criteria for assessing the performance of both managerial staff and production workers rather than adopting dual criteria ('soft and hard'); offering feedback to employees for further improvement of performance; using the appraisal to identify training needs; and seeking better assessment methods. These findings from the case studies were consistent with both survey results and the 2001–2 results clearly showed more enterprises except SOEs had implemented performance appraisal (see Table 8.4). Table 8.17 demonstrates an increase in the use of this practice for three different purposes across nearly all enterprises in 2001–2. However, a substantial increase was still expected in the use of appraisal for these purposes in the second survey, especially for communication and development.

The case studies indicate that progress in performance appraisal is dependent on the development of other HR activities such as job analysis, training and compensation. Without job analysis the appraisal is left to the subjective impression of the appraiser, as observed in TeleCo for its managerial staff. Similarly, without communication between appraisers and appraisees, employees are left ignorant of the criteria and purposes of assessment, as occurred in CableCo. Training is thus required not only for managers to acquire assessment skills, but also for employees to understand how to establish goals for their performance and how to communicate with appraisers. Furthermore, the practice of performance appraisal would be of little use if there was no close link between performance and compensation. The phenomenon of 'eating from the same small rice pot' (*chi xiaoguo fan*, equally distributed bonuses within a small working unit such as a department) as observed in TeleCo and RadioCo is a typical example of poor linkage between pay and performance and its detrimental impact on the effectiveness of performance appraisal. The 2001–2 survey results indicate increased use of written job analyses, formal assessment criteria and methods (see Table 8.15), more individual related performance bonuses in the private sector (see Table 8.23) and training being offered for management development. All of these may contribute to the closer correlation between the purposes of performance appraisal and the three measures of effectiveness shown in 2001–2 than in 1994–5 in the situation of 'is now' (see Table 8.18).

Compensation

In all the case enterprises, the pay system was undergoing reform, with the aim of offering incentives to employees. Different pay practices and various ways of distributing bonuses were experimented with. However, none of the enterprises was satisfied with their current compensation practice and various suggestions for improvements were put forward.

The first suggestion was to link pay and bonuses to the performance of each individual rather than the department so as to alleviate the problem of 'eating from the same small rice pot' (see Chapters 4 and 5). The second suggestion was to introduce a non-transparent compensation system (see discussion about 'unpredictable' and 'confidential' bonuses or wages in Chapters 5–7) to increase the gap between high and low performers' packages as an incentive while avoiding unnecessary jealousy (called 'red eyes' in Chinese) among workers. The research findings from both the quantitative and qualitative studies in 1994–5 indicate that future compensation practice should be developed with a greater focus on individual performance and non-transparency. One major issue faced by an individual-based and money-oriented compensation practice is that it may lead to higher staff turnover and a lack of commitment as has occurred in many FIEs (Tomlinson, 1997).

The respondents in both surveys indicated that material incentives were important in both current and future compensation practices. These included wages and welfare benefits such as social insurance and various allowances. However, the decrease in the number of enterprises that pay pension insurance, especially in POEs in the second survey after the implementation of the *Labour Law* in 1995 (see Table 8.24), has raised the issue of the strength of the regulatory regime to deal with free-riders. Seniority was still regarded as one of the determinants of a wage package but expected to have less weight in the 2001–2 survey. The use of job analyses for determining position salary was increasing greatly in all types of enterprise in the second survey (see item 6 in Table 8.8). Respondents preferred future payments to be individual performance-linked and long-term oriented. The 2001–2 survey results also indicate that compensation is much more strongly and positively related to an enterprise's overall performance than it was in 1994–5 (see Table 8.20). The changes that occurred between the two surveys could well indicate a tendency for compensation practices to provide more motivation or incentive to employees.

Training and development

Various training programmes were evident in the case enterprises and surveys, although these programmes were oriented to new recruits or existing workers needing to update their technical knowledge and skills. This suggests that training has been used as a means of implementing enterprise reform and therefore indicates progress in this HR activity. However, as indicated by the item 7 in Table 8.4, of all the HR activities, training and development is the one respondents expect to increase the most in the future in both surveys although this practice did have an increase in 2001–2. The respondents from both surveys expected specific training (technical knowledge and related skills) to increase from the current moderate level to a much higher level, and behavioural training (e.g. interpersonal skills and adaptability in a changing working environment) to increase from a relatively low level to a high level (see Table 8.26). These expectations were also evident in the four case studies, where people expressed dissatisfaction towards their senior managers' reluctance to invest in training, the lack of training for employees' career development and the reactive approach adopted by enterprises to training.

It has been noted that China still suffers from a shortage of highly skilled workers and experts, as well as a scarcity of qualified managers (Benson, 1996; *China Daily*, 26 March 2002; Zhang *et al.*, 2002; Zhu, C. J., 1997). The lack of adequately trained management was also identified by the government as a major problem in achieving modernization and the implementation of industrial reform (Schlevogt, 2002; Shang, 2003; Warner, 1995). Since the reform programme began, government and education institutes have offered various training programmes for managers. The findings of our study indicate that in 1994–5 only a low level of training was offered to managers, which had greatly improved in 2001–2 (see Chapters 5–7 and Table 8.25). The expectation of survey respondents for employees with better interpersonal skills and a stronger commitment to the enterprise supported the findings of other researchers that greater emphasis should be placed on behavioural training in China (Dalton and Austen, 1995). Greater emphasis on training, especially in the area of behavioural and managerial practice, is likely to develop in the future.

The trend for enterprises to increase their commitment and investment in employee training and development has also been facilitated by the *Labour Law*, which came into effect on 1 January 1995. Although the requirements for training set out in the *Labour Law* are not specific and procedures of enforcement are not established, it is still the first time since the PRC was founded that China has had a legal requirement for employee training and development. The *Labour Law* requires that:

> The employing unit shall establish a system for vocational training, raise and use funds for vocational training in accordance with the provisions of the state, and provide labourers with vocational training in a planned way and in the light of the actual situation of the unit.
>
> (Article 68)

Apart from this requirement, the government policy to deploy (or re-employ or reallocate) rather than retrench surplus employees has become another driving force for enterprises to offer training pro-grammes to increase employee employability. Another factor contribut-ing to the trend is the transition towards a more market-driven economy. Increasing competition within markets (as indicated by Table 8.1) has forced enterprises to raise productivity through training. The low level of employee productivity in many Chinese enterprises was directly related to the low level of workforce education and technical training, as well as to inadequate enterprise management. As China is now facing more rig-orous competition in the world economy as a member of the WTO, it is crucial for China to create a competitive workforce. Such pressure will push enterprises to invest in employee training and development.

Labour relations

The state has changed the requirement in the *Trade Union Law* regarding setting up a trade union committee: in 1950 a committee 'may be' estab-lished in any type of organization with 25 or more employees; this was altered to 'must be' in 1992 and re-emphasized in 2001. However, the findings of this study indicate that the density of union membership in public enterprises may continue in future to be much higher than in other enterprises. During Mao's regime, only full-time employees could be union members and SOEs used to offer lifetime employment to many more employees than any other type of enterprise. As most SOEs have remained 'mini-welfare states' (Thompson and Smith, 1992: 8), they had trade unions to deal with social issues such as the distribution of housing and other welfare items (see Chapter 4). With continuous reform in the state sector, SOEs have been pushed into the market and have to become competitive. Nevertheless, the 2001–2 survey results indicate that SOEs still had more permanent and fewer contract employees than other types of enterprises, reflecting a legacy of their lifetime employment tradition (see Table 8.29). Although employees in the non-public sector have the legal right to form unions, trade unions are still subordinated to the over-all interests of the Party and still focus on social welfare issues, as eco-nomic reform has not touched the political system in China (see Chapters 4, 5 and 7; also Howell, 1992; Story, 2003; Thompson, 1992).

The research results also disclose a low rate of employee participation in management across the four types of enterprises although FIEs showed some increase in the 2001–2 survey (Table 8.30), which may partly reflect the 'weak' position held by trade unions within enterprises. In the case studies of TeleCo, RadioCo and CableCo, trade unions played similar roles of han-dling employee welfare and assisting management. The only exception observed was in the case of CableCo, an FIE, where the trade unions assisted the Chinese managers to negotiate better welfare benefits for its Chinese employees with the foreign partner. Protecting the interests of Chinese employees may become a new role for trade unions in foreign-invested enterprises.

In the private sector, employees have less power to negotiate with management and their rights may not be protected as in ElectroCo. This situation is unlikely to change in the foreseeable future for several reasons. First, with the increasing number of retrenched (or to be reallocated) employees and surplus labour in rural areas, the labour market will be abundantly supplied, giving employers greater bargaining power. Second, the paternalistic style of management in private enterprises, as indicated in the literature and the ElectroCo case study (Chapter 6), may hinder the establishment of trade unions. Furthermore, the turnover rates of employees in the non-public sector tend to be higher as these workers have fewer welfare benefits such as enterprise-supplied housing or supplementary pension insurance tied up with their enterprises. This may reduce the incentive for employees to form unions. Given these influences, it is questionable that trade unions are able to represent workers' interests, in terms of their rights and power, to any great extent. As long as trade unions continue to be subordinate to the Party, their nature will largely remain unchanged.

Summary

The research results indicate possible future development paths for HRM in Chinese industrial enterprises. These include the adoption of the HR activities discussed above; further improvement of current activities such as more use of job analysis for HR planning, which should be linked more to business strategy; greater emphasis on job-related competency in hiring practices; utilizing performance appraisal more for the purposes of communication and development; emphasizing individual performance-related reward and performance-differentiated pay as well as long-term oriented pay practices; and integrating HR reforms into other areas such as the establishment of a nationwide social security system.

IMPLICATIONS OF THE RESEARCH FINDINGS

Government regulation of enterprises

The findings of this study raise the first major implication concerning government regulation of enterprises in their HRM development. The specific issues regarding government regulation include the enforcement of social security policies for different types of enterprises, power over and policies concerning managerial appointments, and further improvement of the business environment for HRM development in the private sector. These three aspects are discussed in the following sections.

The enforcement of social security policies

Prior to the introduction of market-oriented reforms, China's social security system was characterized by separation of urban and rural areas and segmentation of urban enterprises based on their ownership status. As private industry was negligible before the economic reform, no social security programmes existed in the private sector. The system in urban areas was predominantly an organization-based (*danwei*-based), defined-benefit, pay-as-you-go type, primarily covering the employees in the public sector, especially state-owned organizations such as SOEs. Coverage was comprehensive, and included pension insurance, free health services and paid sickness leave, insurance for injury, maternity benefits and funeral subsidies (see Wang, 2001). As a consequence, each organization in the state sector operated like a small society, providing not only social security but also hospitals, housing, schools and retail outlets for their employees (Roy and Chai, 1999). However, the *danwei*-based welfare system proved problematic for the public sector as it hindered labour mobility and represented a huge financial burden on SOEs. That is why up to the mid-1990s the lack of a society-based social security system became a critical problem for public enterprises, especially SOEs, as they were unable to retrench redundant employees and to reduce their heavy burden of maintaining a mini-society. Meanwhile, the non-existence of a social security system in the private sector was incompatible with the rapidly developed private sector and the increased opening up of the economy in the lead-up to China joining the WTO.

In the early 2000s this issue seemed less urgent as the state had adopted a series of social security reforms. These reforms have centred on the implementation of a number of social insurance programmes designed to cover the major risks confronting individuals working in both public and private sectors in a market economy (Saunders and Shang, 2001; Zhu, 2002; Whiteford, 2003). The new social insurance regime, underpinned by welfare pluralism (it is financed by individuals, enterprises and government) (Gu, 2001), has two major objectives. One is to mitigate the responsibility of enterprises in the public sector for welfare provision and to ensure that the burden is shouldered fairly between the major stakeholders. The other is to establish the same social security system in the private sector to protect employees and to contain free-riding as many private employers fail to offer their workers any insurance. Free-riding or contribution evasion problems in the private sector, especially POEs, have been identified in both the 1994–5 and the 2001–2 survey results.

Ensuring that employers meet their social security obligations is a central requirement as the government of China is undertaking this social security regime to assist the country's evolution to a market economy and its further integration into the global market. No matter how well designed a social security regime is, if employers are able to evade mandated contributions the scheme will not fulfil its basic function of providing for the security needs of individuals and the community. Free-riding enterprises are engaging in unfair competition in that they pass on to the community the costs that will have to be met when workers without pensions retire. Ensuring that employees' interests and rights are protected, and that enterprises do not evade their responsibilities but comply with legal requirements is a challenge for the government. The government has to intervene by developing countervailing regulations to restrain this behaviour and to strengthen compliance.

Enforcing the social security policies has also become a challenge for HR managers as they are normally the ones who handle the current social security system within enterprises while the traditional 'direct-planned welfare provision' is being replaced by a 're-distributive process' (Guan, 2000: 119). As social security reform has facilitated personal risk management (e.g. individuals match the job to their own skills rather than being placed in a selected sector of enterprises) and consequently labour mobility between public and private sectors, it has a profound impact on the management of workforce, such as HR planning and the incentive schemes to be applied (Zhu and Nyland, 2004). Furthermore, since non-public ownership is now regarded as not only an important component in China's socialist market economy, but also a motivation for economic development, it will be critical for HR managers in the non-public sector to deal with this issue to help attract and retain their employees.

From managerial appointments to the market of professional managers

The second aspect regarding government regulation of enterprises concerns the changeover from the appointment of senior enterprise managers to the nurturing of a market of professional managers. Research has shown that enterprise performance is directly affected by the competence of its senior managers, especially general managers (Schlevogt, 2002). In 1993, the State Planning Committee conducted a study of 2,586 loss-making enterprises and found that the lack of business competence of their senior managers was the main reason for failure in 81.71 per cent of enterprises investigated (2,102 enterprises) (Zhao and Ni, 1997: 69). Although the government had started open and fair competition in the selection of cadres working in the public sector, senior managers of medium and large SOEs or COEs were still appointed by the government in the early 1990s as revealed in our findings from the case studies.

This situation started to change in the mid-1990s when enterprises began to adopt shareholding systems where the board of directors could appoint the general managers. According to a survey conducted by the State Planning Committee in 1998, among 3,180 respondents (who were all senior managers from industrial enterprises across all four types of ownership), 48.2 per cent of them had been appointed by the government in 1998, and 40.2 per cent by the board of directors (Xie *et al.*, 1999: 70). However, the data indicate that among all the senior managers surveyed who were from SOEs, 92.2 per cent of them were appointed by the government in 1993 and 89.0 per cent in 1998. Meanwhile, of the senior managers surveyed who were from COEs, 60.9 per cent were appointed by the government in 1998. Similarly, a research project conducted by the State Planning Committee in 2000 reported that 75 per cent of the senior managers from state-controlled share-holding firms were appointed by the government while only 7 per cent of them were appointed by the chairperson of the board (Xin, 2001).

The nomenclature system not only impedes the establishment of an open market for professional managers, it also reduces the opportunity for enterprises to recruit competent managers and would also discourage senior managers from striving for excellence, as their promotion might depend on their relationship with the government rather than on their merit or performance (Li, 2003; Zhu and Li, 2002). In 2001 the State Economics and Trade Committee (SETC), the Ministry of Personnel and the Ministry of Labour and Social Security jointly issued a document on the SOEs reform with respect to their personnel system, labour force management and compensation practices (*SETC Enterprise Reform Document No. 230*, 2001). The document emphasized the reform of the previously used nomenclature system by eliminating the differences between 'cadres' and 'workers', advertising senior manager positions and selecting qualified candidates through open and fair competition including written tests, public defence, objective evaluation and publicity of selection results. However, it has been reported that senior managers are being drained from SOEs due to the lack of incentives caused by reasons such as SOEs' restricted right to claim residual earnings, an incompatible performance system and limited wage differentials (Di, 2002; Liu, D.W. 2000; Liu, L. 2003). Consequently, the government needs to nurture a free market of professional enterprise managers by adopting a free competition approach to the selection of senior managers and also to encourage further reform in the public enterprises including the further separation of state ownership from business operations and HR practices.

HRM development in POEs

Our study conducted in the mid-1990s indicated that POEs experienced the least government interference but their HR practices appeared to be the most informal and non-systematic compared with other types of enterprises. One of the reasons for this informality at that time might have been POEs' lack of confidence in government policies towards business development in the private sector as revealed in the ElectroCo case study (see Chapter 6). If owners and managers of POEs still feared policy changes or were uncertain of their political and social status (Chen and Shi, 1998), they could be reluctant to devise a long-term strategy for their business and invest in human resources (Murphy, 1996; Sabin, 1994).

The constitutional amendments of 1999 have upgraded the role of private business from 'a supplementary' to 'an important component' of the socialist market economy, and POEs created new jobs at the rate of nearly 30 per cent per annum from 1990 to 2000 (Story, 2003: 194), which means about 22 million people were working in POEs in 2000 (*China Labour and Social Security Year Book*, 2001: 524). Our 2001–2 survey results indicated that POEs conducted more HR practices than they did in the mid-1990s, but when compared with other types of enterprises, they still fell far behind in some aspects such as training, social insurance supplying and formalized performance assessment. The implication that can be drawn here is that the government needs to further improve the business environment for the private sector through the introduction of consistent policies for all business, with changes such as the lifting of all inherited restrictions discriminating against private businesses as announced by the State Planning Commission in 2000 (*Asian Wall Street Journal*, 2000); and to encourage the improvement of private sector management, especially in the area of HRM. Such support may promote confidence in owners of POEs to invest in their business and human resources, and to further develop their HR practices.

Research on HRM in China

The second major implication drawn from the findings of this study is regarding research on HRM in China. This section discusses the contribution of this study to the literature on HRM in China, a transitional HRM model proposed for Chinese industrial enterprises, and identifies areas for further research and some research issues and lessons of the study.

Contribution to theory development

Many researchers have reported the development of HR practices in China as a result of the economic reform (e.g. Brown and Porter, 1996; Child, 1994; Jackson, 1992; Warner, 1995; 2000; Whiteley *et al.*, 2000), but few studies have reported empirical evidence of current HR practices in terms of all the major HR activities. Furthermore, little research has been conducted to explore the impact of ownership type on HR practices, even though ownership reform has brought a wider range of ownership structures into the Chinese industrial sector. The research findings of this study contribute to the current literature on HRM in China by supplying empirical evidence of current HR practices in a systematic way and examining the impact of ownership form on HR practices across four types of ownership during the transitional period of the reform from the mid-1990s to the early 2000s. The research from this study has demonstrated that some Western HR practices are being used in Chinese enterprises, although often in a mixed or hybrid form with Chinese characteristics.

The literature reviewed in this study, together with our research findings, indicates that the management of human resources is directly affected by the economic system and to some extent by the ownership structure of enterprises. The impact of the economic system is especially powerful in China as its political system has remained intact and its socialist ideology is still being emphasized (e.g. Burns, 1999; Pye, 1999; Starr, 1997; Story, 2003). In addition, the adoption of the 'open-door' policy since economic reforms began has facilitated China's integration into the global network, as reflected by the survey respondents' strong agreement that 'conditions in the business environment are rapidly changing' in both surveys (item 2 in Table 8.1). China's accession to the WTO has also accelerated its economic reforms, a development which has had a direct impact on the separation of enterprise operations from the state ownership and government administration. Under such circumstances, HR practices have 'to be related to directly impinging environmental factors' and there is a need 'to build in external constraints to models of HRM' (Brewster, 1995: 10). This book has thus proposed an HRM model as its major contribution to the literature on Chinese HRM.

A transitional HRM model

Based on the present research, a transitional HRM model is proposed for China's industrial enterprises in Figure 9.1. It includes the key contextual variables in the Chinese economic environment during the reforms, which include the global context, a market-driven economic system, and changes

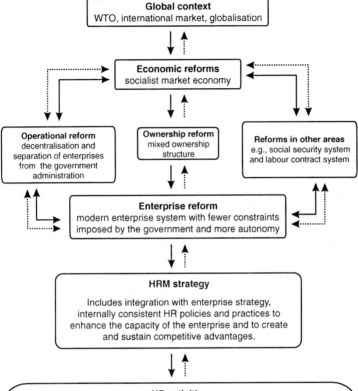

Global context
WTO, international market, globalisation

Economic reforms
socialist market economy

Operational reform
decentralisation and
separation of enterprises
from the government
administration

Ownership reform
mixed ownership
structure

Reforms in other areas
e.g., social security system
and labour contract system

Enterprise reform
modern enterprise system with fewer constraints
imposed by the government and more autonomy

HRM strategy

Includes integration with enterprise strategy,
internally consistent HR policies and practices to
enhance the capacity of the enterprise and to create
and sustain competitive advantages.

HR activities

Job analysis: for managerial and non-managerial employees, to be used for other HR practices such as HR planning, selection and performance appraisal;
HR planning: linked to business strategy, planning for both recruitment and retrenchment;
Recruitment and selection: job position to be advertised, two-way and merit-based selection, emphasis on the match between job and candidate, expert-selected with assistance from HR department, labour contract system;
Performance appraisal: performance criteria set on the basis of job description by both appraiser and appraisee, used more for communication and training in addition to administration purpose;
Compensation and welfare: Enterprise-determined and job-related wage scales, more individual-performance-related bonuses, reduced welfare benefits supplied by enterprises; with adoption of the shareholding system, part of a manager's compensation may be in the form of shares;
Training and development: for improvement of skills and behaviours, including leadership styles, communication for interview and feedback of performance assessment, career development of managers and employees;
Labour relations: liaison between management and employees, supervision of managers in non-public sector enterprises to protect employee interests and rights.

→ direct impact   ⋯⋯▶ mutual interaction

Figure 9.1 Proposed transitional HRM model for Chinese industrial enterprises

in government regulation of enterprises as the result of the operational reform, changes in the patterns of ownership due to the ownership reform and changes in the labour market because of reforms in other areas such as the social security system and labour contract system. The model first presents the context in which changes in the management of human resources have occurred, indicating that China is in transition from a planned economy to a socialist market economy. The model also recognizes the interdependence of HRM with the external international and domestic economic systems and related reforms as shown by arrows with both solid and dotted lines in Figure 9.1 (a solid line indicates a direct impact; a dotted line indicates a mutual interaction). The arrows in the model also show that an enterprise's management and its HRM strategy interact with one another with subsequent impact on the HR practices.

The model places HRM strategy and practices in close interaction with the modern enterprise system and the external environment, emphasizing that all the contextual variables are part of the HRM model rather than merely external factors that may have some incidental influence. The interaction between the HRM model and the external environment results from the major changes that have occurred consequent to the reforms. The first change concerns the domestic economy and its close interaction with global developments. China is moving away from a command economy to a socialist market economy; however, this transition is far from complete and is continuously being affected by global issues, including China's entry into the WTO, competition in the international market and greater participation in globalization. As a member of the WTO, for example, China needs to open up its previously monopolized industries such as banking, insurance and telecommunications to foreign competition and ownership, to reduce its tariffs and subsidies offered to many SOEs, to become subject to international rules and enforcement and to promote market-oriented reforms. China has made, and continues to make, considerable progress towards integration with the rest of the world, which has a direct impact on Chinese enterprises, as more enterprises have to compete in the global market rather than remaining in the protected domestic market. China's economic development has in turn had considerable impact in the global context as it is emerging as an economic giant in the world economy and is the largest recipient of foreign direct investment in the developing world.

Another major change lies in reduced government control over enterprises as a result of the operational reform. The economy is now moving away from highly centralized planning to decentralization and deregulation and cessation of government administration of enterprises. The third change is the result of ownership reform. The ownership structure has changed from being public dominated to mixed with coexistence of both public and non-public enterprises. More state enterprises have been reorganized into limited liability entities owned by government, corporate and private shareholders, and some have been listed on the stock market. As the result of the changes in ownership structure and the government's endeavour to establish a modern enterprise system, enterprises are experiencing fewer government constraints and have more autonomy to compete against others with different types of ownership. The final major change as a consequence of reforms in other areas, such as social security systems and labour contract systems, is the emergence of a free labour market and an increasingly mobile skilled labour force, particularly of those workers in the non-state sector. Ongoing reforms have led to subsequent changes in HR practices and also facilitated HRM development in China's industrial enterprises as presented in the model in Figure 9.1.

The proposed HRM model also indicates that in the future HRM will be conducted at a more strategic rather than operational level and will be linked more closely to the business strategy of the enterprise. Therefore, HRM strategy includes better integration with the business strategy of the enterprise and the development of internally consistent HR policies to enhance the capacity of the enterprise and to create and sustain its competitive advantages. HR activities that flow from the strategy may reciprocally influence the development of management practices in the enterprise, which may then influence the government to allow further reforms at a macro-level. For example, if enterprises are able to evade paying insurance for their employees, the government needs to strengthen its enforcement to protect those disadvantaged employees. Also, the literature reviewed in this study noted that SOEs were striving for more autonomy and employing different types of joint stock ownership in order to survive and/or compete with other types of enterprises. In view of this, the government must offer further guidance and facilitate reforms in the ownership structure. Therefore, in the proposed HRM model, all the variables are shown to interact with each other and the adoption of certain HR activities is interdependent upon other contextual factors. The major features of HR activities are outlined in Figure 9.1 and bear greater resemblance to Western HR practices than they had before.

Areas for further research on Chinese HRM

As HRM in China is an under-researched area and the current literature has offered few hypotheses to test, the aim of this study was to conduct an exploratory study for theory development. The research conducted for the study has provided empirical evidence of current HR practices in Chinese industrial enterprises with four types of ownership, and explored the impact of ownership forms on HRM at two time periods.

Based on this research, a transitional HRM model has been proposed to indicate probable future paths of HRM in China. However, there are still many areas for further research in Chinese HRM, and, as many researchers have noted, it is premature to pronounce that HR practices in China have definitely moved closer to a Western style of HRM (Warner, 1999; Zhu *et al.*, 2004).

One area for further research could be to examine the utilization of the HR activities presented in the HRM model (Figure 9.1) in industrial enterprises with different types of ownership. Empirical testing could be conducted to explore how HRM strategy and its activities interact with each other, and how HRM *per se* is interrelated with other parts of the model, such as the interaction between HRM strategy and the deregulation of government policies, changes in the enterprise ownership structure and further integration of China into the global market. Future research could also examine HR activities that have contributed to, or impeded enterprise effectiveness, and how and why this could happen. In this study only the production output value and correlation between some HR practices and respondents' perceptions were employed as parameters of the effectiveness of HR practices. Future studies could use measures such as sales value, profit and productivity to test the links between HR practices and enterprise performance. In addition, further comparisons could be made to investigate the convergence or divergence of HRM in different types of enterprises towards Western-style HRM in terms of concept, strategy and practices.

Furthermore, the size and location of the enterprise could be considered as a variable in future research. This study focused mainly on small- and medium-sized enterprises located in four well-developed and highly industrialized metropolitan cities. However, Lo (1997) has argued that large-scale SOEs in China are performing much better than other SOEs, which raises the question as to whether size has an impact on an enterprise's HRM practices. This is especially relevant given that the government has adopted the strategy of 'grasping the largest enterprises and releasing the small' (*zhuada fangxiao*) to facilitate the implementation of the ninth five-year plan (1995–2000) and long-term planning for 2010 in China (Wan, 1997: 32). *Zhuada fangxiao* means that the state will focus its reform efforts on the largest 1000 state enterprises, while relaxing its control over other enterprises and letting them survive, develop or go bankrupt. It is worth investigating whether HRM is conducted differently in the large enterprises that remain under direct control of the state. In addition, the geographic region in China may influence HR practices because of the different levels of education, industrialization and access to advanced technology in different regions (Grewal and Sun, 2002; Zhao *et al.*, 1998). The shortage of educated and skilled people in inland and remote areas of China is a major consideration for foreign companies in their site selection for a joint venture.

A longitudinal study could also be conducted in future based on the results of this study. Although two surveys were utilized in this study, they were cross-sectional in nature. Sekaran (1992: 111) argues that longitudinal studies can offer valuable insights and help to identify cause and effect relationships. This is especially relevant as China is still in a transitional stage and will continue its economic restructuring and reforms. A longitudinal design would assist the study of change by providing a baseline for comparison and help identify changes in HRM in China and in the contextual environment as well as the reasons behind such changes.

Some research issues and lessons of the study

This study used an exploratory approach that combined qualitative case studies and quantitative survey questionnaires. The methodology utilized in the mid-1990s achieved the synergy effect noted by Eisenhardt (1989), because quantitative survey data were used to support findings from the qualitative case studies (Merriam, 1988). In-depth and multifaceted investigation and multiple sources of data (triangulation) as suggested by Orum and his colleagues (1991) were consistently used in the four case studies, which enabled the researcher to describe and analyse HR practices in Chinese industrial enterprises. However, there are some methodological issues that need to be considered. First, in regards to the case studies, each type of enterprise had only one case study, which may not allow 'findings to be replicated within categories' so as to 'control extraneous variation and help to define the limits for generalizing the findings' (Eisenhardt, 1989: 537). Although the survey results from respondents in the same type of enterprise have partially overcome this limitation, multiple case studies within the same category could be conducted to allow researchers to follow replication logic of the impact of ownership, with each case serving to confirm or disconfirm the inferences drawn from previous cases (Yin, 1994). Another methodological limitation is that in 2001–2, a survey was conducted only to upgrade findings identified in 1994–5. Moreover, sample size varies for some survey questions because of some respondents had little knowledge of current and ideal HR practices. This limitation may be overcome in future studies when HRM becomes more developed in China and employees acquire greater understanding of HR activities.

From the empirical investigations in this study there are also some lessons to be learned. First, the design and distribution of survey questionnaires are critical to achieve a satisfactory response rate. In this study, all the survey questions were double-checked and back translated by the author with bilingual skills to ensure the suitability of questions in the Chinese context. As the survey is a relatively new research instrument in China, the researcher needs to personally explain the purpose of the survey and to guarantee the ano- nymity and confidentiality of responses. Eliminating the fears of respondents due to political or cultural concerns is crucial and will encourage them to give honest answers to questions and to return the questionnaires. As well, the survey response rate can be improved if the survey questionnaire is offered to respondents together with a self-seal envelope and collected per- sonally by the researcher as carried out in this study. Second, it is important to ensure the confidentiality of the information supplied by interviewees during the interviews. Obtaining the trust of interviewees increases their will- ingness to be interviewed. The researcher noted that interviewees preferred to have individual or very small group interviews with two to three persons of similar status. Under these circumstances, they were usually prepared to be outspoken and critical of their enterprise, superior(s) and management prac- tices. Their reluctance to be involved in any political discussion about so- called 'internal matters' has also been noted by Shenkar (1994: 11).

HR practices in China

The last major implication drawn from the findings of this study is for HR practice in China. One aspect of this implication is training the Chi- nese workforce to prepare for the future development of HRM and the other aspect concerns the strategic role of the HR function.

Training the Chinese workforce

The HRM model proposed in Figure 9.1 indicates that China is in transi- tion from the traditional PRC model (see Figure 2.1) to a new model of workforce management. During this transition period, enterprises have been and will be granted more autonomy to operate their own businesses and to compete in local and international markets. In the early 1990s Child (1990: 150) noted that 'the shortage of managerial and profes- sional expertise [in Chinese enterprises] tends to constrain the de- concentration of authority and delegation of decision making within industrial and other structures', which indicates the significance of train- ing for managers and employees. In our 2001–2 survey the practice of training and development received more attention than it had in 1994–5 among all the HR practices surveyed. However, it still needs to be aug- mented as the results indicated that the amount of further training and career development offered to employees was insufficient especially in POEs. This could be partly attributed to selection criteria of managers, managers' lack of interest in training, lack of support from other man- agement practices and lack of knowledge on strategic HRM.

The traditional way of selecting managers, whether through the nomenclature system or through promotion, has often impeded the development of managerial skills. Political reliability as a prime requirement for HR managers was still being emphasized after over two decades of reform, especially in state sector enterprises, as evident in our second survey results. This emphasis undermines the importance of managerial skills. The proposed HRM model stresses that HR activities need cooperation and joint efforts from managers at all levels rather than being left entirely to HR managers. This raises the issue of training for all managers, especially line managers, in regards to the formulation of HRM strategy and conduct of HR activities, such as attracting qualified job applicants through HR planning and recruitment and selection; effectively utilizing employees with the help of performance appraisal and compensation; developing employee potential via education and training; raising employee initiative by adopting motivational practices; and retaining key employees by integrating and implementing HR practices, especially training and development. With the free labour market for professional managers still being nurtured and developed in China, with more foreign companies tending to localize their management team in China to develop a large corporate presence, and with China's accession to the WTO, management training is all the more urgent. Current managers need to update their knowledge and skills, especially in regards to HRM.

Emphasis on the training of workers is also significant for HR practice in China due to its economic boom and the increasingly complicated job skills required given the development of technology and industrialization. Since the 1980s, the growth rate of GDP in China was in double-digits, until the late 1990s when it was curtailed by the Asian financial crisis. Even so China is still regarded as the fastest growing market in the world (*McKinsey Quarterly*, March 2004). This boom in China's economy has facilitated more foreign investment and technological development than in any other developing country. Foreign investment has brought in advanced technology and sped up changes in the nature of employment (Selmer *et al.*, 1999; Tsang, 1998). To catch up with this change and to prepare for the future, enterprises have to invest in training and development.

However, the research findings of this study indicate that training offered by the enterprises was often focused upon preparing new recruits and remedying current performance deficiencies rather than on changing behaviours or developing future careers for employees. Training is often seen as costly and risky by many Chinese managers, because their enterprises may not receive immediate returns and employees may leave the enterprise after training. The reluctance of managers to offer training and the insufficient number of training programmes offered could impede further reform in China because a highly skilled, committed and competitive workforce will be crucial for enterprises to face more rigorous competition in both the local and world economy. Training and development is undoubtedly one of the key factors in determining China's ability to compete in world markets, and its role is expected to increase in the future as indicated by our two survey results and other researchers (Liu and Shi, 2001; Zhao and Wu, 2003). Creating effective training and development activities to develop such a workforce will be a new challenge to managers, as they need to identify both short- and long-term training needs, design training programmes which address technical and behavioural issues, and have an evaluation system in place to determine if the training and development programme has met its objectives.

The strategic role of the HR function

Another issue raised by the research findings concerns the strategic role of the HR department or HR function. Changes in the business environment in China have had several implications for the HR function and HRM practices (e.g. Braun and Warner, 2002; Sun, 2000; Zhu, 1997; Zhu and Dowling, 1994). As Beer (1997: 49) has noted: 'Competition, globalization and continuous change in markets and technology are the principal reasons for the transformation of human resource management'. Although Beer was probably referring to industrialized nations, this transformation is also increasingly evident in China. In enterprises in China in the past, the HR function was limited to policy implementation or focused on administrative and welfare tasks in the public sector, especially in SOEs. The author postulates that the further integration of China into the global economy, the flourishing of enterprises in the private sector and the decentralization of decision-making to enterprise-level have brought the need for more strategic involvement of the HR function (e.g. Braun and Warner, 2002; Whiteley *et al.*, 2000; Zhao and Ni, 1997). There is broad consensus that strategic HRM involves the development and implementation of internally consistent policies and practices which will enhance the capacity of an organization to create and sustain improved performance and a competitive advantage (Becker and Gerhart, 1996; Boxall and Purcell, 2003; Huselid *et al.*, 1997; Wright *et al.*, 2001). Strategic integration of the HR function is a key step in the development of strategic HRM.

Beer (1997: 51) has argued that for the HR function to be effective in the twenty-first century, it 'will have to shed its traditional administrative, compliance and service role and adopt a new strategic role concerned with developing the organization and capabilities of its managers'. In China, recognition of poor enterprise efficiency and productivity, linked with relatively low education levels, created a need for HR development and strategic

HRM. Some research (e.g. Deng *et al.*, 2003; Mitsuhashi *et al.*, 1999) has begun to explore the implications of the HR function and HRM practices for firms in the Chinese context. For example, Ding and Akhtar (2001) found that the strategic role of the HR function, combined with ownership, has an impact on the choice of HRM practices in Chinese enterprises. Similarly, Braun and Warner (2002) found that a large majority of multinational enterprises operating in China reported that the HR function is of high strategic importance in that environment.

If organizations in China seek to follow the example of HR functions in the West in performing a strategic organizational role, several characteristics could be anticipated to emerge. Enterprises would be likely to introduce an HR function (or department) (Ding and Akhtar, 2001) and will demand various competencies in HR managers (Beer, 1997; Benson and Zhu, 2002). The HR function would seek to participate in strategic decision-making (i.e. decision-making by senior executives) (Braun and Warner, 2002; Truss *et al.*, 2002), be linked to business strategies and be perceived as effective in the organization (Braun and Warner, 2002; Mitsuhashi *et al.*, 1999; Truss *et al.*, 2002; Wright *et al.*, 2001). The research findings of this study indicate that a strategic role for the HR function and adoption of HRM practices often employed in market economies was becoming more prevalent in China in 2001–2 than in the mid-1990s and a considerable improvement in the HR function was observed in the second survey. For example, more enterprises surveyed had an HR department in 2001–2 than in 1994–5, and more of them used the term 'human resource department' rather than personnel or labour department. There is also evidence of a continuing push towards enhancing the competencies (i.e. qualifications and work experience) of HR managers and their participation in senior executive decision-making across all types of enterprises. Furthermore, more HR departments used HR planning for the whole enterprise's business strategy, though such departments were mainly in the non-state sector.

While more enterprises surveyed had a HR function and more were conducting HR practices, the effectiveness of HR departments is perceived at a relatively low level compared with its perceived importance in both surveys. Survey respondents expected the HR function to become less involved in routine work such as record keeping and wage administration, and more involved in other HR activities including HR planning and training and development. The question that arises here is whether the HR function is really integrated with business strategies to help firms become corporate entities and competitors adaptable to the market. Along with the deepening reforms and changing business environment in China, a more level playing field has been created for the enterprise ownership types. This appears to be a recent development, as it contrasts with our earlier studies that have documented differences between ownership types. This development creates a challenge for the HR function to play a strategic role, in order to deal with the complex demands of the dynamic Chinese context. As HR practices are expected to increase in the future, it will be a challenge for the HR function to play a strategic role, that is, to integrate different HR practices with business strategies and to conduct HR practices at the strategic level.

CONCLUSIONS

This book provides an exploratory empirical study of the emerging role of HRM in China's industrial enterprises. Through a review of extant literature, case studies, surveys and a comparative analysis of research findings from both qualitative and quantitative studies, this research has systematically examined major HR practices across enterprises with four major types of ownership and explored the impact of these ownership types on HR practices. Based on the study, a transitional HRM model is proposed for Chinese industrial enterprises. This model has integrated contextual variables that are relevant to the Chinese setting which interact dynamically with HRM strategy and activities. It illustrates a model of HRM in China during its transitional period which is distinct from the traditional PRC model of personnel and labour administration, and suggests possible future paths of HRM development in China as a result of the ongoing reform process.

Some key distinctions between the transitional HRM model and the traditional PRC model clearly demonstrate an emerging role of HRM in China's industrial enterprises, one which appears to bear more resemblance to Western HRM practices in the early 2000s than it had in the mid-1990s. The first key distinction is the change in the name of the model from personnel and labour administration to HRM, which reveals not only the wider acceptance and adoption of the term of HRM, but also the dramatic change of blurring the demarcation between cadres and workers as commonly practised during Mao's regime, and the beginnings of managing a workforce with emphasis on the attraction, retention and development of competent and committed human capitals.

The second key distinction is the significant contextual changes that have occurred in China as it moved from a closed to an open economic system and from an isolated self-reliant country to a member of the WTO. These changes have inevitably created impetus for the reforms in the central planning system, public-dominant ownership structure and other areas such as the *danwei*-based social security system and the labour contract system. These reforms in turn have pushed industrial enterprises into an intense competition in both domestic and global markets regardless of their types of ownership, and have consequently brought fundamental changes in the enterprise's business operations, management practices in general and HRM in particular.

As a result, other key distinctions between the two models include the adoption of HRM strategy, even though it might be in name only, and radical changes in HR practices. Many of these changes may have occurred in a reactive way to address issues such as an increasing labour mobility, shortage of competent managers and skilled workers, and lack of commitment of employees to create or sustain the enterprise's competitiveness. However, the empirical study of this book, especially the development of HR practices observed between the two surveys, strongly indicates that the concept and practices of Western HRM have become more prevalent in China, although the legacy of traditional practices endures and new challenges are emerging along with further reforms for China to be more market-oriented.

The study results from both surveys have consistently demonstrated the leading role of FIEs in the practice of HRM. Many foreign companies surveyed have brought their HR practices into their Chinese subsidiaries to help them compete against other types of enterprises and improve their performance. Though the extent to which foreign companies can transfer the Western-style HR practices into China can still be argued and their effectiveness cannot be overgeneralized, it is essential for foreign managers to understand how Chinese employees were managed in the past so as to understand Chinese managers' difficulty or inertia in accepting non-traditional or Western-style HR practices. While FDI into China is still on the increase and more multinational companies have expanded or are expanding their businesses in the country, it is critical to regard the training of Chinese managers as an urgent issue if Western-style HR practices are to be transferred and developed.

The last chapter has also highlighted the relevance of the research findings for HRM development in Chinese industrial enterprises, particularly in regards to the implications for government regulation of enterprises and for HR practices in China. In particular, it emphasizes the significance of training the Chinese workforce in preparation for the new model of HRM and challenges the HR function to play a strategic role. To conclude, this study has addressed the dearth of research on HRM in China by providing empirical evidence on the emerging role of HRM and the impact of ownership types on HRM. It has therefore achieved its three specific aims. That is, it has enhanced the understanding of HRM in China's industrial sector, contributed to the current theory of HRM by exploring the impact of ownership forms on HRM, and proposed a transitional HRM model to show the emerging role of HRM and possible paths of its development in China.

Notes

3 Research methodology

1 The companies in this research have been disguised to respect confidentiality and protect the anonymity of the parties concerned.
2 A new (also called simplified) set of Chinese characters has been developed and utilized by Chinese of the PRC since the 1950s. The previous translated questionnaire of Von Glinow *et al.* used the traditional (also called complicated) Chinese characters that are still used by Chinese people outside the mainland of China, such as in Hong Kong, Taiwan and Singapore.
3 A more detailed description of the factor analysis can be found in Zhu (2000).

6 Case study 3

1 As Mao Zedong advocated 'red and expert', red is often related to political reliability, and 'to wear a red hat' in this context means to have political protection.
2 In the mid-1990s, enterprises invested in by Hong Kong businesspeople were classified as FIEs.

7 Case study 4

1 At an exchange rate of 6 yuan to $A1 in 1994–5, each stand was $A50 per day.

9 The role of HRM in transition

1 This comment was made in addition to the questionnaire by the General Manager of a Sino–Australian joint venture in Shanghai in late 1994.

Appendix I

Case study interview questions

Enterprise name:

Interviewee name:

1 Briefly describe your job duties.
2 How long have you held this present position?
3 What was your previous job and why did you leave the job?
4 How long have you been working with the current enterprise?
5 Briefly describe your current enterprise in terms of its ownership type, history, business strategy and operation, size and structure, and the changes that have occurred within the enterprise since economic reform?
6 How are employees of this enterprise categorized (e.g. categorized as cadres and workers or managerial and non-managerial employees)?
7 Which department of the enterprise manages its employees?
8 How does this department manage its employees with respect to human resource planning, recruitment and selection, performance appraisal, compensation and welfare, training and development, and labour relations?
9 How were these HR activities conducted before the reform?
10 Are there any major changes in these HR practices since economic reform?
11 Why have these changes occurred?
12 What do you think of the HR practices conducted by your enterprise?
13 Do you think these HR practices are effective in attracting, motivating, retaining and developing employees? Why?
14 How would you like these HR activities to be conducted? Why?
15 Any additional comments?

Appendix II

Survey questionnaire

Human resource management (HRM) practices in Chinese industrial enterprises

Please place a tick beside or circle the most appropriate answer to each of the following questions. In a few cases please fill in the blank.

BACKGROUND INFORMATION

About your enterprise

1 When was the enterprise set up? . . . .

2 Ownership:

State . . . . . . Collective . . . . . .

Private . . . . . . Foreign joint venture . . . . . .

3 Approximately how many employees are there in your company? Please write down . . . . . .

4 The enterprise's total output value in 1993: . . . . . .

5 The percentage of contract employees . . . . . ., and the percentage of permanent employees . . . . . .

6 Do you have employees belonging to unions in your enterprise?

Yes . . . . . . No . . . . . .

If yes, do you know approximately what proportion of employees are members of unions?

. . . . . .Less than half . . . . . . About half . . . . . . More than half

7 Please identify the description below which most accurately describes how your enterprise derives most of its revenue (check only *one* below on A–D).

A Manufacturing products (e.g. durable consumer products. . . . . . or manufacturing of components into finished products)

B Services (doing things for customers rather than . . . . . .
manufacturing things, e.g. airlines, financial services,
retail stores, food preparation)

C Government . . . . . .

D Other (please specify) . . . . . .

8 Please place a check beside *one* of the following three descriptions (A,
B, C) which most accurately reflects how many products your
enterprise has?

Your enterprise obtains *nearly all* (e.g. 70% or more) of its revenue
from:

    A *one* product . . . . . .

Your enterprise obtains less than 70% of its revenue from one
product and the rest from:

    B *related* products . . . . . .

or C *unrelated* products . . . . . .

    D don't know . . . . . .

9 How accurately do each of the following describes the business
environment that your enterprise faces?

	Very false				Very true
Market place competition has increased dramatically	1	2	3	4	5
Conditions in our business environment are rapidly changing	1	2	3	4	5
Government regulations are rapidly changing	1	2	3	4	5
The technology in our product/services is complex	1	2	3	4	5
Abundant supply of skilled people in the labour market	1	2	3	4	5

About yourself

1 Age

   . . . . . .Less than 30   40–49   . . . . . .   60 or older

  30–39   50–59

2 Gender

   . . . . . . Male   . . . . . . Female

3   Please indicate the highest grade in school you have completed:

. . . . . .High school degree or less . . . . . . Some graduate education

. . . . . .Some college education   . . . . . . Graduate degree

. . . . . .Bachelor's degree   . . . . . . Other

4   What is your ethnicity? . . . .

5   What is your job title? . . . .

6   How long have you been in your current job? . . . . . . years

7   How long have you been with your current enterprise? . . . . . .

8   What is your current monthly salary (including all take-home pay)?

Less than 400 yuan . . . . . . 601 to 700 . . . . . . 901 to 1,000 . . . . . .

400 to 500   . . . . . . 701 to 800 . . . . . . Above 1,000 . . . . . .

501 to 600   . . . . . . 801 to 900 . . . . . .

YOUR ENTERPRISE'S PERSONNEL/HUMAN RESOURCE DEPARTMENT

1   Does your enterprise have a separate Personnel Department (or Labour Department or both) that has control of employee personnel records, training programmes, salary and performance appraisal guidelines, and so on, for the rest of the enterprise?

. . . . . . Yes . . . . . . No

If 'Yes', what is the name of that department in your company?

Name of department: . . . .

2   Think of your enterprise's Personnel Department or Labour Department or both Departments. How accurately do the following statements describe that Department, overall?

Please use the following scale for the questions below:

	Very false				Very true	Don't know
It is viewed as an important department in the enterprise.	1	2	3	4	5	6
It tends to *imitate* the human resource practices (e.g. in hiring, pay, etc.) used by other firms in our industry.	1	2	3	4	5	6

It works closely with the senior management group on the key strategic issues facing the enterprise.

    1   2   3   4   5   6

It is viewed as an effective department.

    1   2   3   4   5   6

3   This Department carries out the following activities at present. Please tick those that apply in the left column:

What kind of activities do you think should be involved by the HR Department? Please tick those that apply in the right column.

	Current activities	Should be involved
HR planning for the company's business strategy	. . . . . .	. . . . . .
Being responsible for HR policies	. . . . . .	. . . . . .
Recruitment and selection	. . . . . .	. . . . . .
Job analysis and evaluation	. . . . . .	. . . . . .
Performance appraisal	. . . . . .	. . . . . .
Wage administration	. . . . . .	. . . . . .
Training and career development	. . . . . .	. . . . . .
Record keeping	. . . . . .	. . . . . .
Health and safety	. . . . . .	. . . . . .
Employees' welfare, recreation and sports	. . . . . .	. . . . . .
Organize political studies	. . . . . .	. . . . . .
Contact local Labour Bureau for potential labour supply	. . . . . .	. . . . . .
Other (please specify)	. . . . . .	. . . . . .

4   To be a human resource manager, the person needs to meet the following requirements (tick those that apply):

Having formal qualifications in the area of:
management . . . . . . or . . . . (please specify);

At the level of
university . . . . . . college . . . . . . above Year 12 . . . . . .

Having work experience . . . . . .

Politically reliable (e.g. must be a Party member) . . . . . .

Other (please specify) . . . .

HUMAN RESOURCE (HR) PLANNING

1 Has formal (written) HR forecasting and planning:
   Yes . . . . . .   No . . . . . .
   If 'Yes', it is short-term (1–2 years)   . . . . . .
   and/or long-term (2–5 years)?   . . . . . .

2 In your enterprise, who is involved in HR planning?
   General manager . . . . . .   Department managers   . . . . . .
   Line managers   . . . . . .   Human resource manager   . . . . . .
   Other (please specify)   . . . .

3 What are the main reasons for HR planning?
   Part of the whole enterprise's business strategy   . . . . . .
   Required by the enterprise's own staffing needs   . . . . . .
   Required by the local government (e.g. Labour Bureau) . . . . . .
   Other (please specify) . . . .

4 How significant is HR planning?

1	2	3	4	5
Not important at all	Unimportant	Neutral	Important	Very important

JOB ANALYSIS

1 Does your enterprise conduct written job analysis?
   Yes . . . . . .   No . . . . . .
   If 'Yes', who conducts job analysis?
   HR manager   . . . . . .
   Line manager   . . . . . .
   Other (please specify) . . . .

2 The job analysis process focuses on the following factors (tick those that apply):
   Person – Requirements of the people involved in the job, e.g.
            Education   . . . . . .
            Skills   . . . . . .
            Physical   . . . . . .
            Other (please specify)   . . . .

Task – Brief description of the work to be done   . . . . . .

Brief description of the tools or machines   . . . . . .
to be used

Production standard   . . . . . .

Production quota (e.g. number of products. . . . . .
to be produced per hour/shift)

Other (please specify)   . . . . . .

3   What are the uses of job analysis in the enterprise?

Classify job responsibility and authority   . . . . . .

Basis for HR planning   . . . . . .

Basis for recruitment and selection   . . . . . .

Basis for performance standards   . . . . . .

Basis for job evaluation   . . . . . .

Basis for determining post salary   . . . . . .

Other (please specify)   . . . .

HIRING PRACTICES

1   External employee sources are from:

Local labour market offices   . . . . . .

Job applicants through advertising   . . . . . .

Government employee allocation   . . . . . .

Other (please specify)   . . . .

2   Internal employee sources are from:

The enterprise's HR data bank   . . . . . .

Internal transfer or promotion   . . . . . .

Own employees' children or relatives (*dingti*)   . . . . . .

Other (please specify)   . . . .

3   How accurately do the following statements describe your enterprise's
hiring practices? For each statement provide two responses.

First, use the left column to indicate to what extent the statements below
describe the way Hiring Practices currently are conducted (*is now*).

Second, use the right column to indicate to what extent the statements
below describe the way Hiring Practices ought to be conducted to
promote organizational effectiveness (*should be*).

Please use the following scale for the questions below:

1	2	3	4	5
Not at all		To a moderate extent		To a very great extent

Hiring decisions here are influenced by:

	is now	*should be*
A person's ability to perform the technical requirements of the job.	1 2 3 4 5	1 2 3 4 5
A personal interview.	1 2 3 4 5	1 2 3 4 5
A person's ability to get along well with others already working here.	1 2 3 4 5	1 2 3 4 5
Having the right connections (e.g. school, family, friends, region, government, etc.).	1 2 3 4 5	1 2 3 4 5
The company's belief that the person will stay with the company (e.g. 5 years or longer).	1 2 3 4 5	1 2 3 4 5
An employment test in which the person needs to demonstrate their skills.	1 2 3 4 5	1 2 3 4 5
Proven work experience in a similar job.	1 2 3 4 5	1 2 3 4 5
A person's potential to do a good job, even if the person is not that good when they first start.	1 2 3 4 5	1 2 3 4 5
How well the person will fit the enterprise's values and ways of doing things.	1 2 3 4 5	1 2 3 4 5
Future co-workers' opinions about whether the person should be hired.	1 2 3 4 5	1 2 3 4 5
Personal qualifications.	1 2 3 4 5	1 2 3 4 5
Political background.	1 2 3 4 5	1 2 3 4 5
Personal file records.	1 2 3 4 5	1 2 3 4 5

Please use the same scale to indicate to what extent your enterprise's hiring practices are effective.

The hiring practices help our enterprise to have   1 2 3 4 5
high-performing employees.

The hiring practices help our enterprise to have   1 2 3 4 5
employees who are satisfied with their job.

The hiring practices make a positive contribution 1 2 3 4 5
to the overall effectiveness of the organization.

PERFORMANCE APPRAISAL PRACTICES

1   Does your enterprise have standardized criteria and methods of the appraisal?

Yes . . . . . .   No . . . . . .

If 'Yes', what is the frequency of appraisal?

Once a year . . . . . .   Twice a year . . . . . .   Monthly . . . . . .

2   Who conducts the appraisal?

Department managers   . . . . . .

Line managers   . . . . . .

Peer group   . . . . . .

Individuals to be evaluated   . . . . . .

Other (please specify)   . . . .

3   Method of appraisal:

Self evaluation by using a standardized form   . . . . . .

Discussion within the work group   . . . . . .

Supervisor's comments   . . . . . .

Other (please specify)   . . . .

4   The purpose of performance appraisal practices.

How accurately do the following statements describe the purposes of your company's performance appraisal practices? For each statement provide two responses.

First, use the left column to indicate the extent to which the statements below describe the way Performance Appraisal Practices currently are conducted (*is now*).

Second, use the right column to indicate to what extent the statements below describe the way Performance Appraisal Practices ought to be conducted to promote organizational effectiveness (*should be*).

Please use the following scale for the questions below:

1	2	3	4	5
Not at all		To a moderate extent		To a very great extent

What purposes do you think should be for Performance Appraisal (tick those that apply in the right column):

	is now	*should be*
Determine appropriate pay.	1 2 3 4 5	1 2 3 4 5
Document subordinate's performance.	1 2 3 4 5	1 2 3 4 5
Plan development activities for subordinate (e.g. training, new duties).	1 2 3 4 5	1 2 3 4 5
For salary administration.	1 2 3 4 5	1 2 3 4 5
Recognize subordinate for things well done.	1 2 3 4 5	1 2 3 4 5
Lay out specific ways in which subordinate can improve performance.	1 2 3 4 5	1 2 3 4 5
Discuss subordinate's views.	1 2 3 4 5	1 2 3 4 5
Evaluate subordinate's goal achievement.	1 2 3 4 5	1 2 3 4 5
Identify subordinate's strengths and weaknesses.	1 2 3 4 5	1 2 3 4 5
Allow subordinate to express feelings.	1 2 3 4 5	1 2 3 4 5
Determine subordinate's promotability.	1 2 3 4 5	1 2 3 4 5
Basis for bonus distribution.	1 2 3 4 5	1 2 3 4 5

5   Please indicate to what extent your enterprise's performance appraisal practices are effective.

The performance appraisal helps our enterprise have high-performing employees.	1 2 3 4 5
The appraisal practices help our enterprise to have employees who are satisfied with their jobs.	1 2 3 4 5

The appraisal practices make a positive contribution   1   2   3   4   5
to the overall effectiveness of the organization.

EMPLOYEE COMPENSATION PRACTICES

1   Does your enterprise have a pension plan?
Yes . . . . . .   No . . . . . .
If 'Yes', the plan is decided by the enterprise   . . . . . .
or according to the government's regulations? . . . . . .

2   What is the percentage of pension in the average monthly wage?
Less than 5% . . . . . .   10 to 15 . . . . . .
5 to 10 . . . . . .   More than 15% . . . . . .

3   Does your enterprise have a medical plan?
Yes . . . . . .   No . . . . . .
If 'Yes', the plan is decided by the enterprise . . . . . .
or according to the government's regulations? . . . . . .

4   What is the percentage of medical fee in the average monthly wage?
Less than 5% . . . . . . 10 to 15 . . . . . .
5 to 10 . . . . . .   More than 15% . . . . . .

5   The components of wage and their percentage in the wage:

Base pay	Percentage . . . . . .
Floating wage	Percentage . . . . . .
Positional allowances	Percentage . . . . . .
Other (please specify)	Percentage . . . . . .

6   Bonus is distributed on the basis of:

Individual performance	. . . . . .
Group performance	. . . . . .
Attendance	. . . . . .
Profitability	. . . . . .
Consumer Price Index (CPI)	. . . . . .
Other (please specify)	. . . . . .

7   The items of subsidies and their percentage in the monthly take-home pay:

Non-staple food	Percentage . . . . . .

Housing fund . . . . . .   Percentage . . . . . .

Personal hygiene allowance . . . . . .   Percentage . . . . . .

Books and newspapers . . . . . .   Percentage . . . . . .

Other (please specify) . . . . . .   Percentage . . . . . .

8   Is there a profit-sharing plan in your enterprise?

Yes . . . . . .   No . . . . . .

If 'Yes', what is the percentage of profit-sharing in 1993?

9   How accurately do the following statements describe your enterprise's
pay practices? For each statement provide two responses.

First, use the left column to indicate the extent to which the statements below describe the way Pay Practices currently are conducted
(*is now*).

Second, use the right column to indicate to what extent the statements
below describe the way Pay Practices ought to be conducted to promote organizational effectiveness (*should be*).

Please use the following scale for the questions below:

1	2	3	4	5
Not at all		To a moderate extent		To a very great extent

	is now	*should be*
Pay incentives, such as bonus or profit sharing, are an important part of the compensation strategy in this enterprise.	1 2 3 4 5	1 2 3 4 5
The benefits are an important part of the total pay package.	1 2 3 4 5	1 2 3 4 5
In this enterprise a portion of an employee's earnings is contingent on group or enterprise performance goals being achieved.	1 2 3 4 5	1 2 3 4 5
Our pay policies recognize that long-term results are more important than short-term results.	1 2 3 4 5	1 2 3 4 5

An employee's seniority does   1 2 3 4 5   1 2 3 4 5
enter into pay decisions.

Pay incentives are designed to   1 2 3 4 5   1 2 3 4 5
provide significant amount of
an employee's total earnings
in this organization.

The employee benefits   1 2 3 4 5   1 2 3 4 5
package is very generous
compared to what it could be.

The pay system in this   1 2 3 4 5   1 2 3 4 5
enterprise has a futuristic
orientation. It focuses
employees' attention on long-
term (2 or more years) goals.

In this enterprise pay rises are 1 2 3 4 5   1 2 3 4 5
determined by an employee's
job performance. There is a
large pay spread between low
performers and high
performers in a given job.

10   Please indicate to what extent your enterprise's pay practices are
     effective.

The pay practices help our enterprise have   1 2 3 4 5
high-performing employees.

The pay practices help our enterprise to have   1 2 3 4 5
employees who are satisfied with their jobs.

The pay practices make a positive contribution   1 2 3 4 5
to the overall effectiveness of the organization.

TRAINING AND DEVELOPMENT PRACTICES

1   Does your enterprise have on-the-job training?
    Yes . . . . . .   No . . . . . .

2   Does your enterprise have off-the-job training?
    Yes . . . . . .   No . . . . . .

3   Types of Training Programmes include:
    Induction and orientation   . . . . . .

Occupational skills . . . . . .

Technical/professional . . . . . .

Management development for administrative staff . . . . . .

4 Who is responsible for Training?

In-house training staff . . . . . .

Outside training agencies . . . . . .

5 How accurately do the following statements describe the purposes of your enterprise's Training and Development practices? For each statement provide two responses.

First, use the left column to indicate the extent to which the statements below describe the way Training and Development practices are currently (*is now*).

Second, use the right column to indicate to what extent the statements below describe the way Training and Development practices ought to be conducted to promote organizational effectiveness (*should be*).

Please use the following scale for the questions below:

1	2	3	4	5
Not at all		To a moderate extent		To a very great extent

Possible purposes of Training Practices:

	is now	*should be*
Provide a reward to employees.	1 2 3 4 5	1 2 3 4 5
Improve their technical job abilities.	1 2 3 4 5	1 2 3 4 5
Improve employees' interpersonal abilities, i.e. how well they relate to others.	1 2 3 4 5	1 2 3 4 5
Remedy employees' past poor performance.	1 2 3 4 5	1 2 3 4 5
Prepare employees for future job assignments.	1 2 3 4 5	1 2 3 4 5
Build teamwork within the enterprise.	1 2 3 4 5	1 2 3 4 5

Provide substantial training
when employees first start
working in the enterprise.　　1　2　3　4　5　　1　2　3　4　5

Help employees understand　1　2　3　4　5　　1　2　3　4　5
the business, e.g. knowledge
of competitors, new
technologies, etc.

Provide employees with the　1　2　3　4　5.　1　2　3　4　5
skills needed to do a number
of different jobs, not just one
particular job.

Teach employees about the　1　2　3　4　5　　1　2　3　4　5
enterprise's values and ways
of doing things.

6　Please use the same scale to indicate to what extent your enterprise's
training and development practices are effective.

The training practices help our enterprise to　1　2　3　4　5
have high-performing employees.

The training practices help our enterprise to　1　2　3　4　5
have employees who are satisfied with their jobs.

The training practices make a positive　1　2　3　4　5
contribution to the overall effectiveness of the
organization.

EMPLOYEE PARTICIPATION

1　Employees are encouraged to participate in the management process
by:

Using a suggestion box　　　　　　　　　. . . . . .

Encouraging suggestions　　　　　　　　. . . . . .

Accepting suggestions and offering rewards　　. . . . . .

Employees participating in management decisions　. . . . . .

Other (please specify) . . . .

2　What is the approximate percentage of employees who participate in
management decisions?

Less than 30% . . . . . .　About 50% . . . . . .　Over 60% . . . . . .

Is there anything else you would like to tell us about the human resource (HR) practices in your organization? For example, you may wish to identify what, in your opinion, are remarkable HR practices or HR practices you would like to change. Please feel free to comment in the remaining space.

Thank you very much for your participation and cooperation

Glossary

ACFTU	All-China Federation of Trade Unions
ANOVA	Analysis of variance
CMRS	Contract management responsibility system
COE	Collective-owned enterprise
CPC	Communist Party of China
CPI	Consumer price index
FDI	Foreign direct investment
FDRS	Factory director responsibility system
FIE	Foreign-invested enterprise
HOD	Head of department
HR	Human resource
HRM	Human resource management
MANOVA	Multivariate analysis of variance
MBA	Master of Business Administration
MBO	Management of objective
MRC	Municipal Radio Conglomerate (in Nanjing, China)
ODCC	Organization Department of the Central Committee (*zhongyang zuzhi bu*)
PLA	People's Liberation Army
POE	Private-owned enterprise
PRC	People's Republic of China
R&D	Research and development
SETC	State Economics and Trade Committee
SOE	State-owned enterprise
WTO	World Trade Organization

References

An, M. and Feng, T. Q. 1991. *Gonghui Xue (Unionology)*. Shengyang, China: Liaoning People's Publishing House (in Chinese).

Ann, L. Z. 1996. 'Discussion on labour relations under the transition'. *Laodong Jinji yu Renli Ziyuan Guanli (Labour Economy and Human Resource Management)*, 2: 8–9, Beijing: Renmin University Press (in Chinese).

Asian Wall Street Journal, 20 January 2000. 'State power caused China's decline', *Wall Street Journal*, New York, 6 January 2000.

Battat, J. Y. 1986. *Management in Post-Mao China: An Insider's View*. Michigan: UMI Research Press.

Beamish, P. W. 1993. 'The characteristics of joint ventures in the People's Republic of China', *Journal of International Marketing*, 1(2): 29–48.

Becker, B. and Gerhart, B. 1996. 'The impact of human resource management on organizational performance: progress and prospects', *Academy of Management Journal*, 39(4): 779–801.

Beer, M. 1997. 'The transformation of the human resource function: Resolving the tension between a traditional administrative and a new strategic role', *Human Resource Management*, 36(1): 49–56.

Beijing Review, references in text.

Benson, J. 1996. 'The sleeping giant slumbers no more', *People Management*, 13 June: 22–6.

Benson, J. and Zhu, Y. 1999. 'Markets, firms and workers: The transformation of HRM in Chinese state-owned enterprises', *Human Resource Management Journal*, 9(4): 58–74.

Benson, J. and Zhu, Y. 2002. 'The emerging external labour market and the impact on enterprise's human resource development in China', *Human Resource Development Quarterly*, 13: 449–66.

Benson, J., Debroux, P. and Yuasa, M. 1998. 'Labour management in Chinese-based enterprises: The challenge of flexibility', Working Paper No. 2, Department of Management, the University of Melbourne.

Bian, Y. J. 1994. '*Guanxi* and the allocation of urban jobs in China', *The China Quarterly*, 140: 971–99.

Boisot, M. and Child, J. 1996. 'The institutional nature of China's emerging economic order'. In Brown, D. H. and Porter, R. (eds), *Management Issues In China: Domestic Enterprises*. London: Routledge, pp. 35–60.

Borgonjon, J. and Vanhonacker, W. R. 1992. 'Modernising China's managers'. *The China Business Review*, September–October, Special Report: 12–18.

Boxall, P. and Purcell, J. 2003. *Strategy and Human Resource Management*. Basingstoke: Palgrave Macmillan.

Branine, M. 1997. 'Change and continuity in Chinese employment relationships', *New Zealand Journal of Industrial Relations*, 22(1): 77–94.

Braun, W. H. and Warner, M. 2002. 'Strategic human resource management in Western multinationals in China', *Personnel Review*, 31(5): 553–79.

Brewster, C. 1995. 'Towards a "European" model of human resource management', *Journal of International Business Studies*, 26(1): 1–22.

Brosseau, M. 1995. 'The individual and entrepreneurship in the Chinese economic reforms'. In Kin, L. C., Pepper, S. and Yuen, T. K. (eds), *China Review 1995*. Hong Kong: The Chinese University Press.

Brown, D. H. and Branine, M. 1995. 'Managing people in China's foreign trade corporations: Some evidence of change', *The International Journal of Human Resource Management*, 6(1), February: 159–75.

Brown, D. H. and Porter, R. (eds). 1996. *Management Issues in China: Volume I*. New York: Routledge.

Burns, J. P. 1999. 'The People's Republic of China at 50: National political reform'. *The China Quarterly*, 159: 580–94.

Butler, J. E., Ferris, G. R. and Napier, N. K. 1991. *Strategy and Human Resource Management*. Mason, OH: South-Western Publishing Co.

Cardy, R. L. and Dobbins, G. H. 1994. *Performance Appraisal: Alternative Perspectives*. Ohio: South-Western Publishing Co.

Chai, J. C. H. and Docwra, G. 1997. 'Reform of large and medium state industrial enterprises: Corporatisation and restructure of state ownership'. In Brosseau, M., Hsin-chi, K. and Kueh, Y. Y. (eds), *China Review: 1997*. Hong Kong: The Chinese University Press, pp. 161–80.

Chan, A. 1995. 'The emerging patterns of industrial relations in China and the rise of two new labour movements', *China Information*, IX(4): 36–59.

Chan, A. 1996. 'Chinese enterprise reforms: Convergence with the Japanese model?' In McCormick, B. L. and Unger, J. (eds), *China After Socialism: In the Footsteps of Eastern Europe or East Asia*. New York: M. E. Sharpe, pp. 181–202.

Chan, A. 2001. *China's Workers Under Assault: The Exploitation of Labour in a Globalizing Economy*. Armonk, New York: M. E. Sharpe.

Chan, A. and Unger, J. 1990. 'Voice from the protest movement, Chongqing, Sichuan', *The Australian Journal of Chinese Affairs*, vol. 24 (July): 1–21.

Chan, A. and Senser, R. A. 1997. 'China's troubled workers', *Foreign Affairs*, March/April: 104–17.

Chen, D. R. 1995. *Chinese Firms Between Hierarchy and Market: The Contract Management Responsibility System In China*. New York: St. Martin's Press.

Chen, Jia Gui. (ed.). 2001. *China Social Security System Development Report*. Beijing: Social Science Documents Publishing House.

Chen, J. X. and Shi, W. 1998. 'Zhongguo siying qiye fazhan toushi' (Perspective on the development of private-owned enterprises in China). *Working Paper* (CP 98010). School of Business, Hong Kong Baptist University, Hong Kong (in Chinese).

Chen, K. 1995. *The Chinese Economy In Transition: Micro Changes and Macro Implications*. Singapore: Singapore University Press.

Chen, Qintai. 1995. 'Deepening experiment, striving for the effectiveness, and further facilitating the reform of state-owned enterprises', *Gongye Qiye Guanli (Industrial Enterprise Management)*. Beijing: Renmin University Press (in Chinese),12: 65–9.

Chen, S. (ed.). 1990. *Xiandai Laodong Renshi Gongzuo Shiyong Shouce (Contemporary Labour and Personnel Administration Handbook)*. Shanghai, China: People Publishing House (in Chinese).

Child, J. 1990. 'Introduction: The character of Chinese enterprise management'. In Child, J. and Lockett, M. (eds), *Advances In Chinese Industrial Studies*. London: Jai Press, 1: 137–52.

Child, J. 1993. 'A foreign perspective on the management of people in China'. In Blunt, P. and Richards, D. (eds), *Readings In Management, Organisation and Culture In East and Southeast Asia*. Darwin: Northern Territory University Press., 213–25.

Child, J. 1994. *Management In China During the Age of Reform*. Cambridge: Cambridge University Press.

Child, J. 1995. 'Changes in the structure and prediction of earnings in Chinese state enterprises during the economic reform', *International Journal of Human Resource Management*, 6(1): 1–30.

Child, J. and Lu, Y. (eds). 1996. *Management Issues in China: Volume II*. New York: Routledge.

China Daily, references in text.

China Labour and Social Security Yearbook. 2000, 2001. Beijing: China Labour and Social Security Publishing House.

China Statistical Yearbook. 1990–2002. Beijing: State Statistical Bureau Publishing House.

Chow, G. C. 1994. *Understanding China's Economy*. Singapore: World Scientific Press.

Cleveland, J. N., Murphy, K. R. and Williams, R. E. 1989. 'Multiple uses of performance appraisal: Prevalence and correlates', *Journal of Applied Psychology*, 74: 130–5.

CPC Central Committee. 1993. *Documents of the 14th CPC Central Committee*. Zhonggong Zhongyang Wenxian Yanjiushi (CPC Central Committee, Documentation and Research Office). Beijing: People's Press (in Chinese).

Cronbach, L. J. 1951. 'Coefficient alpha and the internal structure of tests'. *Psychometrika*, 16: 297–334.

CVQDV (China Vocational Qualification Development and Verification). 1994. *Enhancing China's Vocational Qualification Verification System*, vol. 7. Beijing: Vocational Qualification Verification Centre of the Ministry of Labour (in Chinese).

Cyr, D. J. and Frost, P. J. 1991. 'Human resource management practice in China: A future perspective'. *Human Resource Management*, 30(2): 199–215.

Dalton, T. and Austen, G. 1995. *Operating Successfully In China: Lessons From Leading Australian Companies*. Melbourne: International Market Assessment.

Dang, X. J. 1991. 'The model of reforming fixed-term employment system'. In Xia, J. Z. and Dang, X. J. (eds), *Zhongguo De Jiuye Yu Shiye (Employment and Unemployment In China)*. Beijing: China Labour Press House (in Chinese), pp. 220–5.

Davidson, W. H. 1987. 'Creating and managing joint ventures in China', *California Management Review*, 29: 77–94.

Deng, Hongxun. 1998. 'Thoughts on the estimation that to turn around the difficult situation of state-owned enterprises within three years'. *Gongye Qiye Guanli (Industrial Enterprise Management)*. Beijing: Renmin University Press (in Chinese), 2: 47–55.

Deng, J., Menguc, B. and Benson, J. 2003. 'The impact of human resource management on export performance of Chinese manufacturing enterprises', *Thunderbird International Business Review*, 45: 409–29.

Deng, P. 2001. 'WFOEs: The most popular entry mode into China', *Business Horizons*, 44(17): 63–77.

Deng, P. 2003. 'Determinants of full-control mode in China: An integrative approach', *American Business Review*. West Haven: January, 21(1): 113–24.

Dernberger, R. F. 1982. 'The Chinese search for the path of self-sustained growth in the 1980s: An assessment'. In US Congress Joint Economic Committee's Compendium: *China Under the Four Modernisations*. Washington, DC, US Government Printing Office, Part 1: 19–76.

Dernberger, R. F. 1997. 'China's transition to a market economy: Back to the future, mired in the present, or through the looking glass to the market economy?' In Babkina, A. M. (ed.), *Domestic Economic Modernisation In China*. New York: Nova Science Publishers, pp. 1–14.

Di, Feng. 2002. 'How state enterprises to manage personnel after the accession to the WTO', *Renli Ziyuan Kaifa yu Guanli (Development and Management of Human Resources)*. Beijing: Renmin University Press (in Chinese), vol. 2: 11–14.

Ding, D., Fields, D. and Akhtar, S. 1997. 'An empirical study of human resource management policies and practices in foreign-invested enterprises in China: The case of Shenzen Special Economic Zone', *The International Journal of Human Resource Management*, 8(5): 595–613.

Ding, Z. D. and Akhtar, S. 2001. 'The organisational choice of human resource management practices: A study of Chinese enterprises in three cities in the PRC', *International Journal of Human Resource Management*, 12(6): 946–64.

Dixon, J. 1981. *The Chinese Welfare System: 1949–1979*. New York: Praeger Publishers.

Documents. 1997. 'Jiang Zemin's report – Hold high the great banner of Deng Xiaoping theory for an all-round advancement of the cause of building socialism with Chinese characteristics into the 21st century', *Beijing Review*, October 6–12.

Dong, F. R. 1982. 'The Chinese economy in the process of great transformation'. In Wang, G. C. (ed. and translated), *Economic Reform in The PRC: In Which China's Economists Make Known What Went Wrong, Why, and What Should Be Done About It*. Boulder, CO: Westview Press, pp. 125–38.

Dong, F. R. 1992. 'Forward'. In Hay, D., Morris, D., Liu, G. and Yao, S. J. (eds), *Economic Reform and State-owned Enterprises In China, 1979–1987*. Oxford: Clarendon Press, pp. v–viii.

Easterby-Smith, M., Malina, D. and Yuan, L. 1995. 'How culture-sensitive is HRM? A comparative analysis of practice in Chinese and UK companies', *International Journal of Human Resource Management*, 6(1): 31–60.

Eisenhardt, K. M. 1989. 'Building theories from case study research', *Academy of Management Review*, 14: 532–50.

Eisenhardt, K. M. 1991. 'Better stories and better constructs: The case for rigour and comparative logic', *Academy of Management Review*, 16: 620–7.

EIU (The Economist Intelligence Unit). 1997. *China: Country Forecast*, 3rd Quarter, London: EIU Ltd.

Feng, L. R. 1996. 'The situation and strategy of China's third tide of unemployment'. *Laodong Jingji yu Renli Ziyuan Guanli (Labour Economy and Human Resource Management)*, 11: 51–61. Beijing: Chinese People's University Press (in Chinese).

Fung, R. J. 1995. *Organisational Strategies For Cross-cultural Cooperation: Management of Personnel in International Joint Ventures in Hong Kong and China*. Delft: Eburon Publishers.

Gamble, J. 2000. 'Localizing management in foreign-invested enterprises in China: practical, cultural, and strategic perspectives', *International Journal of Human Resource Management*, 11(5): 883–903.

Gao, S. Q. and Chi, F. L. (eds). 1996. *The Development of China's Nongovernmentally and Privately Operated Economy*. Beijing: Foreign Language Press.

Geringer, J. M. and Frayne, C. A. 1990. 'Human resource management and international joint venture control: A parent company perspective', *Management International Review*, 30, Special Issue: 103–20.

Geringer, J. M., Frayne, C. A. and Milliman, J. F. 2002. 'In search of "best practices" in international human resource management: Research design and methodology', *Human Resource Management*, 41(1): 67–86.

Glover, L. and Siu, N. Y. M. 2000. 'The human resource barriers to managing quality in China', *International Journal of Human Resource Management*, 11(5): 867–82.

Goodall, K. and Warner, M. 1997. 'Human resources in Sino-foreign joint ventures: Selected case studies in Shanghai, compared with Beijing', *The International Journal of Human Resource Management*, 8(5): 569–94.

Goodall, K. and Warner, M. 2002 'Corporate governance in Sino-foreign joint ventures in the PRC: The view of Chinese directors'. *Journal of General Management*, 27(3): 77–92

Goss, D. 1994. *Principles of Human Resource Management*. London: Routledge.

Grewal, B. and Sun, F. 2002. 'Extending the frontier of high growth inland: Implications for China's regional policy'. In Grewal, B., Xue, L., Sheehan, P. and Sun, F. (eds), *China's Future in the Knowledge Economy: Engaging the New World*. Melbourne: Centre for Strategic Economic Studies, Victoria University and Tsinghua University Press.

Gu, E. X. 2001. 'Dismantling the Chinese mini-welfare state? Marketization and the politics of institutional transformation, 1979–1999', *Communist and Post-Communist Studies*, 34, 91–111.

Guan, Xinping, 2000. 'China's social policy: Reform and development in the context of marketization and globalization'. *Social Policy and Administration*, 34(1): 115–30.

Guan, Y. T. (ed.). 1990. *Zhiye Peixun Gailun (An Introduction to Vocational Training)*. Beijing: China's Labour Press (in Chinese).

Hai, X. 1998. 'Making an endeavour to achieve the target of re-employing sixty percent of retrenched employees', *Laodong Jingji yu Renli Ziyuan Guanli (Labour Economy and Human Resource Management)*. Beijing: Renmin University Press (in Chinese), 4: pp. 32–3.

Hanser, A. 2002. 'Youth job searches in urban China: The use of social connections in a changing labour market'. In Gold, T., Guthrie, D. and Wank, D. (eds), *Social Connections in China: Institutions, Culture and Changing Nature of Guanxi*. Cambridge: Cambridge University Press, pp. 137–62.

Harding, H. 1987. *China's Second Revolution: Reform After Mao*. Sydney: Allen & Unwin.

Hay, D., Morris, D., Liu, G. and Yao, S.J. 1994. *Economic Reform and State-owned Enterprises in China, 1979–1987*. Oxford: Clarendon Press.

Hoffmann, C. 1974. *The Chinese Worker*. Albany: State University of New York Press.

Holton, R. H. 1990. 'Human resource management in the People's Republic of China', *Management International Review*, 30, Special Issue: 121–36.

Howard, P. 1991. 'Rice bowls and job security: The urban contract labour system', *The Australian Journal of Chinese Affairs*, 25: 93–114.

Howe, C. 1992. 'Foreword'. In Korzec, M. (ed.), *Labour and the Failure of Reform in China*. London: Macmillan, pp. vii–x.

Howell, J. 1992. 'The myth of autonomy: The foreign enterprise in China'. In Smith, C. and Thompson, P. (eds), *Labour in Transition: The Labour Process in Eastern Europe and China*. London and New York: Routledge, pp. 205–26.

Hsu, R. C. 1991. *Economic Theories in China, 1979–1988*. Cambridge: Cambridge University Press.

Hu, X. Y. and He, P. (eds). 1992. *Gangwei Jineng Gongzi Shishi Wenda (The Implementation of Post-plus-skills Wage System)*. Beijing: Wage Research Institute of the Ministry of Labour of China (in Chinese).

Hughes, N. C. 1998. 'Smashing the iron rice bowl', *Foreign Affairs*, 77(4): 67–77.

Huo, Y. P. and Von Glinow, M. A. 1995. 'On transplanting human resource practices to China: A culture-driven approach', *International Journal of Manpower*, 16(9): 3–15.

Huo, Y. P., Huang, J. H. and Napier, N. K. 1999. *Divergence or Convergence?: A Cross-national Comparison of Personnel Selection Practices*. Paper presented to the Annual Meeting of Academy of Management, Chicago, 6–11 August 1999.

Huo, Y. P., Sakano, T., Tsai, S. D. and Von Glinow, M. A. 1996. 'Searching for effective hiring practices: a comparison of Japan and Taiwan', *Working paper* No. 96–014, Center for International Business Education and Research, Florida International University, Miami.

Huselid, M. A., Jackson, S. E. and Schuler, R. S. 1997. 'Technical and strategic human resource management effectiveness as determinants of firm performance', *Academy of Management Journal*, 40: 171–88.

Hussain, A. 2000. 'The social role of the Chinese state enterprise'. In Warner, M. (ed.), *Changing Workplace Relations in the Chinese Economy*. London: Macmillan, pp. 57–76.

Ishihara, K. 1993. *China's Conversion to a Market Economy*. Tokyo: Institute of Developing Economies.

Jackson, S. 1988. 'Management and labour in Chinese industry: A review of the literature'. *Labour and Industry*, June, 1(2): 335–63.

Jackson, S. 1992. *Chinese Enterprise Management: Reforms in Economic Perspective*. Berlin: Walter de Gruyter.

Kaple, D. A. 1994. *Dream of a Red Factory: The Legacy of High Stalinism in China.* Oxford: Oxford University Press.

Kline, P. 1994. *An Easy Guide to Factor Analysis.* London and New York: Routledge.

Kornai, J. 1986. *Contradictions and Dilemmas: Studies on the Socialist Economy and Society.* Cambridge, MA: MIT Press.

Korzec, M. 1988. 'Contract labour, the "right to work" and new labour laws in the People's Republic of China'. *Comparative Economic Studies* (ASE), 30(2): 117–49.

Kraus, W. 1991. *Private Business in China: Revival Between Ideology and Pragmatism* (translated from German by Holz, E.). London: Hurst & Company.

Laaksonen, O. 1988. *Management in China During and After Mao.* Berlin, New York: Walter de Gruyter.

Lau, C. M., Ngo, H. Y. and Chow, C. K. W. 1999. 'Private businesses in China: Emerging environment and managerial behaviour'. In Kelley, L. and Luo, Y. D. (eds), *China 2000: Emerging Business Issues.* Thousand Oaks, CA: Sage Publications, pp. 25–48.

Lee, L. T. 1986. *Trade Unions in China: 1949 to the Present.* Singapore: Singapore University Press.

Lee, P. N. S. 1987. *Industrial Management and Economic Reform in China, 1949–1984.* Oxford: Oxford University Press.

Leung, K., Wang, Z. and Smith, P. B. 2001. 'Job attitudes and organisational justice in joint venture hotels in China: The role of expatriate managers'. *International Journal of Human Resource Management,* 12(6): 926–45.

Leung, T. W. 1989. 'Workers for democracy'. *International Labour Reports,* 34(5) (July–October), 7–11.

Li, C. Q. 2003. 'A study on the problem of managers' reputation incentive in state-owned enterprises'. *Gongye Qiye Guanli (Management of Industrial Enterprises).* Vol. 4. Beijing: Renmin University Press (in Chinese), pp. 57–62.

Li, W. Y. 1991. *Zhongguo Gongzi Zhidu (China's Wage System).* Beijing: China Labour Press (in Chinese).

Liew, L. 1997. *The Chinese Economy in Transition: From Plan to Market.* Cheltenham: Edward Elgar Publishing Ltd.

Lin, J. Y., Cai, F. and Li, Z. 1996. *The China Miracle: Development Strategy and Economic Reform.* Hong Kong: The Chinese University Press.

Lindholm, N., Tahvanainen, M. and Bjorkman, I. 1999. 'Performance appraisal of host country employees: Western MNCs in China'. In Brewster, C. and Harris, H. (eds), *International HRM: Contemporary Issues in Europe.* New York: Routledge, pp. 143–61.

Liu, C. L. and Shi, J. J. 2001. 'To set up a new HRM paradigm'. *Gongye Qiye Guanli (Management of Industrial Enterprises).* Vol. 8. Beijing: Renmin University Press (in Chinese), pp. 75–80.

Liu, D. W. 2000. 'Difficulties in the reform of the personnel system in state enterprises'. *Laodong Jingji yu Renli Ziyuan Guanli (Labour Economics and Management of Human Resources).* Vol. 8. Beijing: Renmin University Press (in Chinese), pp. 13–16.

Liu, J. Q. 1994. 'New approaches to the issue of unemployment'. *Laodong Jinji yu Renli Ziyuan Guanli (Labour Economy and Human Resource Management),* 12: 25–7. Beijing: Renmin University Press (in Chinese).

Liu, Lian. 2003. 'Preliminary analysis on the system of professional managers in contemporary China'. *Gongye Qiye Guanli* (*Management of Industrial Enterprises*). Vol. 1: 52–4. Beijing: Renmin University Press (in Chinese).

Liu, Y. H. 1996. 'Achievements following the implementation of the Labour Law'. *Laodong Jingji yu Renli Ziyuan Guanli (Labour Economy and Human Resource Management)*, Vol. 8: 5–6. Beijing: Renmin University Press (in Chinese).

Lo, D. 1997. *Market and Institutional Regulation in Chinese Industrialisation, 1978–94*. London: Macmillan Press Ltd.

Lockett, M. 1988. 'The urban collective economy'. In Feuchtwang, S., Hussain, A. and Pairault, T. (eds), *Transforming China's Economy in the Eighties, Volume II: Management, Industry and the Urban Economy*, London: Zed Books Ltd., pp. 118–37.

Lu, Y. and Bjorkman, I. 1997. 'MNC standardization versus localization: HRM practices in China–Western joint ventures'. *The International Journal of Human Resource Management*, 8(5): 614–28.

Mackerras, C., Taneja, P. and Young, G. 1994. *China Since 1978: Reform, Modernisation and "Socialism with Chinese Characteristics"*. New York: St. Martin's Press.

Mai, Y. H. and Perkins, F. 1997. *China's State Owned Enterprises: Nine Case Studies*. Department of Foreign Affairs and Trade, Australia.

Marshall, C. and Rossman, G. 1989. *Designing Qualitative Research*. Newbury Park, CA: Sage.

May, T. 1997. *Social Research: Issues, Methods and Process* (2nd edn). Buckingham: Open University Press.

McKinsey Quarterly (McKinsey & Company), references in text.

Melvin, S. and Sylvester, K. 1997. 'Shipping out'. *The China Business Review*, May–June, 30–4.

Merriam, S. B. 1988. *Case Study Research in Education: A Qualitative Approach*. San Francisco: Jossey-Bass Publishers.

Merriam, S. B. 1998. *Qualitative Research and Case Study Application in Education*. San Francisco, CA: Jossey-Bass Publishers.

Miles, M. B. and Huberman, A. M. 1994. *Qualitative Data Analysis: An Expanded Sourcebook* (2nd edn). Thousand Oaks, CA: Sage.

Mitsuhashi, H., Park, H. J., Wright, P.M. and Chua, R. S. 1999. 'Line and HR executives' perceptions of HR effectiveness in firms in the People's Republic of China'. *The International Journal of Human Resource Management*, 11: 197–216.

Murphy, R. 1996. 'A dependent private sector: No prospects for civil society in China'. *Working paper* No. 62, April 1996. The Asia Research Centre, Murdoch University, Australia.

Naughton, B. 1996. *Growing Out of the Plan: Chinese Economic Reform, 1978–1993*. Cambridge: Cambridge University Press.

Noe, R. A., Hollenbeck, J. R., Gerhart, B. and Wright, P. M. 1997. *Human Resource Management: Gaining a Competitive Advantage* (2nd edn). Chicago: Irwin.

Nunnally, J. C. 1978. *Psychometric Theory*. New York: McGraw-Hill.

Nyaw, M. K. 1991. 'The significance and managerial roles of trade unions in joint ventures in China'. In Shenkar, O. (ed.), *Organisation and Management in China: 1979–1990*. New York/London: M. E. Sharpe Inc., pp. 109–24.

Nyaw, M. K. 1995. 'Human resource management in the People's Republic of China'. In Moore, L. F. and Jennings, P. D. (eds), *Human Resource Management on the Pacific Rim*. Berlin: Walter de Gruyter, pp. 185–216.

Nyland, C., Smyth, R. and Zhu, C. J. (In press). 'Globalisation and occupational health and safety regulation in China'. In Smyth, R., Tam, O. K., Warner, M. and Zhu, C. J. (eds), *China's Business Reforms: Institutional Challenges in a Globalised Economy*. London: Routledge, pp. 177–98.

O'Leary, G. 1992. 'Chinese trade unions and economic reform'. In Chen, E. K. Y., Lansbury, R., Ng, S. H. and Stewart, S. (eds), *Labour-Management Relations in the Asia-Pacific Region*. Hong Kong: Centre of Asian Studies, University of Hong Kong.

O'Leary, G. 1994. 'The contemporary role of Chinese trade unions'. In Jackson, S. (ed.), *Contemporary Developments in Asian Industrial Relations*. Hong Kong: Centre of Asian Studies, University of Hong Kong, pp. 26–54.

Orum, A. M., Feagin, J. R. and Sjoberg, G. 1991. 'Introduction: the nature of the case study'. In Feagin, J. R., Orum, A. M. and Sjoberg, G. (eds), *A Case for the Case Study*. Chapel Hill, NC: The University of North Carolina Press, pp. 1–26.

Paik, Y., Vance, C. M. and Stage, H. D. 1996. 'The extent of divergence in human resource practice across three Chinese national cultures: Hong Kong, Taiwan and Singapore'. *Human Resource Management Journal*, 6(2): 20–31.

Panitchpakdi, S. and Clifford, M. L. 2002. *China and the WTO: Changing China, Changing World Trade*. Singapore: John Wiley & Sons (Asia) Pte Ltd.

Pearson, M. M. 1997. *China's New Business Elite: The Political Consequences of Economic Reform*. Berkeley, CA: University of California Press.

People's Daily (Renming Ribao), references in text.

Perkins, D. H. 1996. 'China's future: Economic and social development scenarios for the twenty-first century'. In *OECD 1996: China in the 21st century*. Paris: Head of Publication Service, OECD, pp. 21–35.

Poole, M. 1986. *Industrial Relations: Origins and Patterns of National Identity*. London: Routledge.

Poole, M. 1998. 'Industrial and labour relations'. In Poole, M. and Warner, M. (eds), *The IEBM Handbook of Human Resource Management*. Boston, MA: International Thomson Business Press, pp. 772–90.

Porket, J. L. 1995. *Unemployment in Capitalist, Communist and Post-Communist Economies*. Oxford: St. Martin's Press.

Pu, Shan. 1990. 'Comment: Planning and the market'. In Dorn, J. A. and Wang Xi (eds), *Economic Reform in China: Problems and Prospects*. Chicago, IL: The University of Chicago Press, pp. 17–20.

Putterman, L. 1996. 'The role of ownership and property rights in China's economic transition'. In Walder, A. (ed.). *China's Transitional Economy*. Oxford: Oxford University Press, pp. 85–102.

Pye, L. W. 1999. 'An overview of 50 years of the People's Republic of China: Some progress, but big problems remain'. *The China Quarterly*, 159: 569–79.

Qian, Y. and Xu, C. 1993. 'Why China's economic reforms differ: The M-form hierarchy and entry/expansion of the non-state sector'. *Discussion Paper* No. 154, Centre for Economic Performance, The London School of Economics.

Qian, Y. Y. and Weingast, B. R. 1997. 'Institutions, state activism and economic development: A comparison of state-owned and township-village enterprises in China'. In Aoki, M., Kim, H. K. and Okuno-Fujiwara, M. (eds), *The Role of Government in East Asian Economic Development*. Oxford: Oxford University Press, pp. 254–78.

Qin, L. 1995. 'Policies and strategies of human resource development in China's enterprises'. *Laodong Jinji yu Renli Ziyuan Guanli (Labour Economy and Human Resource Management)*, 6: 16–19. Beijing: Renmin University Press (in Chinese).

Rawski, T. G. 1995. 'Implications of China's reform experience'. *The China Quarterly*: 144: 1150–73.

Redding, G. 1993. *The Spirit of Chinese Capitalism*. Berlin: Walter de Gruyter.

Riskin, C. 1987. *China's Political Economy: The Quest for Development Since 1949*. Oxford: Oxford University Press.

Riskin, C. 1995. 'Reform and system change in China'. In Schor, J. and You, J. (eds), *Capital, the State and Labour*. Aldershot: Edward Elgar. Tokyo: United Nations University Press.

Roy, K. C. and Chai, J. C. H. 1999. 'Economic reforms, public transfers and social security nets for the poor: A study of India and China'. *International Journal of Social Economics*, 26(1/2/3): 222–38.

Sabin, L. 1994. 'New bosses in the workers' state: The growth of non-state sector employment in China'. *The China Quarterly*, 140: 944–70.

Saunders, P. and Shang, X. 2001. 'Social security reform in China's transition to a market economy'. *Social Policy and Administration*, 35(3): 274–89.

Schlevogt, K. 2002. *The Art of Chinese Management: Theory, Evidence and Applications*. Oxford: Oxford University Press.

Schmitt, N. W. and Klimoski, R. J. 1991. *Research Methods in Human Resources Management*. Cincinnati, OH: South-Western Publishing Co..

Schuler, R. S. 2001. 'Human resource issues and activities in international joint ventures'. *International Journal of Human Resource Management*, 12(1): 1–52.

Schuler, R. S., Dowling, P. J., Smart, J. P., and Huber, V. L. 1992. *Human Resource Management in Australia* (2nd edn). Sydney: Harper Educational.

Sekaran, U. 1992. *Research Methods for Business: A Skill-Building Approach* (2nd edn.). New York: Wiley & Sons, Inc..

Selmer, J., Erdener, C., Tung, R. L., Worm, V. and Simon, D. F. 1999. 'Managerial adaptation in a transitional economy: China'. In Warner, M. (ed.), *China's Managerial Revolution*. London: Frank Cass.

SETC Enterprise Reform Document (No. 230), 2001. *Renli Ziyuan Kaifa yu Guanli (Development and Management of Human Resources)*. Vol. 8: 4–7. Beijing: Renmin University Press (in Chinese).

Sha, Y. 1987. 'The role of China's managing directors in the current economic reform'. *International Labour Review*, 26(6): 691–701.

Shang, L. 2003. 'Quality and changes of enterprises leaders in 1990s'. *Gongye Qiye Guanli (Industrial Enterprise Management)*, Vol. 2: 87–98. Beijing: Renmin University Press (in Chinese).

Shaw, J. B., Tang, F. Y. T., Fisher, C. D. and Kirkbride, P. S. 1993. 'Organisational and environmental factors related to HRM practices in Hong Kong: A cross-cultural expanded replication'. *The International Journal of Human Resource Management*, 4(4): 785–815.

Shenkar, O. 1994. 'The People's Republic of China: Raising the bamboo screen through international management research'. *International Studies of Management and Organization*, 24(1–2): 9–34.

Shenkar, O. and Chow, I. H. 1989. 'From political praise to stock options: Reforming compensation systems in the People's Republic of China'. *Human Resource Management*, 28(1), Spring: 65–85.

Shenkar, O. and Von Glinow, M. A. 1994. 'Paradoxes of organizational theory and research: Using the case of China to illustrate national contingency'. *Management Science*, 40(1): 56–71.

Shirk, S. 1993. *The Political Logic of Economic Reform in China*. Berkeley: University of California Press.

Sieber, S. D. 1982. 'The integration of fieldwork and survey methods'. In Burgess, R. G. (ed.), *Field Research: A Source Book and Field Manual*. London: Allen & Unwin.

Silverman, S. B. 1989. 'Individual development through performance appraisal'. In Wexley, K. N. (ed.), *SHRM. BNA Series 5: Developing Human Resources*. Washington, DC: The Bureau of National Affairs Inc., pp. 121–51.

Siu, Wai-sum. 1995. 'Entrepreneurial typology: The case of owner-managers in China'. *International Small Business Journal*, 14(1): 53–64.

Skopal, A. and Zhu, C. J. 2003. 'Entry strategy development in China: Some empirical evidence'. In Zhao, S. M. (ed.), *Multinational Business Management in the New Economy*. Nanjing: Nanjing University Press, pp. 463–78.

Smyth, R. 2002. 'Enterprise bankruptcies and the restructuring of China's state-owned sector: A review of some recent problems and prospects for future success'. In Pieke, F. N. (ed.), *People's Republic of China, Policies and Implications of Structural Reform*. Aldershot: Ashgate Publishing.

Smyth, R. and Zhai, Q. G. 2003. 'Economic restructuring in China's large and medium-sized state-owned enterprises – evidence from Liaoning'. *Journal of Contemporary China*, 12(34): 173–205.

Starr, J. 1997. *Understanding China*. New York: Hill and Wang.

Stevenson-Yang, A. 1996. 'Re-vamping the welfare state'. *The China Business Review*, January–February: 8–17.

Story, J. 2003. *China: The Race To Market*. London: Pearson Education Ltd.

Strange, R. (ed.). 1998. *Management in China: The Experience of Foreign Businesses*. London: Frank Cass Publisher.

Su, T. L. and Zhu, Q. F. (eds). 1992. *Ren Shi Xue Dao Lun (Fundamentals of Personnel)*. Beijing: Beijing Normal College Press (in Chinese).

Sun, B. 2000. 'Pay and motivation in Chinese enterprises'. In Warner, M. (ed.), *Changing Workplace Relations in the Chinese Economy*. London: Macmillan.

Takahara, A. 1992. *The Politics of Wage Policy in Post-Revolutionary China*. London: The Macmillan Press Ltd.

Talas, B. 1991. *Economic Reforms and Political Attempts in China 1979–89*. Springer-Verlag Berlin: Heidelberg.

Tan, J. J. and Li, M. F. 1996. 'Effects of ownership types on environment: Strategy configuration in China's emerging transitional economy'. *Advances in International Comparative Management*, 11: 217–50.

Tang, J. Z. and Ma, L. J. C. 1985. 'Evolution of urban collective enterprises in China'. *The China Quarterly*, 104: 614–40.

Teagarden, M. B., Von Glinow, M. A., Bowen, D. E., Frayne, C. A., Nason, S., Huo, Y. P., Milliman, J., Arias, M. A., Butler, M. C., Geringer, J. M., Kim, N. K., Scullion, H., Lowe, K. B. and Drost, E. A. 1995. 'Towards building a theory of comparative management research methodology: An ideographic case study of the Best International Human Resources Management Project'. *Academy of Management Journal*, 38: 1261–87.

The Labour Law of the People's Republic of China. 1994. Beijing: The Publisher of the Ministry of Labour of the People's Republic of China.

Thompson, P. 1992. 'Disorganised socialism: State and enterprise in modern China'. In Smith, C. and Thompson, P. (eds), *Labour in Transition: The Labour Process in Eastern Europe and China*. London and New York: Routledge, pp. 227–59.

Thompson, P. and Smith, C. 1992. 'Socialism and the labour process in theory and practice'. In Smith, C. and Thompson, P. (eds), *Labour in Transition: The Labour Process in Eastern Europe and China*. London and New York: Routledge, pp. 3–36.

Tomlinson, R. 1997. 'You get what you pay for, corporate recruiters in China find'. *Fortune*, April 28: 218–19.

Truss, C., Gratton, L., Hope-Hailey, V., Stiles, P. and Zaleska, J. 2002. 'Paying the piper: choice and constraint in changing HR functional roles'. *Human Resource Management Journal*, 12(2): 39–63.

Tsang, E. W. K. 1998. 'Foreign direct investment in China: A consideration of some strategic options'. *Journal of General Management*, 24(1): 15–34.

Tu, H. S. and Jones, C. A. 1991. 'Human resource management issues in Sino–US business ventures'. *Akron Business and Economic Review*, 22(4) Winter: 18–28.

Tung, R. L. 1982. *Chinese Industrial Society After Mao*. MA, Toronto: Lexington Books, DC. Heath and Company.

Ulrich, D. 1997. *HR Champions*. Boston: Harvard Business School Press.

Unger, J. and Chan, A. 1996. 'Corporatism in China: A developmental state in an East Asian context'. In McCormick, B. L. and Unger, J. (eds), *China After Socialism: In the Footsteps of Eastern Europe or East Asia?* New York: M. E. Sharpe, Inc.

Vanhonacker, W. R. 1997. 'Entering China: An unconventional approach'. *Harvard Business Review*, March–April: 130–40.

Von Glinow, M. A. 1993. 'Diagnosing "best practice" in human resource management practices'. *Research in Personnel and Human Resource Management*, Supplement 3: 95–112.

Von Glinow, M. A. 2002. 'Guest editor's note: Best practices in IHRM: Lessons learned from a ten country/regional analysis'. *Human Resource Management*, 41(1): 3–4.

Von Glinow, M. A. and Teagarden, M. B. 1990. 'Contextual determinants of human resource management effectiveness in international cooperative alliances: Evidence from the People's Republic of China. In Nedd, A. (ed.), *International Human Resource Management Review*, Vol. 1: 75–94. Singapore: McGraw-Hill Book Co.

Walder, A. G. 1986. *Communist Neo-Traditionalism: Work and Authority in Chinese Industry.* Berkeley: University of California Press.

Walder, A. G. 1995. 'China's transitional economy: Interpreting its significance'. *The China Quarterly,* 114: 963–79.

Wan, Yi. 1997. 'General comments on the issue of "controlling large enterprises and relaxing the control of small enterprises"'. *Gongye Qiye Guanli (Industrial Enterprise Management),* 2: 32–5. Beijing: Renmin University Press (in Chinese).

Wang, F. Y. 1993. 'Young people's working attitudes and expectations in China's urban areas'. *Laodong Jinji yu Renli Ziyuan Guanli (Labour Economy and Human Resource Management),* 7: 27–34. Beijing: China's People's University Press (in Chinese).

Wang, M. K. (ed.). 1994. *Woguo Suoyouzhi Jiegou Biange De Qushi He Duice (The Development Trends and Relevant Policies for Changes in Ownership Structure in China).* Beijing: China's Economy Press (in Chinese).

Wang, M. K. (ed.). 2001. *Restructuring China's Social Security System: Funding, Operation and Governance.* Beijing: China Development Publishing House.

Warner, M. 1993. 'Human resource management "with Chinese characteristics"'. *The International Journal of Human Resource Management,* 4(1): 45–65.

Warner, M. 1995. *The Management of Human Resources in Chinese Industry.* New York: St. Martin's Press.

Warner, M. 1996a. 'Human resources in the People's Republic of China: The "three systems" reforms'. *Human Resource Management Journal,* 6(2): 32–43.

Warner, M. 1996b. 'Beyond the iron rice-bowl: Comprehensive labour reform in state-owned enterprises in North-East China'. In Brown, D. H. and Porter, R. (eds), *Management Issues in China: Domestic Enterprises.* London and New York: Routledge, pp. 214–36.

Warner, M. 1997. 'Management-labour relations in the new Chinese economy'. *Human Resource Management Journal,* 7(4): 30–43.

Warner, M. 1998a. 'Human resource management practices in international joint ventures versus state-owned enterprises in China'. In Selmer, J. (ed.), *International Management in China: Cross-cultural Issues.* London and New York: Routledge, pp. 83–97.

Warner, M. 1998b. 'China's HRM in transition: towards relative convergence?' In Rowley, C. (ed.), *Human Resource Management in the Asia Pacific Region: Convergence Questioned.* London: Frank Cass, pp. 19–33.

Warner, M. 1999. 'Human resources and management in China's "hi-tech" revolution: A study of selected computer hardware, software and related firms in the PRC'. *The International Journal of Human Resource Management,* 10(1): 1–20.

Warner, M. (ed.). 2000. *Changing Workplace Relations in the Chinese Economy.* London: Macmillan Press.

Weldon, E. and Jehn, K. A. 1993. 'Work goals and work-related beliefs among managers and professionals in the United States and the People's Republic of China'. *Asia Pacific Journal of Human Resources,* 31(1): 57–70.

White, G. D. 1993. *Riding the Tiger: The Politics of Economic Reform in Post-Mao China.* London: Macmillan.

White, G., Howell, J. and Shang, X. Y. 1996. *In Search of Civil Society: Market Reform and Social Change in Contemporary China.* Oxford: Clarendon Press.

Whiteford, P. 2003. 'From enterprise protection to social protection: Pension reform in China'. *Global Social Policy*, 3(1), 45–77.

Whiteley, A., Cheung, S. and Zhang, S. Q. 2000. *Human Resource Strategies in China*. Singapore: World Scientific.

Williams, M. R. 1972. *Performance Appraisal in Management*. London: Heinemann.

Wong, C. P. W., Heady, C. and Woo, W. T. 1995. *Fiscal Management and Economic Reform in the People's Republic of China*. Oxford: Oxford University Press.

Wong, J. 1993. *Understanding China's Socialist Market Economy*. Singapore: Times Academic Press.

Wong, J. and Chan, S. 2003. 'China's outward direct investment: Expanding worldwide'. *China: An International Journal*, 1, 2 (Sept. 2003): 273–301 (ISSN 0219–8614).

Wong, Siulun. 1996. 'Chinese entrepreneurship and economic development'. In McCormick, B. L. and Unger, J. (eds), *China After Socialism: In the Footsteps of Eastern Europe or East Asia*. New York: M. E. Sharpe, pp. 130–48.

Woo, W. T. 1997. 'Crises and institutional evolution in China's industrial sector'. In Babkina, A. M. (ed.), *Domestic Economic Modernization in China*. New York: Nova Science Publishers, pp. 97–110.

Wright, P. M., Dunford, B. B. and Snell, S. A. 2001. 'Human resources and the resource based view of the firm'. *Journal of Management*, 27:701–21.

Wu, Yanrui. 1996. *Productive Performance in Chinese Enterprises: An Empirical Study*. New York: St. Martin's Press, Inc..

Xia, J. Z. (ed.). 1991. *Laodong Xinzheng Guanli Zhishi Daquan (Encyclopedia of Labour Administration)*. Beijing: China Labour Press (in Chinese).

Xiao, Z. J. 2001. 'Strategic restructuring of state economy and the development of non-state economy'. *China Review*, 41(5): 16–18 (in Chinese).

Xie, F. Z., Lu, Z. Y., Shao, N., Qiu, X. H. and Chen, Z. 1999. 'A large scale investigation of top senior managers of enterprises in China'. *Gongye Qiye Guanli (Industrial Enterprise Management)*, 5: 70–5. Beijing: Renmin University Press (in Chinese).

Xie, J. L. 1995. 'Research on Chinese organizational behavior and human resource management: Conceptual and methodological considerations'. *Advances in International Comparative Management*, 10: 15–42.

Xin, X. B. 2001. 'Analysis on the income of executives in state enterprises'. *Renli Ziyuan Kaifa yu Guanli (Development and Management of Human Resources)*. Vol. 4: 39–44. Beijing: Renmin University Press (in Chinese).

Xu, Feng. 1997. 'The analysis on barriers of the current implementation of re-employment project and some recommendations'. *Laodong Jingji yu Renli Ziyuan Guanli (Labour Economy and Human Resource Management)*, 12: 24–7, Beijing: Renmin University Press (in Chinese).

Xu, Y. C. 1996. 'Deepening and widening the economic reform in China: from enterprise reform to macroeconomic stability'. *The Journal of Developing Areas*, 30 (April): 361–84.

Xue, Muoqiao. 1981. *China's Socialist Economy*. Beijing: Foreign Language Press.

Yabuki, S. 1995. *China's New Political Economy: The Giant Awakes*. Harner, S. M. (trans.). Oxford: Westview Press.

Yang, B. Z. and Wu, S. 1993. *Zhongguo Quanyuan Laodong Hetongzhi Zonglan (The Overview of Chinese Workforce Labour Contract System)*. Beijing: Contemporary China Press.

Yang, M. 1992. 'Management of industrial enterprise owned by the whole people'. In Totten, G. and Zhou, S. L. (eds), *China's Economic Reform: Administering the Introduction of the Market Mechanism*. Boulder, San Francisco, Oxford: Westview Press, pp. 51–66.

Yang, Y. 1995 'The analysis of employment policies and strategies: 1995 to 2000'. *Laodong Jinji yu Renli Ziyuan Guanli (Labour Economy and Human Resource Management)*, 9: 30–4. Beijing: Renmin University Press (in Chinese).

Yao, Y. Q. 1998. 'The issue of retrenchment: Reasons, current situation and suggestions. *Laodong Jingji yu Renli Ziyuan Guanli (Labour Economy and Human Resource Management)*, 2: 57–60. Beijing: Renmin University Press (in Chinese).

Yin, R. K. 1994. *Case Study Research: Design and Methods* (2nd edn). Thousand Oaks, CA: Sage.

Young, S. 1991. 'Private business and the state in China's reforming economy'. *Working paper*, No. 91/12, Chinese Economy Research Unit, The University of Adelaide, Australia.

Young, S. 1995. *Private Business and Economic Reform in China*. Armonk, New York: M. E. Sharpe.

Yu, L. J. and Xin, Z. X. (eds). 1994. *Qiye Laodong Guanlixue Jichu (Introduction to Enterprise Labour Management)*, Beijing: China Labour Press. (in Chinese).

Yuan, Enzheng (ed.). 1993. *Zhongguo Siying Jingji: Xianzhuang, Fazan yu Pinggu (China's Private Economy: Current Situation, Development and Assessment)*. Shanghai: Shanghai People's Publishing House (in Chinese).

Zhang, D. Z. 1996. 'Enterprise disease and its treatment for state-owned enterprises'. *Gongye Qiye Guanli (Industrial Enterprise Management)*, 1: 39–42. Beijing: Renmin University Press (in Chinese).

Zhang, X. Q., Huang, Z. J. and Meng, S. D. 2002. 'How to manage knowledgeable employee under the information economy era'. *Gongye Qiye Guanli (Industrial Enterprise Management)*, Vol. 4: 47–51. Beijing: Renmin University Press (in Chinese).

Zhao, L. K. (ed.). 1986. *Renshi Guanlixue Gaiyao (Introduction to Personnel Management)*, Beijing: China Labour Press (in Chinese).

Zhao, S. M. 1994. 'Human resource management in China'. *Asia Pacific Journal of Human Resources*, 32(2): 3–12.

Zhao, S. M. 1995. *Zhongguo Qiye Renli Ziyuan Guanli (Human Resource Management in China's Enterprises)*, Nanjing, China: Nanjing University Press (in Chinese).

Zhao, S. M. 1998. 'The development of state-owned enterprises and the investment in human capital'. *Laodong Jinji yu Renli Ziyuan Guanli (Labour Economy and Human Resource Management)*, 5: 5–7. Beijing: Renmin University Press (in Chinese).

Zhao, S. M. and Ni, W. 1997. 'Human resource management and development in China's state-owned enterprises'. *Gongye Qiye Guanli (Industrial Enterprise Management)*, 2: 68–71. Beijing: Renmin University Press (in Chinese).

Zhao, S. M. and Wu, C. S. 2003. 'Research on the current HRM in China's enterprise groups'. *Renli Ziyuan Kaifa yu Guanli (Development and Management of Human Resources)*. Vol. 7: 27–35. Beijing: Renmin University Press (in Chinese).

Zhao, S. M., Zhe, J. S., Tan, Y. M. and Xun, H. P. 1998. 'Studies on the strategies of human resource management in state-owned enterprises'. *Laodong Jingji yu Renli Ziyuan Guanli (Labour Economy and Human Resource Management)*, 9: 62–67, Beijing: Renmin University Press (in Chinese).

Zhao, Y. W. 1995. 'Chinese motivation theory and application in China: An overview'. In Kao, H. S. R., Sinha, D. and Ng, S. H. (eds), *Effective Organizations and Social Values*. New Delhi/Thousand Oaks/London: Sage, pp. 117–131.

Zhou, X. Z. 1995. 'Industry and the urban economy'. In Benewick, R. and Wingrove, P. (eds), *China in the 1990s*. Vancouver: University of British Columbia Press, pp. 145–57.

Zhu, C. J. 1997. 'Human resource development in China during the transition to a new economic system'. *Asia Pacific Journal of Human Resources*, 35(3): 19–44.

Zhu, C. J. 2000. 'The emerging role of human resource management in industrial enterprises in China: Past, current and future HR practices'. *Unpublished PhD dissertation*, University of Tasmania, Australia.

Zhu, C. J. and Dowling, P. J. 1994. 'The impact of the economic system upon human resource management practices in China'. *Human Resource Planning*, 17(4): 1–21.

Zhu, C. J. and Dowling, P. 2000. 'Managing people during economic transition: The development of HR practices in China'. *Asia Pacific Journal of Human Resources*, 38(3): 84–106.

Zhu, C. J. and Nyland, C. 2004. 'Globalization and social protection reform: Emerging HRM issues in China'. *The International Journal of Human Resource Management*, 15(4) and 15(5): 853–77.

Zhu, C. J., De Cieri, H. and Dowling, P. J. 1998. 'The reform of employee compensation in China's industrial enterprises'. *Management International Review*, Special Issue 1998/2: 65–87.

Zhu, C. J., Nyland C. and Yang Z. C. (In press). 'Marketization, globalization and social protection reform in China: Implications for the global social protection debate and foreign investors'. *Thunderbird International Business Review*, 47(1).

Zhu, C. J., Cooper, B., De Cieri, H. And Dowling, P. J. 2004. 'The human resource management role in transition: Evidence from industrial enterprises in China'. *Working paper* series 5/04, March 2004, Department of Management. ISSN 1327-5216.

Zhu, M. And Li, Y. L. 2002. 'A comparative study on job satisfaction and motivators between entrepreneurs in China's state-owned enterprises and overseas'. *Gongye Qiye Guanli (Management of Industrial Enterprises)*, Vol, 4: 58–65. Beijing Renmin University Press (in Chinese).

Zhu, Y. 1997. 'The impact of foreign direct investment on labour relations: The case of China'. *Paper presented at International Labour Organisation international seminar*, Geneva, 21 May 1997.

Zhu, Y. 2002. 'Recent developments in China's social security reforms'. *International Social Security Review*, 55(4), 39–54.

Index